High School Homilies

High School Homilies

by Gideon Rappaport

One Mind Good Press
San Diego, California

One Mind Good Press
San Diego, CA 92117

ISBN: 979-8-218-39192-8

Contents

Preface

This is a collection of prepared talks, book and film reviews, letters to former students, and other pieces written during the period of thirty-two years during which I was teaching high school English and intermittently working as a theatrical dramaturge, mostly on productions of Shakespeare. As must be the case, some themes repeat and some pieces I might phrase differently today. I hope they remain worth reading. In a few places I have included updates in square brackets.

Of the formal talks in the first section many were delivered as homilies during the weekly chapel meetings at which attendance was required for students and faculty at The Bishop's School. One was first given to the Headmaster's Advisory Council and another to the Board of Trustees of that school. Two were given at Cum Laude induction ceremonies, one at The Bishop's School and one at La Jolla Country Day School. The commencement address was given at the latter school. For the invitations to give these talks I am grateful to the Bishop's School chaplains and administration, the Cum Laude committees of both schools, and the graduating seniors of the Class of 2012 at La Jolla Country Day School. My gratitude also goes to the editors who at various times have invited me to write reviews for *Ararat*, *Independent School*, *The San Diego Union Tribune*, and the Washington Independent Review of Books. Those reviews appear among others in the middle section. Some of the pieces in the last section were written in response to letters from former students, and I am grateful to those students both for their questions and for permission to quote their words. Many pieces have appeared previously on my weblog at www.raplog.blogspot.com. My thanks go also to the copyeditor, Tom Feltham, the book designer, Chuck Eng, and the proofreader, Mark Swift.

I remain deeply grateful to the students of all ages who over the years have valued these offerings. For a teacher there is no greater reward than contributing to the education of his or her students; their appreciation of it is the icing on that cake.

High School Homilies

Finger Food for Thought
[February 22, 1986]

A group of fingers was sitting around after philosophy class one day discussing the body.

"The body is the bones and the bones are the body," said a materialist middle finger, who was taller than the others and a bit proud of his height. "It's obvious. Without the bones what would we be? A drooping flap of nothing." Then he added, "Bones and nails, of course."

An index finger, aware of his neighbor's crudity, said, "Yours is too shallow a definition. The truth of the body is in sensation. What are the bones without the capacity of our tips to feel, and not only that but by feeling to distinguish among the subtlest of differences?"

"But we can all do that," said an individualist thumb. "The real body is what is unique to each of us, never duplicated in a universe of fingers *and* thumbs. (I wish you'd remember to include us too. Thumbs are thumbs, not fingers.) The prints of our skin are our real bodies—no two alike."

"All three of you have such mechanistic ideas about the body!" shouted the romantic ring finger, reddening with emotion. "Our bones and nails and skin are vessels for relating to others. It's working together with others that being a finger is for, and all your structures and sensations and individuality are nothing without that. Our relationships are our true body."

"Dreamer," said the middle finger.

"You can always spot a ring finger," said the thumb to the group. "It thinks it's nothing till three or four other fingers put a ring on it and then it's instantly the be-all and end-all and expects to live happily ever after." And turning to the ring finger, he demanded, "Where's your self-respect, man?"

"Anyway," added the index finger, "the whole point of being with other fingers is feeling with them. That's the body of your so-called relationship. The rest is just cultural conditioning."

The four went on wrangling for a while until, during a lull in the argument, a pinky said, "I'm not really sure, but I think none of us can say what the body is. After all, our vantage point is so limited. And if we *could* say, why would we be disagreeing about it? Why would we even need to *discuss* it? I think there's more to it than fingers can grasp."

When the chorus of guffaws died down, the middle finger observed, "Obviously the wishful thinking of a pip-squeak, about as convincing as the non-violence of a sissy."

"All I'm saying," continued the pinky, undaunted, "is that we can't know what our true body is. Maybe we don't have a body at all," he added. "Maybe the true body has us."

"Ha, ha, ha," said the others as the bell rang, sending them all to their next lesson.

Seeker, Snooper, Teacher, Tale
[November 1, 1986]

During class one Friday I was in the midst of explaining how to punctuate the line references for verse quotations when a hand went up.

"Yes?"

"Can I ask a question?"

"Yes."

"Do you believe in God? And if you do, why? I mean what proof do you have that he exists?"

I said, "That's two questions. I can answer the first pretty easily. The answer is yes. Answering the second might take some time. You aren't on the point of committing suicide or suffering some other catastrophe if you don't have an immediate answer, are you?" I said it half-jokingly, but it was a serious question. I've known some who would have answered differently.

"No," the student said.

"Then let's discuss it over lunch today."

"I have an away game this afternoon."

"How about Monday?"

"It's a deal."

"Anyone else who wants to can join us," I said to the rest of the class, who, after their initial laughter at the apparent inappropriateness of the question, had become uncharacteristically quiet awaiting my response. "I'll try to have a decent answer by then."

Lying in bed on Saturday morning, I recalled the question. The difficulty, of course, was not to offer a proof where none was possible, but to demonstrate the impossibility of the proof while affirming the value of the questioner's continued seeking. But I had not even formulated it that clearly in my mind before Snooper, as she has many a time, came to my aid. (Snooper was my beloved companion of over twelve years, a mixed border collie who meant to me more than anyone but our common Maker can know.) She didn't *do* anything, you understand, but continue sleeping nearby. But she came to mind and, with the help of our Founding Fathers, brought with her an analogy that might serve.

"Proving to a human being that God exists," I said to the two or three gathered at lunch on the following Monday, "is like proving to my dog Snooper that the United States of America exists. It can't be done. The U.S.A. includes her as one of its inhabitants, obviously. She must abide by its laws. It allows her to live and, if she proves in certain ways troublesome, may put her to death. Her territory, from her napping place under the table to the park of her excursions, is contained within it. And yet its existence can by no method be demonstrated to her. I could walk her from San Diego to Bangor, Maine; I could take her to Washington, D.C., to sniff the parchment of the Constitution itself. Proof of the existence of the nation would remain, to her, unattainable. She simply lacks the organ to perceive it.

"In the same way, we lack the organ by which the divine may be directly perceived and proven. Since we are a part of it, it cannot become a part of us, even as an idea, certainly not as a proof to any organs we do have—the senses, the intellect, the imagination. But does the nation cease to exist or cease to strive for the welfare of its citizens and their dependents, including Snooper, because for her it is invisible?"

From there the conversation was carried in various directions. Some argued that the analogy breaks down, and of course it does eventually. But its good was harvested before it did, and I felt that through the two of us, Snooper in her being and I in my thought, something valuable had been accomplished. Only later did I realize that we had incarnated James Joyce's famous *jeu d'esprit*: God is dog spelled backwards (an anagram Joyce may have read in Aubrey's brief life of Sir Walter Raleigh).

The following week ended the quarter, and on its last day I indulged the impulse to tell this story and to draw from it one more lesson.

"It is true that we cannot encompass and know the divine. It is great and we are small. But it can shrink itself down to become for a moment known to us—not through expansion of our organs of knowing but through its own contraction into perceivability—as, the Jewish mystics say, it did in the beginning to make room for creation. The presence in the Burning Bush and at Sinai, the Sermon on the Mount, the inner voice of Socrates and the enlightenment of Buddha, the vast universe of space and time itself, and the instantaneous and subtle shift in comprehension that can change one's life—all these are contractions of the divine to fit into our narrow sphere of experience. We call them revelations. God, when he wills, can reveal himself to us as the U.S. of A. cannot to a dog.

"And this is why I am here teaching poetry to you and why I think it important that you should be here learning it. Because a great poem or play or novel, too, is a revelation. It comes, as the poets report, from somewhere beyond the self, and the poet, like every artist, is not a creator but a maker of forms in which to convey what is demanding to be revealed (which is why the word *creative* as usually used seems so absurd). Every work I will teach you this year I teach because I know it can become, for a moment, a small window on the vast, unfathomable, living reality of which we are all parts—a revelation of the divine."

The bell rang, and at the end of the day I went home to write progress reports. But I carried with me the experience of a small revelation of my own: A student is one who raises his hand under invisible compulsion to ask a question and is never quite satisfied with the answer. A teacher is one who in seeing that raised hand hears the voice of his calling. And when two or three such are gathered together to discuss the existence of God, who do you suppose is there in the midst of them?

"Embalm All the Brutes!"
[March 10, 1987]

Listening to National Public Radio a few weeks ago, I heard about a man in Washington State who has invented a fluid that, when injected into plants of various kinds, preserves them in their green and living beauty for up to three years. Of course it kills them in the process, but no one looking at them, we are told, can tell that they aren't alive. Since the fluid is not in fact a universal mixture but must be adjusted to the particular chemical makeup of each species, it is difficult to market, so its inventor is marketing instead the various plants that the fluid has successfully preserved. His clientele consists of florists who see that there is profit to be made in having their stock in trade shipped from the nursery by way of the embalmer.

Noah Adams, the NPR interviewer, suggested that there was something about this process that didn't seem right. "I'm not sure just what it is," he said coyly, "but something about it bothers me." With no detectable irony the inventor replied, "Most people feel that way when they hear about it, but when they actually see the plants we've preserved, they're so amazed and excited that the feeling disappears."

No doubt seeing a dead plant that looks alive is quite wonderful. But is it more wonderful than seeing a plant that is alive? Most of us have experienced the precious beauty of a perfect rose. And we've felt the desire for it to last longer. But would its beauty mean as much to us if we knew we were looking at the preserved corpse of a rose? Isn't its life essential to its beauty? Something about this embalming process bothers me too. It is like what bothers me about the voice-driven mechanical dogs, cats, and birds recently advertised in a New York City newspaper not as toys but as pets: "They respond to the sound of your voice," runs the ad more or less, "just like real, live animals, but you'll have no mess to clean up, no veterinary bills, and no worries about what to do with them during vacations. Just put them in a closet when you leave. They'll be there whenever you return, ready to come or stay, purr, bark, or chirp on command." *Pets*, the ad calls them!

When I described these latest "advances in civilization" to my great teacher, Mary Holmes, her response was this: "The one thing I find even more distressing than the greed of our age is its love of death." And I knew that she had named what bothers us about these inventions. In a hundred ways our age prefers the actually or artistically dead to the living. And why? Because the dead we can control. Attaching our attention to what is dead, we need not confront the mysterious temporariness of things living—their reminder to us of our own mortality.

When I considered pointing this out in chapel one day, examples began competing for attention. I remembered the shoppers' abandonment of Clinton, New York, a small upstate village where I lived for a year. Its shops, housed in graceful eighteenth-century wood-frame buildings with gabled windows, were always going out of business because most people preferred to drive eight miles to the Utica shopping mall. The rotunda of the mall was decorated with—guess what?—tawdry pasteboard imitations of eighteenth-century gabled windows.

I thought of the highschoolized American prose version of *Macbeth*, which pretends to offer Shakespeare to those who can't or won't learn to read the original. Everything in the older play is retained in the modernization—plot, characters, the moving of Birnam Wood—everything, that is, but Shakespeare's living poetry, which has been as resolutely murdered as ever King Duncan was.

I thought of the plan to save the Parthenon from the rapid corrosion of Athenian smog by removing it to a museum and putting an incorruptible plastic replica in its place. I thought of the computer program I am told about with which you can have a real conversation: it is called "Friends." (Don't you bet that someone is working right now on one to be called "Lovers"?)[1] I thought of fast food, of indoor tanning centers, of Muzak.

All these modernisms show bad taste, of course. But they show something worse. They show that many people value artificiality above both art and life. Thinking about all this, I was reminded of Mammon, whom some of you will remember from John Milton's *Paradise Lost*. He is the fallen angel, now a demon, who believes he can build in hell a magnificence to rival that of heaven. We have gems, gold, and the skill with which to do it, he argues, "and what can heav'n show more?" Or, as C. S. Lewis paraphrases it in *A Preface to Paradise Lost*, "What do you mean by saying we have lost love? There is an excellent brothel round the corner." In other words, the imitation is just as good as the real thing.

---

1 This was written before Myspace and Facebook, before "friend" became a verb.

Or better. Consider AI, artificial intelligence, so-called. Like Mary Shelley's Dr. Frankenstein, who longed to create a man, the pursuers of artificial intelligence, the highest tech of all, also long to create a man, but a mechanical man without life, a mind without a body or a heart. In short, like Dr. Frankenstein's creation, a monster. There is mastery for you. There is the triumph of the will to control. Only suppose the inventors *could* make such a consciousness out of wires and silicon chips (which I don't for a moment believe they can). What would their moral obligations be? Should they worship it? Should they expect it to worship them? Can they be sure it would be any more obedient to them than Adam was to God? Would they be entitled to unplug it because its hardware was faulty or because it disagreed with them about something? Would it thank them for giving it a permanent but lifeless consciousness that might very well be worse than death?

These moral questions led me from considering artificiality, which is the dead in art, to something immeasurably worse—the various kinds of actual death our culture engages in. The embalming of plants is innocence itself compared to the intentional maiming and killing of animals to satisfy the lust for control that too often masquerades as scientific research. And when we look honestly at the difficult questions of abortion and euthanasia, we uncover more than a single motive. There is of course the wish to ease people's suffering. But there is also the hunger to have control over even those events that are hidden deepest in mystery.

The most extreme example of the love of death that springs from the lust for control is that of the tyrant. The tyrant wants humanity itself to be his object. He wants it to submit to his will like a dead thing. As a result, he treats people as the plant embalmer treats living plants. You might remember the way Kurtz in Conrad's *Heart of Darkness* treats the Africans, for example. He thought he wanted to better the lives of the natives. Really he wanted to be their god. Those who frustrated him in that desire he would murder.

And finally, all of us fear that the whole world might be put to death by some Russian [or Communist Chinese] ideologue or American [or World Economic Forum] technocrat or Third World terrorist proclaiming some passionate conviction or another. Such a destroyer would rather see the death of everything than be reminded by everything living that his own will is not absolute.

All these errors, both the artificial imitations and the immoral killings, spring, I believe, from one thing: our fear of death, the ultimate uncontrollable. In response to this fear we despair. We suicidally embrace death itself in order to avoid the fear of death, or we vainly seek to control death by becoming dealers of it.

But despair is only one response to this fear of death. There are two other responses available: one is patience—willingly accepting the prospect of death so that, for a time, we can enjoy life; the other is faith—recognizing that death is as much part of God's will as life is and that therefore death must be as meaningful as life, even if it is a mystery to the living. Few of us can claim more than occasional moments of faith of this kind, the faith that Socrates and St. Francis and the Baal Shem Tov held for a lifetime, the faith that removes mountains of doubt from others who know of their saintly lives. But all of us whose faith is less than theirs must choose daily between despair and patience. We can pretend that it is possible to avoid or control death. Or we can consent to find what meaning there is in our mortal lives before death does whatever it does to us, whether it ends us or releases us.

Thus, though eventually we must all die, we are not doomed while we live to loving death more than life. However much we must suffer their presence, we are not doomed to attaching ourselves to embalmed plants, mechanical pets, cheap replicas, and artificial intelligence, or to the tyrannies of research, repression, and terror. We have a choice. In spite of inevitable death we can surrender the pretense of control and choose to receive, share, and love the gifts of life. It is the same choice God gave to Moses and the Children of Israel: "This day I have set before you life and death, the blessing and the curse—therefore choose life."

We cannot, even for the noblest of motives, both make the world over in our image and live in it. A world frozen in our idea of perfection, no less than in that of the Dr. Frankensteins and the Kurtzes, is a world made dead, or worse than dead. To live in it we would have to deaden what lives in us. But we can, as individual souls, cherish the living flowers and the mortal pets God has given us. We can celebrate the graceful buildings and the true poetry given us by inspired artists. And we can love both friends and strangers, and, if we want to enough, even enemies. For every one of them is a temporary and therefore precious bearer of the uncontrollable, mysterious, and sacred gift of life.

Ceremony
[Spring, 1988]

In a few days, many will process into bleachers and participate in a traditional commencement ceremony. Many may imagine that they would prefer to receive their diplomas in the mail (and to put them in a drawer instead of in a frame on the wall). There may be similar resistance for many who attend Eagle Scout Courts of Honor, weddings, funerals, inaugurations, church, chapel, and synagogue services, and other ritual ceremonies.

Why are we so resistant to this kind of activity, which human beings have been practicing since they have been known to be human? Part of the answer lies in two big chips we carry on our shoulders when we enter into ceremonial occasions.

On our left shoulder is the unexamined assumption that anything that is not spontaneous, arising from immediate visceral instinct, is artificial and therefore false. This chip we inherit from the Romantic movement of the nineteenth century, still very much with us. The spokesman for that movement, Jean-Jacques Rousseau, in many pages of argument, articulated the premise that man is naturally good and that it is society that corrupts him. The conclusion drawn by many was and is that in order to recover goodness, we must depart from the group and become entirely individual, which in practice means getting in touch with the most natural parts of ourselves: our bodies, spontaneous impulses, feelings, gut. The enemy is every fraternal, political, or religious institution, every tradition, every form of social conditioning or societal influence (except that which tells us to resist societal influence!).

With this chip on our shoulder, we experience any ceremony as a compromise of our sacred individuality, a succumbing to corrupting external pressure, a surrender. And so we resist. The moment our elders tell us "This ritual is what we do and how we do it," we inwardly rebel. ("Who are you to tell me what to do? Nature is my guide to the good. You are society, trying to corrupt me.") The romantic enters the place of ceremony believing his best (natural) self is under attack by society in the form of artificiality.

On our right shoulder is the unexamined assumption that anything that cannot be scientifically demonstrated to our rational intellect is likely to be at best inadvertent error and at worst intentional deception. This chip we inherit from the Enlightenment of the eighteenth century, still very much with us too. Here the premise is that man's intellect is constantly growing in its mastery of reality and, given time and sufficient experimentation, will eventually comprehend all things that have in the past seemed to be mysterious. The conclusion drawn by many was and is that in order to attain to truth, we must examine everything with the eye of objective and skeptical rational observation supported by experiment. The enemy is every attempt to appeal to non-objective modes of experience: tradition, imagination, faith, revelation, obedience to authority (except the authority of science!).

With this chip on our shoulder, we experience any ceremony as a compromise of our sacred reason, a succumbing to corrupting superstition, a surrender. And so we resist. The moment our elders tell us "This ritual is what we do and how we do it," we inwardly rebel. ("Do you really expect me to believe this is real? Reason is my instrument of truth. You are the ignorant past, trying to bamboozle me.") The rationalist enters the place of ceremony believing his true (rational) self is under attack by the past in the form of superstition.

We are all both romantics and rationalists—all of us. We can't help it. We came to consciousness being trained to be both, and reinforcement is all around us. Except in our ceremonies.

Despite the inherited burden of those two chips on our shoulders, we nonetheless keep participating in ceremonies. We go to weddings and funerals; we look forward to the prom and commencement; we watch the ball dropping on New Year's Eve or the President taking his oath of office. Why? Because we are not *only* romantics and rationalists. We are also mysterious whole beings that transcend our own categories and prejudices. As it turns out, we *want* something besides the satisfaction of our impulses or the observation of facts. We *crave* it.

What is this mysterious other thing that we crave, this thing that we willingly participate in ceremonies in order to find? The answer is meaning—which lies in the experience of being or becoming part of something bigger than we are—bigger than our impulses and our individual natures, bigger than our facts and our explanations. We crave the meaning of being taken up and absorbed into something even more real than ourselves. And we simply will not live without it.

As a result, despite the weight of those chips on our shoulders, we participate in ceremonies—because lurking within us, out of range of the romantic longing for freedom from constraint, out of range of the all-examining eye of reason, is the hope that yet once more we may be granted participation in the experience of something real. This is why those of you who will graduate this spring will be at baccalaureate and commencement wearing your caps and gowns. You will be hoping to experience meaning.

But because this experience of meaning is mysterious, ceremony comes with a warning: There are no guarantees. There is no guarantee that even if you give yourself wholeheartedly to the experience you will be deeply moved by it. Ceremony invites meaning; it can't command it. But you can bet that if you *withhold* your willing participation, you will almost certainly *not* be moved.

How can we lose ourselves in what is bigger than we are if we are anchored to ourselves by those heavy chips? If the left chip tells us that the most important thing is our separateness, and the right chip that it is our detachment, how can we let these overly precious selves go and actually join in the ceremony?

There is a way, of course, and it is the way of faith that things can happen that we are not masters of, faith in the wisdom of our forebears who established the ceremony for our benefit. It is the way of hope in the power of something outside ourselves to reach in and change us, hope in the integrity and authenticity built into the ceremonial forms. It is the way of love of our own good that longs to be, even for a moment, redeemed from the prison of our mere selves, love of our neighbors' good that wills them to be moved even if we ourselves are not. It is the way of surrendering the will to that otherwise inaccessible reality which the ceremony exists to draw into the here-and-now world of time and space.

So as you are marching to the tune of "Pomp and Circumstance," or stepping under the wedding canopy, or singing a hymn, or saluting the flag, know that if you let the chips govern you and keep your mental distance, the potential meaning will surely elude you, because you have closed the door and left it no way to come in. But if you choose to participate in the ceremony with your whole self, if you open that door and invite the meaning in, it may or may not enter, but you have done your part. And if it does enter, the reward will be the fulfillment of your longing for meaning, a spirit that blows those chips off your shoulders like the dust of the earth and lifts you toward the stars.

My Karma Ran Over My Dogma
[October 13, 1988]

I'm going to keep two promises today, and to do so I will have to repeat myself. But since keeping both promises involves telling stories of the Hasidim, and since they are the kinds of stories that bear repeating, I hope those of you who have heard them before will not suffer too much. I've promised to explain the bumper sticker on my bulletin board, and I've promised to tell what I said to a few of the guys late one night at Senior Retreat.

On my bulletin board in Bentham is a bumper sticker, the only one that has never bored me, however often I notice it. It says, "My karma ran over my dogma." I should warn you that there is a bastard version of it running around that turns the wisdom of the original into a polite form of aggression: It says, "Excuse me, but my karma just ran over your dogma." But karma is nobody's ego machine. We'll keep to the humbler version—"My karma ran over my dogma." What does it mean?

The sentence is a double pun, and both its senses challenge me. First, I have a dog, as some of you know, whom I love very much, and a car that could easily crush her if she and I were not careful. Such a disaster could even happen, God forbid, though we *are* careful. And that brings me to the second sense of the pun: "Dogma" is a Greek word meaning an established opinion or tenet or a body of doctrines. It comes from *dokein*, to seem or to seem good, and from it we get the adjective "dogmatic" and the noun "dogmatism," that is, inflexibility in asserting opinions or in holding doctrines. "Karma" comes from Sanskrit, the ancient language of India, and means a combination of something like destiny and something like divine justice. It is, in Hinduism and Buddhism, the force of the ethical consequences of one's actions, which determine one's destiny and the conditions of one's next incarnation. It is, in other words, what you've got coming to you. (In the Eastern religions, perfection of life leads to nirvana, which is the release from karma into bliss.)

We all know the experience that the bumper sticker names: You want to and are pretty sure that you will go to Stanford. Your parents are absolutely sure you will go to Stanford. Even one or two of your teachers think that you'll probably go to Stanford. Your grades are good, your sports, arts, prizes, service, SATs, and college essay are all in order. You've already been accepted at Berkeley, Harvard, and Oxford. But Stanford rejects you. What has happened? Your karma has run over your dogma.

Or you run away from Corinth to be certain that you will never kill your father or marry your mother, and you end up in Thebes, where you discover that you have already done just that.

Or you spend ten years assuming that you are going to be a college professor of Shakespeare. The scarcity of jobs doesn't deter you. That career is just right for you. You are just right for it. What *else* would you do for a living, after all? Then one day you find yourself struggling to explain reference of pronouns to a gaggle of tenth graders with an unconquerable Pavlovian hunger for the ringing of a bell. What has happened? Why is a Jew telling Hasidic tales in an Episcopal chapel? His karma has run over his dogma. And so has yours.

Dogma is what we *think* is true. Karma is what will *be* true because of who and what we are and what reality is, whether we predict it or desire it or accept it or not. Dogma need not be bad, but it is partial. Karma is whole.

The Hasidim, of course, did not know of karma by that name, but they knew very well what it is that runs over your dogma. The Hasidim are those passionately mystical Orthodox Jews, originally of Eastern Europe, followers of the eighteenth-century tzaddik—that is, sage and righteous man—the Baal Shem Tov, the Master of the Good Name, who taught that God is to be worshipped in joy as well as in understanding and obedience. The Hasidim praise God not only in prayer but in singing and dancing—and in stories.

Here are three stories told by the holy Rabbi Simcha Bunam. In the first, his own karma runs over his dogma:

Rabbi Bunam said: "Once when I was on the road near Warsaw, I felt that I had to tell a certain joke. But this joke was a worldly one, and I knew that it would rouse only laughter and ridicule among the many people who had gathered about me. The Evil Impulse in me tried very hard to dissuade me, saying that I would alienate all those people because once they heard this joke they would no longer consider me a rabbi. But I said to my heart, 'Why should you be concerned about the secret ways of God?' And I remembered the words of Rabbi Pinchas of Koretz: 'All joys come from paradise, and

jokes too, provided they are uttered in true joy.' And so in my heart
of hearts I renounced my rabbi's office and told the joke. The whole
gathering burst out laughing. And instead of my followers becoming
alienated, even those who had before been distant from me now drew
near and attached themselves to me."[1]

Sometimes, if your dogma is pure bred, a collision is averted:

Rabbi Simcha Bunam said: "Rabbi Eleazar of Amsterdam was at sea
on a journey to the Holy Land when, on the eve of Rosh Hashanah,
a storm almost sank the ship. Before dawn Rabbi Eleazar told all his
people to go on deck and blow the ram's horn at the first ray of light.
When they had done this, the storm died down. But do not think,"
Rabbi Bunam added, "that Rabbi Eleazar intended to save the ship.
On the contrary, he was quite certain it would go down. But before
dying with his people he wanted to fulfill the holy commandment of
blowing the ram's horn. Had he intended to save the ship through a
miracle, he would not have succeeded."[2]

Sometimes, as seniors discovered on retreat, you go a long way to find
that your karma has been parked at home all along, not far from your
dogma's house:

Rabbi Simcha Bunam used to tell young men who came to him for the
first time the story of Rabbi Eisik, the son of Rabbi Yekel in Cracow.
After many years of great poverty which had never shaken his faith
in God, he dreamed someone bade him look for a treasure in Prague,
under the bridge which leads to the king's palace. When the dream
recurred a third time, Rabbi Eisik prepared for the journey and set
out for Prague. But the bridge was guarded day and night and he
did not dare to start digging. Nevertheless he went to the bridge
every morning and kept walking around it until evening. Finally the
captain of the guards, who had been watching him, asked in a kindly
way whether he was looking for something or waiting for somebody.
Rabbi Eisik told him of the dream which had brought him here from
a faraway country. The captain laughed. "And so to please the dream

---

1   Martin Buber, *Tales of the Hasidim: The Later Masters* (New York: Schocken, 1948; 7th pr.
1974), page 248.
2   Buber, pages 247–48.

you poor fellow wore out your shoes to come here! As for having faith in dreams, if I had had it, I should have had to get going when a dream once told me to go to Cracow and dig for treasure under the stove in the room of a Jew—Eisik, son of Yekel, that was the name! Eisik, son of Yekel! I can just imagine what it would be like, how I should have to try every house over there, where one half of the Jews are named Eisik, and the other Yekel!" And he laughed again. Rabbi Eisik bowed, traveled home, dug up the treasure from under the stove, and built the House of Prayer which is called "Reb Eisik's Shul."

"Take this story to heart," Rabbi Bunam used to add, "and make what it says your own: There is something you cannot find anywhere in the world, not even at the zaddik's, and there is, nevertheless, a place where you can find it."[3]

That place, says Martin Buber, is "the place on which one stands."[4] Rabbi Nachman of Bratslav, retelling the story, would say: "The treasure is at home, but the knowledge of it is in Prague."

3   Buber, pages 245–46.
4   Martin Buber, The Way of Man According to the Teaching of Hasidism (New York: Citadel Press, 1966; Repr. Carol Pub. Group, 1990), page 37.

On Teaching Morality[1]
[April 13, 1989]

Our topic for the headmaster's advisory council was "What do we mean by 'preparing students for college'?" I decided to focus on morality. Students need to learn to be moral if they are to be prepared for college. College, like life, will challenge them with innumerable temptations to immorality. And, what with academic professionalism, the detachment of so-called objectivity, and specialization, [and ideological propagandizing,] most colleges and universities will do little to teach students moral behavior or foster it in them. And we know that most television programs, movies, rock music, and magazines are to moral education what Pop-Tarts are to breakfast.

So in addition to developing knowledge, reasoning ability, artistry, and physical prowess, a college preparatory school has to teach morality. Fine. But how?

There are three ways. The first is force—exercised, as in the society at large, through the establishment of moral rules, the punishment of wrongdoing, and the consequent fear of punishment. We encourage moral behavior by making the alternative so unpleasant that students will want to avoid it.

Though I came of age in the 1960s, I do not entirely reject this method in favor of nicer ones. Legitimate force and fear are useful and often necessary teaching devices. We depend on them to show that we mean what we say and to give students practice in behaving more or less morally until they can learn to want to do so.

But though sometimes necessary, force is an invasion of the self and fear a corruption of it. Without some other forms of moral education, force and fear can do as much damage as good. So in teaching morality the method of force alone is not enough.

The second method is simply to inform our students about what is moral and what is immoral behavior. It is important not to underestimate the value of such information. We should engage in as much Socratic

1 Published in *Independent School*, Volume 49, Number 1 (Fall 1989), page 45.

dialogue about our own and others' pronouncements as students will put up with. But when all the talking is done, they need to know where we stand. If we hesitate to state the moral principles we hold, whether because we lack conviction, because we overvalue individual freedom, or because we are afraid of alienating our students, our hesitation is nothing less than an invitation to confusion and error.

Speech is influential, and speech arising from conviction is particularly so. Even if students threaten to rebel against our moral instruction, let us at least give them something solid—not tyrannical, but solid—to rebel against. As we all know from our own lives, experience may eventually bring our students to perceive the wisdom in what they rejected in their youth. If it does, they will be thankful for the very clarity and firmness of moral instruction under which they may now chafe.

In times of questioning or crisis, good words can arise in the memory to foster good deeds. But not if they have not been planted there in the first place. The words of parents and certain teachers, experienced early as revelations, return over and over through life, like themes on which are played many variations.

For example, in the first century Rabbi Tarfon said, "It is not up to you to complete the work; neither is it permitted you to abandon it." His teaching is available to anyone who reads the section of the Talmud called *Pirkei Avot*, often called the Ethics of the Fathers. Yet Rabbi Tarfon's teaching would not ring in my mind to guide and console me if my father had not quoted it in a rare and, to me, momentous revelation of the springs of his own action. And one of the reasons that our philosophy, art history, and Latin teacher is so revered in our own school community is that he is not afraid to enter our memories by stating, on an important ceremonial occasion, the moral truth that "nothing is equal to virtue."

The third method of teaching morality is the hardest. When added to the others, it is also the most powerful. My greatest college professor, Mary Holmes, said at commencement one year, "There is no excellence without discipline." This assertion applies to morality as well as to artistic, athletic, intellectual, and every other kind of excellence.

Discipline is the submission of self—not the burying of insight and experience, but the surrender of self-will and whim. Without that submission of the extraneous to the essential, excellence is impossible. And morality is, among other things, a species of discipline. Without the surrender of selfish desire in the name of a higher good, there can be no moral excellence.

But what Professor Holmes went on to say was startling: "There is no excellence without discipline. But," she said, "there is no such thing as self-discipline." What? Was she out to subvert every parental admonition against laziness? Giving students permission to "bail" discipline? To sit around the house all day, waiting for mere inspiration to impel them to do their math homework or take out the garbage?

Her next words were these: "There is only the being disciplined by what we love." (She later revised the last word to "desire.") To me this was one of the most astonishing, liberating, challenging sentences I had ever heard. And I knew it was true.

It is only what we love or desire, what moves us, what we really care about, that can command us to surrender our self-will and whim to discipline. If we love a person, a poetic experience, an A, a prospective college, power, money, or self-abandonment, we will sacrifice everything and submit to whatever discipline is required in order to achieve the particular excellence that our love inspires us to crave. Think of the sacrifices drug addicts make to attain what they most desire. Or of Michelangelo, four years on his back painting the Sistine Ceiling. "There is no excellence without discipline, but there is no such thing as self-discipline. There is only the being disciplined by what we desire."

So the question is, how can we get our students to desire morality, or rather the good itself, so that they will *want* to submit to its discipline?

The answer is we can't. Human beings cannot be made to love something they do not love, to desire something they do not want. If they could, there would be no unrequited love in the world, and no need for pop quizzes. Love invades us and grows in us, as and when *it* chooses; it cannot be invented, constructed, induced, or threatened into us.

But we know that a lovable object may *inspire* love. This means that, while we cannot make students love the morally good and thereby willingly surrender to the discipline of morality, we can offer them the opportunity to experience moral good. And if they experience it, there is always hope that they might be inspired to love it.

How can we provide this opportunity? There is only one way: by being moral. We teach not only what we teach. We teach what we are. Whether we mean to or not, we teach by example. Living morally, then, is the best method we have of fostering in our students that love of the good without which there is no moral discipline, without which, in turn, there is no moral excellence.

This does not mean that we have to be perfect to teach morality, only that we have to be strivers for the good. A moral person is not necessarily a perfect person but one who can respond morally to his or her imperfections.

Though their greatest pleasure may be in sharing, teachers still get a measure of ego gratification from feeling superior in knowledge and experience to their students. As a result, one of the hardest things for a teacher to do is to apologize to a student and to mean it. And yet hardly a better moral lesson can be taught than the one taught by the teacher who humbly admits to a mistake, apologizes, and then gets on with things. In so doing, the teacher demonstrates not only the wrongness of an error but the rightness of confession and the wrongness of uncritical self-justification; the rightness of atonement and the wrongness of dwelling on failure; the rightness of courage and the wrongness of fear.

In teaching morality to students by striving to be moral ourselves, we occasionally find ourselves at odds with certain of our students' parents. These parents by their own behavior may sometimes convey the message that personal gain justifies the abandonment of principles. In such cases we walk a fine line, for we would not ourselves abandon the principle that students should honor their fathers and mothers.

Thus we at times are put in the position of having to teach morality to parents as well as students. And since parents indirectly pay a large portion of our salaries, we may sometimes be challenged to risk our very livelihoods for moral values.

We are certainly not infallible. But when we have the courage to chastise a young offender and then forgive, when we proclaim that our students must do unto others as they would be done by, and when we apologize to one another or to a student, or seem to a parent with Stanford on the brain to be nothing but a gratuitous obstruction, it is often because we have been disciplined in morality by love.

If our students take with them one example of just punishment, one phrase of moral wisdom, or, best of all, the clear image of even one humble gesture by a respected teacher, to that extent we will have prepared them well, and not only for college.

A Good Word about Atheists
[October 19, 1989]

Chapel may seem an odd place for it, but I'm going to say a good word about atheists. One reason I want to do so is that some of my best friends think of themselves as atheists. Another reason is the unsavory images of God held by some people who think of themselves as *theists*: I mean those believers who are certain that God is American, Republican, English-speaking, and white, or anti-American, Democratic, bilingual, and multi-racial; or those who are absolutely certain that God wants them to condemn, terrorize, and kill in his name; or those who are certain that God means for them to serve him by getting rich on the contributions of the faithful poor; or those who are certain that the deepest insight God expects from us is, in the words of the Church Lady (played by Dana Carvey on *Saturday Night Live*), "Isn't that special?"; or those who are certain that God damns those who believe differently from them. Atheists are valuable because they tell these theists a truth they need to hear: No such God exists.

Of course many of us hold much better images of God than those I've just listed. But we too need our atheist friends. In addition to the rest of the good that they do, atheists keep us humble. For one thing, it is humbling to find that we simply cannot convince them of what is so obvious to us, namely that God exists. What a dramatic proof of the limits of our powers of argumentation! For another thing, the resistance of the atheist to our arguments reminds us that it was not through argument that we ourselves came to faith. His conviction shows us that it is not in our power to dictate who will believe in God and who won't. But atheists keep us humble in another way, too. They show us that *all* images of God, even the truest, are limited.

We can all pretty much reject the images of God I mentioned at first. God has no race or political party; he is not a terrorist or a tyrant, a high-pressure salesman or a sentimentalist. But what about the images of him that we embrace—creator and preserver, lawgiver and judge, punisher and destroyer, forgiver and redeemer? We who have these images hold to them on good authority—the authority of revelation. We believe that, in one or more ways, God has revealed himself to humanity, informing us how to imagine him rightly so that we may worship him rightly. The Children of Israel at Mount Sinai, the hearers of the Sermon on the Mount, and other good authorities have testified to meeting face-to-face with the divine. And on their authority, coupled with our own experience, we trust to the images of God that they have passed down to us. They are good images and true ones, and they provide us a path toward God.

But they are not themselves God. Even the best images of the divine are limited because no revelation to man reveals God in his totality. How could it? Who would be able to receive it? If we are ideas in God's mind, so to speak, how could God's fullness be reduced to an idea in ours? No more than Shakespeare could have been conceived of by Hamlet. Revelations reveal God to us as *we* can perceive him, not as he is in himself, because in comparison with the infinite mystery of God our capacity to experience him is minute. He makes himself knowable through images, but no image can contain him.

Now I don't say all this on my own authority: Speaking from the whirlwind, God says to Job, "Where wast thou when I laid the foundations of the earth?" (Job 38:4). In other words, who are you to presume to know what I am up to? The great medieval Jewish philosopher and Torah scholar Maimonides writes, "All people, both of past and present generations, declared that God cannot be the object of human comprehension, that none but Himself comprehends what He is, and that our knowledge consists in knowing that we are unable truly to comprehend Him" (*Guide for the Perplexed*, I.59). Saint Thomas Aquinas says, "God is not to be comprehended, for he is infinite and cannot be contained in any finite being" (*Summa Theologiae*, Ia.xii.7.*ad*1). Dante, in his ultimate allegorical vision of God, cries, "O Light Eternal, that alone abidest in Thyself, alone knowest Thyself" (*Paradiso*, XXXIII.124–25). And Rav Kook, the twentieth-century Talmudic scholar and mystic, says, "All the divine names, whether in Hebrew or in any other language, give us only a tiny and dull spark of the hidden light to which the soul aspires when it utters the word *God*."[1]

---

1 Moses Maimonides, *The Guide for the Perplexed*, translated by M. Friedlander (New York: Dover, 1956), page 85; St. Thomas Aquinas, *Philosophical Texts*, edited by Thomas Gilby (New York: Galaxy, 1960), page 86; Dante Alighieri, *Paradiso*, translated by John D. Sinclair (New York: Galaxy, 1961), page 485; Abraham Isaac Kook, "The Pangs of Cleansing" in *The Lights of Penitence [etc.]*, translated by Ben Zion Bokser (New York: Paulist Press, 1978), page 261.

For this reason, as good as our image of God may be, even if it is a God-given image, we must not mistake it for God himself. And because no image can convey to us God's totality, it cannot give us the power to comprehend fully his purposes or his judgments. We do know, of course, more than enough. We know what he wants us to know: that we should do justice and love mercy, for example, that we should worship only him, that our lives come to judgment, that we are unimaginably loved. But even the purest faith does not justify us in speaking for God on subjects about which only he knows his mind—subjects like which of us will be saved and which will not, or how near to God one may go on a path different from our own. That is why we are told to judge not lest we be judged. Because, not being God, we are fallible, and our judgment, unlike his, is imperfect. Therefore, the true theist is a humble theist. He knows that to have a true path to God is not to have the *only* path to God. As a great Hasidic tzaddik, the Seer of Lublin, put it, what kind of God would it be who could be served in only one way?

Finally, even to apply the word "existence" to God is to reduce his full reality. As Rav Kook says, "[W]hatever we ascribe to the term *existence* is immeasurably remote from the divine... The divine is the activating influence on existence and is, therefore, obviously above existence."[2] This brings us back to the atheists. In arguing against the existence of God, whatever their intentions, the atheists tell a partial truth: namely, there is no such God as *any* of us can picture. For a God whose existence we could imagine would not be God, the source of existence itself. This being so, who are we to say that his path of negation may not lead even the atheist toward God?

Now, having defended the atheists, I have to add that of course their negative images of God too are limited. To say that "existence" is too small a term to be applied to God is not to say there is no God. Atheists help to purify our faith by reminding us that all our images of God fail to convey the fullness of divine reality. But the atheist still has to choose between believing in that infinite, absolute, unfathomable divine reality, a reality with the power to reveal itself to us, and believing in nothingness. If the atheist's rejecting is done in the name of a search for truth, he may well find God at the end of his search. If his rejecting is merely a way to exalt his own ego, he will be left with nothing *but* his ego, and therefore, eventually, with nothing—that is unless God's mercy intervenes. But

2 Kook, pages 266–67.

since we are not God ourselves, the atheist's eternal fate, like our own, remains a mystery. For him, as for ourselves, we can only hope and pray for the best. I think we are also permitted to argue with him, but only so long as we don't permit ourselves to sit in judgment on his soul.

I will conclude with two Hasidic stories about atheism and faith. The first story comes to me from the great tzaddik Rabbi Nachman of Bratslav via Elie Wiesel. It is about getting the facts but missing the point. I should warn you that the meaning of the story is *in* the story, not in any twist at the end.

The king had sent a letter to a wise but skeptical man, who, in his faraway province, refused to accept it. He was one of those men who think too much, who complicate their lives by complicating small things. He couldn't understand, not in the slightest, what the king might want of him: "Why would the sovereign, so powerful and so rich, address himself to me, who am less than nothing? Because he takes me for a philosopher? There are more important ones. Could there be another reason? If so, what reason?"

Unable to answer these questions, he preferred to believe the letter a misunderstanding. Worse: a fraud. Worse yet: a practical joke. "Your king," he said to the messenger, "does not exist." But the messenger insisted: "I am here, and here is the letter; isn't that proof enough?"—"The letter proves nothing at all; besides, I haven't read it. And by the way, who gave it to you? The king in person?"—"No," confessed the messenger. "It was given to me by a royal page. In his name."—"Are you sure of that? And how can you be sure that it comes from the reigning sovereign? Have you ever seen him?"—"Never. My rank does not permit or warrant it."—"Then how do you know that the king is king? You see? You don't know any more than I."

And without unsealing the letter, the sage and the messenger decided to learn the truth once and for all. They would go to the end of the world, they would question the very last of mortals, but they would know.

At the marketplace, they accosted a soldier: "Who are you and what do you do?"—"I am a soldier by trade and I am in the king's service."—"What king?"—"The one to whom we swore allegiance; this land is his. We are all here to serve him."—"Do you know what he looks like?"—"No."—"Then you have never seen him?"—"Never."

The two companions burst into laughter: "Look at him! This man in uniform insists upon serving someone he has never seen and will never see!"

Further on, they met an officer: yes, he would willingly die for the king; no, he had never had the honor of seeing him, neither from close by nor from afar.

A general: same questions, same answers, clear and precise. He, too, thinks of nothing but to serve the king, he lives only for him and by him; and yet, even though he is a general, he cannot boast of ever having set his eyes upon the king.

"You see?" says the skeptical sage to the messenger. "People are naïve and credulous, and rather foolish; they live a lie and are afraid of the truth."[3]

The second story is this:

An atheist and a tzaddik were carrying on a long and complicated debate about the existence of God. As usual, neither was having any success in convincing the other. All of a sudden, the tzaddik became terror-stricken. "My God," he said, "what if what you say is true?" His momentary terror passed, but the atheist was so frightened by the look in the tzaddik's eyes that he was instantly converted.

---

3 Elie Wiesel, *Souls on Fire: Portraits and Legends of Hasidic Masters,* translated by Marion Wiesel (New York: Vintage, 1973), pages 172–74.

One Way of Teaching Morality
[March 28, 1990, delivered at a Board of Trustees meeting]

My subject is whether and how we faculty members promote ethics, morality, and the religious tradition at our school, and I will begin in what is perhaps an odd way—with some case histories. They are the kinds of moral problems that our students are called upon to deal with every day. Some details have been changed, for reasons that will be obvious. After I have presented each problem, take a moment to consider how you would respond to it and how you would use it as an opportunity to teach morality and religion.

Case 1: A student comes to me whose best friend has publicly said things that the community finds offensive. The administration has found the friend guilty and has ordered his punishment. This student asserts that his friend is innocent, that he had a right to say what he thought, which was not that bad, and that the administration is overreacting and being vindictive. He wants to know why his friend should not resist the unfair punishment. Wouldn't it be better to run away in protest? The whole class is arguing about the case. To complicate matters, I personally think the administration has behaved outrageously. What should I say to the students?

Case 2: A student whose father died a while back and whose mother has remarried enters the room in a state of anguish. From various conversations he has discovered that his stepfather, a fairly prominent local official, whom the student can't stand under the best of circumstances, is involved in a scam—in fact, has gained his position by fraud. The student is ashamed of his stepfather. He doesn't want to hurt his mother, but on the other hand he knows people are being hurt by the stepfather's dishonesty. The student feels that, according to the values taught him in school, it is wrong *not* to do something about it. He is afraid and confused and angry and desperate. The more he talks, the more suicidal he sounds. What have I to teach him that will help?

Case 3: A senior boy and a junior girl have been dating for a while, holding hands and smooching in the prayer garden. One day, the boy appears in my room unusually distraught. It seems that in a fit of desire and self-delusion the two of them have lost their innocence. The signs all point to trouble. He begins by blaming the girl—it was her fault, she had assured him it would be okay, she wanted to give him everything she had—in short, she intentionally tempted him. Meanwhile, she is saying that he should have known better, should have controlled himself, should have resisted. They feel their lives are ruined. They're afraid to confess and submit to parental authority, and they've begun to hate one another. What do I tell them?

There are many other cases I could describe: the girl whose boyfriend's father has found out that she's not wealthy enough to attend the school without a scholarship and for that reason is pressuring his son into breaking up with her; the girl who can deal with her tyrannical mother and the mother's abusive live-in boyfriend only by repeatedly fantasizing that her older brother, off at school, will come home and kill both of them; the girl whose neighborhood gang leader has threatened her that if she doesn't sleep with him, he will have her brother killed.

Every day I deal with problems like these, and as you can see, they are not easy. Often they are genuinely frightening. And they cannot be solved with simple platitudes or casual advice. They need to be lived with, struggled over, and suffered through. They are never solved once and for all but resurface in new forms and in different people. And always they are confrontations between the self and the world, confrontations which demand understanding and imagination and courage, and which severely test the deepest convictions that we at the school profess.

Now I know some of you are hoping that I've invented these cases out of whole cloth, because if not, then our students must be going to hell in a handbasket. But I have *not* invented them. And to prove it, I'm going to name names. I'm also going to name those who have helped me to respond to these dilemmas and thereby to learn and teach morality.

Case 1: The student whose friend is about to be punished is named Crito, and his friend is named Socrates. He accepts his friend's unjust punishment with the help of Socrates himself, who, speaking as if to himself in the voice of the Laws of Athens, says, "Do not think more of your children or of your life or of anything else than you think of what is right" (*Crito* 54c).

Case 2: The student whose stepfather is a villain is named Hamlet, and through his tragedy Shakespeare conducts us to the recognition that "There's a divinity that shapes our ends, / Rough-hew them how we will" and that "the readiness is all" (*Hamlet* V.ii.10–11, 222).

Case 3. The young man and woman in trouble are named Adam and Eve, and in *Paradise Lost* John Milton shows that having faith, hope, and love, the penitent Adam and Eve will have a happier paradise within them than that which they have lost.

The girl maligned by the snobbish and greedy father of her boyfriend is named Catherine Morland, and in *Northanger Abbey* Jane Austen shows us how her happiness is preserved by her own honesty and by the reason, conscience, justice, honor, and fidelity of her beloved Henry Tilney. The girl who wants her brother to kill her mother and her mother's lover is named Electra. She gets her wish, but in *The Eumenides*, Aeschylus shows us that, in the end, peace comes to families and to cities only when wisdom, through "holy persuasion," substitutes justice for vengeance and law for violence. And the girl whose brother's life seems to depend on her unchastity is named Isabel. She ends happily, but not before Shakespeare, in *Measure for Measure*, causes her to perform one of the most dramatic acts of mercy in all Christian literature.

Ladies and gentlemen, school is life. It is not a lab experiment. And children are not predictable substances upon whom we can work our preferred transformations. Nor can love of the good and the true be produced by formula. Teaching ethics and morality and spiritual values is a risky, slow, uncertain, often painful, though often rewarding business. Above all, it is a daily business. And it is part of what my colleagues and I do for a living.

How? Through chapel talks, religion courses, and casual conversations, yes. But also through our everyday teaching of philosophy, history, literature, language, and the arts. Contrary to popular opinion, these subjects are not addenda to life. They are not excess baggage which you leave aside when you want to teach values. In the works of the human imagination, just as in daily life, the spirit lives, and in them it can be taught. Plato and Shakespeare and Jane Austen are not merely subject matter. They are voices of the moral, ethical, and spiritual tradition that it is our duty to pass on to the next generation. In teaching them we are teaching how to live.

Billy B.'s Diary
[May 8, 1990]

DATE: Month 5 / Day 10 / Year 2090
TIME: 19:30
OPERATOR: Billy B.
SYSFUNC: Process
MODE: Diarecord

Dear Diarecorder,

This morning I figured out a way to get my carryware pacemaker-microprocessor to access the mainframe of this place. The first thing I did was to use the MINDWARP function to find out what I was doing a hundred years ago today. It was weird. It turns out I was sitting in chapel in high school listening to this:

DATE: Month 5 / Day 10 / Year 1990
TIME: 09:30
SYSFUNC: Mindwarp
MODE: Memoretrieve

START COPY

Because we are spiritual creatures, all human beings hunger for meaning. And because we are also physical creatures, all human beings hunger to experience meaning through the senses. We can define the Garden of Eden as that place where (or time when) this hunger was perfectly satisfied in every moment of perception. For meaning is another word for participation in a reality that is greater than we are, and in Eden sensation itself was a way of participating in the love that joined Adam and Eve to their creator, to one another, and to the rest of creation. But since our exit from the garden, it requires special blessing, and usually also extreme effort, to experience such participation. And yet we cannot live without it. So again and again we try to rediscover

Eden in worship and in art, in work and in play, in the love of people and of nature. And only when we find it, or it finds us, is our hunger for meaning temporarily satisfied.

Today I want to focus on the simplest and most obvious of the paths to meaning, namely the natural world, the one that we take most for gran...
END COPY

It didn't take long to get bored with that, so I left MINDWARP and accessed my medical prognosis. I can't say that deep down I was really surprised, but it was startling to see it in cold LCD: "Billy B.: Life expectancy 30 (±3) days." How fake it made those technomeds seem, who come on the screen in their dailies all nice and smiley as if I were going to live another hundred years. You'd think, since I'm paying $7,850 a day to stay in this godforsaken nursing dome, that the least they could do is tell the truth. But no, always the same boring, phony questions: "And how are we this morning? Have you got your slippers on? All your carryware programs updated? Oh, you've dropped your mini-terminal. Shall we send in your robonurse to get it for you?" Yes, you moron! Can't you see I'm stuck in this damned fusion chair and I'm nearly a hundred and twenty years old and I can't move an inch and I have a month to live?

For some reason I wanted to go outside today. I don't know why. The MINDWARP function was too weird, and I was sick of the hologravideo and the audiochromaton. I just wanted to see the brown sky for a change and breathe the unfiltered air. And anyway, how much can being outside hurt me now? The robonurse was horrified, of course, but I told her I had permission. Naturally she didn't believe me and called up my schedule on the screen. But I had entered the permission myself this morning when I found out I had only a month left. So, covering her intake with one hand, she helped me out through the airlocks, saying she'd be back for me in half an hour.

I don't know what I had hoped to find outside. Everything was silent except for the regular humming of the city's underground central service systems. The heavy atmosphere under the familiar tobaccite-colored sky made the light pretty much uniform. Of course there were no clouds, or anyway none visible. Haven't been any for ten or fifteen years, I guess. But my eyes are still good enough to catch the slightly brighter spot in the sky where the sun occasionally peeked through the billows of thick air. I even detected a shadow once or twice, cast by my fusion chair on the concrete.

All this — the silence, the outside, air, the hint of sun — was refreshing for a moment. But the feeling didn't last. Soon I was sad—terribly sad. I guess that's understandable, considering this morning's discovery. But it wasn't only that. I have my moments of terror about dying. But this sadness had something else in it. I knew no one would miss me, but I also asked myself over and over what in the world I would miss. The answer was nothing. And that thought made me feel like just plain crying, which I haven't done in years, about the emptiness of my life and about its rapidly nearing end. Like the ancient restaurant joke: the food there is terrible, and such small portions! I guess I *was* crying. I kept saying to myself, over and over, "nothing to miss, there's nothing left to miss," and wiping the slow tears.

I sat there for a while, till I almost forgot where I was. Eventually I turned my fusion chair around and was heading back to the airlocks when suddenly I heard a swooshing sound and something dark passed between me and the sky. I turned to find out what it was and saw that a pigeon had landed on the sidewalk near my chair and was prancing around, pecking here and there, looking for something to eat. A pigeon! I thought all the pigeons had disappeared years ago when the food started coming in capsules and all the trees died. I was amazed and sat staring at him, at his sleek feathers, his bobbing head, his eyes searching the barren concrete for a crumb to peck at. What could he have hoped to find by landing *here*? Did he have some vague memory that where there were human beings there might be food?

I tried to think how long it had been since I'd seen a pigeon. In my childhood of course there had still been pigeons — lots of them. They had swarmed around the terrace at school where we ate lunch every day. We used to complain about how they ate garbage, walked around on our tables, dropped surprises from the sky. People always called them filthy and disgusting. Some would even throw things at them. Why? Basking comfortably in the luxuries of real food and sunshine, what could we possibly have had against the pigeons, who innocently risked the menace of our hard shoes to feed themselves by cleaning up our mess? It must have been some school tradition to pretend to hate them, that's all. Prejudice. But why hadn't we seen their beauty as I was seeing it now? I sat gazing at the pigeon's neck, which shimmered pink and blue-green whenever a fleck of sun could reach it, the only natural color for a thousand miles, the sea being black with grime and our skin sallow from a lifetime of indoor lighting. That iridescent neck! Nothing I had seen in fifty years was as beautiful as the feathers in the neck of that pigeon.

It hit me then that the pigeon's beauty was something I would miss, *had* missed without knowing it. I wished I had some bits of capsule to give him, or anything edible, but I had nothing. So I just sat there, trying to remember whether I'd ever fed a pigeon in my life. I didn't think I ever had, at least not intentionally. And that made me sad, and I felt the tears coming again, because I was going to die in a month and had never in my life fed a pigeon.

I think I would have begun sobbing except that the pigeon shocked me out of it by hopping onto my right foot. Feeling his toes through my slipper was startling at first, and then exhilarating. I couldn't get enough of him—his orange eyes and sturdy beak and coral feet. He bobbed and tilted his head a few times, once or twice looking me in the eye with the same sharp attention he gave to everything. Then, all at once, he took off over my shoulder and flew away, disappearing into the brown haze of the sky. I still felt the echoes of sensation: his weight on my foot, the puff of wind his wings had fanned into my hair. But he was gone. I missed him, and missing him hurt. But in a way I couldn't understand I also felt happy. I felt that his visit and his beauty somehow were still in me.

I stopped praying during my last year in high school because I couldn't believe in a God who would allow suffering to exist. Believing in a meaningless universe seemed better than believing in a cruel God. And if the universe was meaningless, I was free to create my own meaning in life. But as I was going out of the murky air into the lighted nothingness of the nursing dome, I said a blessing in my heart for that pigeon, who had struggled to survive partly for my sake, though he couldn't have known it. And I thought I had survived all these long years partly for his sake too, to give his life an added meaning. So what if the meaning was greater than he could realize? I hadn't realized why I was going outside today either, though now I know it was to see him. Maybe our real purposes are different from what we think they are. Maybe we were both part of something that lives on in spite of the apparent emptiness around us, something more real than the world. And for some reason thinking so made me feel it would be easier to die.

When I got back to my niche in the nursing dome, two things happened. One was this: I realized that nothing can ever separate me from the pigeon, not even death, whatever it is, because he is part of reality, and so am I. And reality is not something we can hold on to or lose. Reality holds *us*.

The other thing that happened was that I discovered the pigeon had left me a present. He must have been getting food from somewhere, because when I happened to glance down at my right foot, there on my slipper was a thick white dropping. The instant the robonurse's sensors detected what I was smiling at, she got hysterical and went scurrying for her antibionizing fluid to clean it up. But I overrode her program.

Seniors Chapel[1]
[March 5, 1992]

Rabbi Tarfon, living in the first century, used to say: "It is not your duty to complete the work; neither are you at liberty to give it up." Rightly, your parents and teachers take pains to emphasize the second part of his sentence, putting on your shoulders the weight of practical and moral duties of all kinds. And that's as it should be. But today I want to focus on the first part of Rabbi Tarfon's sentence and help you unload some unnecessary weight. It is your duty to study and to work hard and to be good, paying the right kind of attention to your conscience, to your parents and teachers, to others, to nature, and to God. But it is *not* your duty to know what cannot be known, to be excellent at everything, to invent yourself, or to judge your soul. So your challenge is to discover your own place somewhere between giving up the work of the world (which would be wrong) and completing it (which is impossible).

To illustrate, I'm going to describe three liberations that I have experienced, each presided over by my great and beloved teacher, Mary Holmes.

Once, in graduate school, I was spiritually stuck. I was struggling to figure out how good I had to be to justify my existence. And I felt that to do so I had first to know the extent to which being good depended on my own will. I knew about free will and about providence or grace or whatever you want to call the help that comes from elsewhere. But I didn't know how much of the work of being good I had to do myself and how much God would do. Until I could answer that, I felt, I could not go on. And since I couldn't figure it out, I was miserable. The more I tried to solve the equation, the more frustrated and frightened I became, and the more I hated myself for not being able to solve it. Then one day Mary Holmes had occasion to observe that nothing in the universe happens without the grace of God. So I gathered my courage and asked, "But how much is grace and how much is up to us?" meaning, of course, how much was up to me.

---

1 Published in *The Chaplain's Craft* (a publication of the Council for Religion in Independent Schools), Volume 5, Number 3 (Spring 1993), page 1.

"Well, of course it's a great mystery," she said. "How can we possibly know?" My very soul heaved a sigh of relief. Mary went on to illustrate how people can go wrong in pretending to know the answer. The Calvinist doctrine of predestination ascribed all to grace and nothing to man. Certain pragmatists and existentialists leave nothing up to God. Both doctrines can lead to despair, where I had been headed. But the instant Mary said we couldn't know, I knew she was right, and I experienced liberation. When I realized I had been trying to do the impossible, I could let the job go, breathe again, and get on with my life. Trying to do my best was my business. Knowing how much trying would suffice was not.

But *how* does one do one's best? A second liberation came in a commencement address I heard Mary deliver. Have in mind those swimming lessons or poem analyses or diets or math problems that make life hell. Why can't we just get good at these things, if only to get them over with? In three short sentences Mary unloaded my soul's shoulders again:

"There is no excellence without discipline." You know this already, even if you don't know you know it. The world resists you. That basketball has no desire to go through the hoop. You have to make it go through, and wanting it to isn't enough. You have to practice. The same with writing poems or solving equations or being nice to your kid brother.

"But there is no such thing as self-discipline." What? You mean the over-thirty crowd has been lying to us? What were all those wind sprints if not self-discipline? And if there's no excellence without discipline, but there's no such thing as self-discipline, how does anyone ever achieve excellence at anything?

"There is only being disciplined by what you love." That is, only the passionate desire that we sometimes call love has the power to command the work, attention, and sacrifice necessary to achieving excellence. Whether the object of desire is the perfect shot, the thrill of victory, the adulation of the crowd, the approval of parents, the cash prize, or something secret and inexpressible, no one who is not moved by desire will have the discipline to achieve excellence. This holds as true for junk bond trading and forgery as for piano playing, writing essays, splitting atoms, relating to the opposite sex, and being virtuous. What keeps you drumming with your band in the garage till you get that song right when you should be in the house studying chemistry or reading Jeremy Bentham? It is not self-discipline. It is some passionate desire.

The second of my three liberations lay in knowing that we cannot become excellent at something for which we have no passion. Now be careful. I am not saying you should refuse to practice what you don't enjoy. You can and should become at least competent at all sorts of things. More importantly, you can't know whether or not something will inspire passion in you unless you have given it time and attention. But only passionate desire can make you submit to the discipline required for excellence. So you are hereby liberated from the guilt of not being the greatest _____ (fill in the blank) west of the Mississippi. It's because you don't desire it enough.

Which leads me to liberation number three: How can I get myself to desire what I ought to, or to desire it more? The answer? Impossible.

I hate formal lesson plans. I've never been able to do them, which is pretty absurd for a teacher. I tell myself "This is absurd. A teacher is someone who does lesson plans. I'll just sit down this minute and do a lesson plan." Immediately I have to decide whether to give the junk mail my undivided attention or to mop the kitchen floor. This situation, and many like it, used to fill me with guilt, and also fear. What if the headmaster finds out? But the guilt and the fear come from only one place: my false belief that because I love teaching and "teachers do lesson plans," I ought to want to do lesson plans.

Mary once wrote, "Accept yourself for what you are and reject categories." I looked up the word "category." It comes from the Greek word for accusation. Every category is an accusation. I am in the category "unable to do lesson plans," but so what? Whether it is a weakness or a strength, I have to live with it as best I can. Yet lesson plan or no lesson plan, my passion is to teach. So while other teachers may achieve excellence by doing lesson plans, I have to achieve it *not* doing them. To try to do them in spite of myself is to steal energy from teaching and to waste it. The same holds true for being tall or short, scientific or literary, rich or poor, liberal or conservative, nerdy or cool. To categorize oneself or others so is to reduce by an accusation. But every self in the world is far too complex, and far too mysterious, to fit comfortably into any categories we can think of.

My point is that you cannot choose what you desire or choose not to desire it. Desire is response, not invention. The only questions are whether you will acknowledge with courage and truth what commands your passion, whether you will say yes or no to it, and how you will then behave. This means that you do not need to invent yourself. You are a given. The possibilities for you are many and immeasurable, but they do not include being someone else. You must accept as given your parents and genes, your body and mind, your talents and weaknesses, your feelings and fears, your loves and hates. Now please do not misunderstand. This acceptance does not imply spiritual laziness or despair. Just the opposite. You can only become better, in fact become fully who you are meant to be, if you start from self-acceptance. You will never become a better basketball player by pretending that you're already as good as you need to be, or that you are doomed to being bad, or that the basketball will do the work. The same is true for the moral and for the spiritual life. To get anywhere worth getting, you have to start from where you are.

Finally, while it is important to judge your work, your actions, and your opinions, you do not need to judge your soul. God is a far more just judge of us than we are, but he is also a far more merciful one. We become much better at being ourselves when we stop trying to be him.

To the Class of '93
[April 22, 1993]

Last week the chaplain talked about the leap of faith required of us, and in our *Cum Laude* ceremony we were instructed to give ourselves to something larger than we are. Today I want to take the next step and discuss not the what of faith, but the how. Even if you are not struggling with the question of religious faith just now, all of you are having to make a leap of faith in choosing the best college for you. So I want to ask the question "How does one make a leap of faith?" You can go to only one college, yet you cannot know in advance what being there will actually be like. So how is it possible to choose? Even if in theory you accept that you should serve something bigger than you are, how can you choose it? And if you don't already believe in God, how can you possibly choose to do so? I hope you will be as relieved as I was to learn the answer: You can't. If by choosing a college or choosing what to serve or making a leap of faith you mean inventing the power within yourself to "just do it," the answer is that it simply isn't possible.

Now I will digress a moment to say that from my own experience, and from the glimpses into your lives that you and other students have permitted me, I conclude that a large amount of the world's avoidable suffering is caused by fear. Often we suffer nearly as much over imaginary disasters as we do over actual ones, which for most of us are mercifully fewer. "What if I choose Yoknapatawpha U. and I don't understand the professors' accents and my roommate is a neatness freak?" "What if I'm too sophisticated for Mulligatawny College but not smart enough for Fandango University?" "What if I give myself to what's bigger than me and it crushes me?" "What if my big leap of faith plunges me into the mire of hypocrisy?" Or "What if I *don't* leap and God assigns me a permanent detention?" Do you recognize these inner voices of fear? And do you recognize the parallel inner voices of free-floating guilt? "College? With your pretentious personality, weak will, nervous habits, thin-ice grades, and zits? Get a life!" Or "Something bigger than *you*? Fat chance, you self-absorbed, self-centered, egotistical cloakbag of selfishness." Or "Believe in God? Who are you, Mother Theresa? You can't even believe in

Santa Claus. You can't even believe in recycling. Get a life!" Interesting, that phrase "get a life." As if anyone could.

But we won't leave you alone, will we? We believers, I mean. We begin to sound to you something like this: "Come on, you can do it if you want to, you really can, just try, we know you can, we really really do, we did it, come on, just a little leap, it's for your own good, come on, try." And then two voices within you fight over who's going to answer. The voice of despair whines, "I know I should make a leap, but I just can't. I'm no good. I've never been any good. And I never will be. I've always known I'm hopeless. Please give up on me." And the other inner voice shouts, "Leave me alone, blast you! You tell me to make a leap of faith? I'd rather die and rot. I can't believe the stuff and that's that. And I won't pretend to when I don't. If I'm damned for that, fine. Anything's better than your everlasting bushwa!"

Well, at last a voice of truth. The voice is impolite and the truth is partial, but it is truth, and I will tell you why. I will tell you in the words of my beloved friend Philip Thompson. He was a poet, dedicated to celebrating the divine and human mysteries and to mocking all the false voices of our age. I had written an argument that must have sounded to him very much like the voices I have been quoting to you. His reply worked its way into my soul and has never left it. He wrote, "What has not come from the ego will not be domesticated by the ego… True surrender is not the work of the will but is compelled in the presence of gods, and if it is true surrender, to him who hath (*truly* surrendered) shall be given and from him who hath not shall be taken away…"

Philip's words resolve the question "How does one make oneself believe?" But they don't do so by offering an answer. They don't provide any self-help method. Instead they totally discredit the question itself, and in doing so they transform the questioner. "True surrender is not the work of the will," he writes. You cannot will yourself to serve something bigger than yourself, or to believe in God, or even to pick the right college. "True surrender … is compelled in the presence of gods." That is, every leap of faith is a *response* to a reality outside the self. You cannot make yourself leap into faith, any more than you can make yourself fall in love. You can only *be moved* to do so. You are not called to invent your faith in God out of your mere self. You are not called to create in yourself a devotion to that which is bigger than you. It can't be done. You are not even called to determine what will be the right college for you. How could you, having no such foreknowledge in you? When I say "I chose to go to Santa Cruz," what I really mean is this: "In response to the vision of U.C. Santa Cruz that U.C. Santa Cruz gave birth to in me, I said yes. To say no to it I would have had to be—or to be trying to be—someone else, different from who I was."

May I give you another example from my own life? In 1985 I was invited to this school for an interview. I was also invited to a state college in Massachusetts. I knew I might get offers from both schools, and before the interviews I felt I needed to decide which position I wanted most. It seemed a very difficult choice. Massachusetts meant my dream of college teaching, a tenure-track position, proximity to Boston and to friends. This school meant the unknown of high school teaching but also a more close-knit community, mild winters, and proximity to my family and other friends. Though the pay was about the same then, it would be more at the college in the long run, and I'd have a lighter teaching load. Here, a thousand bureaucratic duties but no publish-or-perish threat. I couldn't decide. So I went out into the woods, crossed the footbridge over the stream, and sat down to think. I balanced every fact, idea, hope, fear, and expectation. And after two full hours of plashing water, natural beauty, and intense mental struggle, I was absolutely stuck. I could decide nothing, except to return to my apartment.

Then, as I was walking back through the woods, defeated, a voice spoke to me. It wasn't an external voice, but it wasn't my voice either. And I did not think up what it said. It just came to me: "You can't decide," it said, "so don't. You really can't decide, so stop trying. Go to the school that wants you most." And my response was, "Of course! Why didn't I think of that? Of course!" Well, the rest, as they say, is history. It soon became obvious where I was most wanted, and though I was frightened when I said yes here—what if high school teaching turned out to be a total disaster and college teaching refused to take me back?—the fear I felt was irrelevant. My leap had been made, and it had been made in response to a reality so clear that not leaping was unimaginable.

My point is that as long as I thought choosing was purely an act of my own will based on my own best interests, I was paralyzed. The direction I must take came clear only when I admitted the truth of my actual condition—that I was stuck. Only then could I hear a voice not my own. Only then could I see that though I could not invent the right choice, I could respond rightly. And seeing that was believing. As soon as that reality was clear to me, the leap was as easy as crossing back over the footbridge.

Now, there is something important that I am *not* saying. I am not saying that we have no free will and no responsibility, that everything is predestined, that we can just snooze on till vision hits. We do have free will and there is work for it to do. But, as I said to the seniors last year, we cannot know, in any act of choosing, how much depends on our own free will and how much is compelled. The border between our freedom and internal or external necessity is a mystery. And it is not our responsibility to solve that mystery, nor is it in our power to do so.

What *is* in our power and what *is* our responsibility is this: to ready ourselves for vision by striving toward right thinking and right action. And we can do that by paying careful attention to the visions that we have already been granted. Not all visions come like tidal waves. Some are simple and familiar, like courtesy in a doorway or a troubled conscience. Have you ever been moved to admiration by someone who has spoken the truth, small or large? Then strive to know and speak the truth. "I plagiarized on that research project because I was afraid of disappointing my father, who wants to think I'm smarter than I really am." Have you ever been overcome by a rush of love for someone who has been unselfish toward you? Then strive to be unselfish. "You take this chair; I'll find another one." Have you ever been filled with joyful wonder at the unfathomable mystery of a flower or a hummingbird or your own mysterious self? Then strive to attend to the mysteries that surround you. In other words, pay attention to what your own experience invites you to see. That is your spiritual homework. I had to sit by that stream debating with myself for those two hours before I could see that my indecision itself was sending me a message. The message was "Stop trying to invent a decision. Listen to what is."

If you are striving to clarify your sight, you are not to blame for not yet wholeheartedly believing that Berkeley is for you or that Shakespeare is great or that money isn't everything or that God is God. Because seeing is believing, and if you haven't seen it yet, there's no way you can make yourself believe it. The college you go to, the person you marry, the faith you make your own—all these can be chosen only in response to the vision of a reality outside your self that compels your self to respond. And then, "to him who hath (*truly* surrendered) shall be given." But you are responsible for looking, not just with your eyes but with all that you are. You are responsible for considering all the elements involved in choosing a college, a career, a mate, a form of worship. You are not permitted to delude yourself by turning to the dice or to the astrology column or to the majority opinion or to the likes of David Koresh or to any other false prophet to make your choices for you. Your job is to pay attention, with courage and patience, to the realities that your experience and conscience and heart reveal. Pay attention to those scriptures and traditions and to those works of art that, for you, make the invisible truth visible. And pay attention to any poet or preacher or teacher or friend who helps you to see for yourself what is. You cannot call reality into being. It calls you. What you can do is listen to what has moved you and strive to be ready.

Machines and Fear
[Chapel Talk for the Senior Class, May 18, 1995]

As a consequence of the death of my friend Philip, I have taken on the task of editing a collection of his works.[1] In order to do that, I have sought the help of a machine. I have bought a computer, so-called, for its capacity to remember and reproduce lots of words and their arrangement in a short time. This purchase has made a huge, though I hope temporary, change in my life. It has turned me into an obsessive-compulsive fanatic.

I used to read literature in spare moments. Now I frantically pore over *Word for Windows for Dummies*. I used to think about good and evil, meaning and futility, time and eternity, the blessing of life and the curse of death. Now I think about directories and menus, formats and fonts, cursors and cursing. The cursing happens because the computer doesn't respond to normal human expectations. If I am to get it to do what I want, I must reformat myself to satisfy *its* expectations. Of course accomplishing anything requires adjustment. Nothing in the world simply obeys our will. But to run my computer I must begin to think like a machine.

This highly frustrating experience of having to conform myself to a machine has reminded me of Jacques Ellul's assertion that ours is the Age of Technique, an age in which we get better and better at answering *"how can it be done?"* and worse and worse at asking *"why should it be done?"* I have learned to play solitaire on my new computer, for example. But why should I pay for the electricity and suffer the muscle tension and radiation pollution when I can play solitaire perfectly well with a harmless deck of cards? Is shuffling such a chore that I need a computer to do it for me? Does the computer's mouse feel nicer to the touch than a playing card? Or consider the radio ad I once heard, in which the Cadillac's air conditioning system was praised as so subtle and automatic that one feels no temperature change when the sun goes behind a cloud. Think of the advance in civilization! Thanks to modern technology, at last no one (at least

---

1 Gideon Rappaport, editor, *Dusk and Dawn: Poems and Prose of Philip Thompson* (San Diego: One Mind Good Press, 2005).

no one who can afford a Cadillac) has to live in terror of the thermostatic torments of a partly cloudy day. What an inspiration to get rich!

The Cadillac ad ominously implies that humanity's ultimate goal is to be effortlessly protected by machines from every uncomfortable natural variation, every uncontrolled sensation. Would that be life? No wonder my generation and yours have swathed themselves in high decibel music and risked their future with narcotic and hallucinogenic drugs. These are understandable (though counterproductive) responses to society's most inventively pursued goal—i.e., total human insensibility. Conditioned air, processed food, processed words, programmed entertainment—are we making machines to serve us or turning ourselves into machines to serve them?

Why *should* we want to avoid feeling the sun go behind a cloud? What the Cadillac ad is really appealing to is our fear of death. I know that sounds extreme, but think about it for a moment. The young don't buy Cadillacs. The ad is appealing to older, wealthier comfort-seekers, who might buy a Cadillac if persuaded it could secure their comfort from the invasion of unwanted forces of nature. And that imaginary security promises relief from the awareness of inevitable death. The trouble is that the more we reduce ourselves to a machine-like state in order to control or avoid the uncontrollable, the more like dead we become. The ad makes sun and clouds seem a nuisance; once we conform ourselves to the air conditioning system, the sun and clouds become entirely irrelevant and yet another bit of our natural life has been abolished from our consciousness. This may partly explain the suicide rate too. When all the subliminal messages of our culture imply that life is a futile attempt to distract us from the fear of the inevitable, why not get the inevitable over with? The dead presumably do not feel the sun's going behind a cloud either, and death has the advantage of being permanent, entirely removing the fear of death—"he that cuts off twenty years of life / Cuts off so many years of fearing death," says Shakespeare's stoical Casca after helping to kill Julius Caesar. And death is less expensive than a Cadillac.

Thank God there is a better alternative. We can have courage. We can courageously turn off the air conditioning, open the windows (not the Microsoft Windows!), and expose ourselves to the cold and the heat of nature a little more. Of course bypassing the machine may result in some surprises from nature's variety, but, in Southern California at least, many of them are likely to be pleasant. In any case, in feeling them are we closer to or further from the death we fear?

Needless to say, I am talking not only about physical sensation. When we ourselves seem stuck in repetitive thoughts, mechanical feelings, automatic behaviors, and begin mangling our daily life to fit them, it is almost always because of an unconscious desire to have the absolute control over our lives that the Cadillac ad promises we can have over our air. And the desire for absolute control not only drives us to reformat ourselves into controllable mechanisms. It also leads inevitably to the fear of *losing* control, and that fear is, in disguise, the fear of death. Nine times out of ten it is this fear that lies behind writer's block, drunkenness, drug abuse, grade grubbing, wallet stealing, hurtful graffiti, cheating, and so on.

What can prevail against such fear? Well, courage. And how do we get courage? Wouldn't you like me to offer you a technique? Wouldn't you pay a lot for a computer or a Cadillac that could deliver you from fear? You see why Jacques Ellul is right?

But courage is no mere technique and cannot be bought. It is a gift of the spirit. It is given to some and not to others. It may be given when we think we don't need it and not given when we think we do. Worst of all, it may be offered but not accepted. And no one can tell you why. But at a crucial time in my life I was given an *image* of courage that has proved extremely helpful, and I thought I would share it with you. Some of you have heard it before.

You are living in a house seemingly happily, going through all the motions of life without visible problems. But day and night, while you are eating and sleeping, talking and thinking, succeeding and failing, you are simultaneously holding the front door closed against a monster that is trying to get in to kill you. You do pretty well at getting everything done while half your attention and energy are devoted to protecting yourself and your world from that unseen monster, but you are beginning to get tired. Yet the more you try to forget about the monster, the harder he pushes on the door.

Pretty soon the quality of your accomplishments and of your attention to other people and to activities suffers, the natural sparkle goes out of things, and living becomes a chore. Your thoughts and actions and feelings become mechanical, spiritless. You may even begin to do things harmful to yourself and perhaps to others. Yet all the while you never question the need to keep that door closed against the monster. Your misery increases until you feel that anything would be better than this life of endless anxiety, and, in a fit of desperation, you throw the door open.

What do you find on the other side? A small child in a Halloween mask saying, "Boo!" You recognize that it is this child who has been pushing on the door the whole time. You tell the child to run along, the game is over. Now the door is open. You can go in and out at will. You can concentrate on what you really care about. When you close the door, it stays closed. When someone knocks, you are not afraid to open it. You feel, at last, free and happy to be alive.

The problem is that before we do it, it feels as though to open the door is to die. Consider what it takes to say, "Doctor R., I feel like a failure because I haven't been able to write a word of my essay. Can you help me?" or "Mrs. M., I'm ashamed to admit it but I'm drinking too much and can't stop. Can you help me?" or "Dear God, I feel like I'd rather be dead. Help me!" These confessions take everything we've got. Because usually what they really mean is "I'm afraid of losing control" or "afraid of being myself" or "afraid of being unloved." Confessing these fears feels like letting happen exactly what we're afraid of, and that is so scary that until we do it, it feels like dying. As a result, most of us avoid facing these monsters until we get so desperate that we feel we have nothing to lose. And some of you, I know, can take a hell of a lot of anguish before getting to that point.

But if we do throw the door open, if we do say "Doctor R., help" or "Mrs. M., help" or "Dear God, help me," suddenly, in the twinkling of an eye, what a liberation we feel! Not that all our problems vanish. But having invited what we fear to declare itself, at last we are free of our imaginary fears (which are usually worse), free to focus our attention, free to enjoy the good in life and to meet its *real* trials with all our resources available. And when we see that the monster is only the leftover phantom of a childhood terror posing no real threat, we can forgive it and ourselves. We may eventually even be able to recognize it as having been a gift. If the monster had been less persistent, would we ever have thrown open the door?

So courage in relation to the kinds of fear I've been discussing turns out to be something like willingness to face the undisguised truth. Of course, we do not come to this moment of truth entirely on our own. We are compelled to it, mostly against our will, by all that we are and have been and by all the rules of reality, from gravitation and ionic bonding to the Ten Commandments to the limit on the patience of our friends. But it is *also* an act of will, and therefore potentially an act of virtue, because at the crucial moment—which may be *any* moment—we can also choose *not* to face the truth. We can choose to continue trusting in the protection of our mechanical denials, as in the Cadillac's air conditioning system, to the end. Yet who of us does not know that even the smallest acknowledgment of truth brings such relief that we wonder why we ever resisted it? After the fact, who would not prefer Doctor R.'s passing jab ("I bet you did your *science* homework!") to the ongoing anxiety about his finding out that you haven't read the literature assignment?

I believe this moment of courage I have been describing is also an image of what life looks like from the viewpoint of eternity. Is the death we fearfully imagine anything more than a phantom monster we have not yet confronted? The dying we are all forced to do one way or another is a final surrender of our will back to the infinite love that gave it to us. What makes it possible to accomplish that surrender with courage is an intuition that we do not contain reality as an idea in our minds as we do our imaginary monsters, but rather reality contains us and means our good. If it were not so, truth would lead only to pain and not also to joy, and fear and self-delusion would lead to happiness. But they don't and can't, and we all know it from experience.

Finally, the image of the whole universe as a machine, a soulless physical entity undergoing a meaningless physical process, an image bequeathed to us by the likes of Descartes and Darwin, is also a phantom, an imaginary monster at the door of the modern world. And fear of it will tend to reduce us more and more to machines until, in a moment of courage, we fling open the door to discover that Dante and Shakespeare and Dickens and my friend Philip in the works I am editing were right, that fear of reality, though understandable and forgivable, is an error, that reality is in fact loving and holds us securely. Granted the courage to discover that, we can enjoy in freedom, even in the face of death, the meaningful natural life and the promise of eternal joy for which we and the world were created.

Three Rules of Life
[1996, revised 1999]

I was asked to talk in chapel about how we at our school behave toward one another. I did so by examining three perhaps familiar rules of life.

If you have not yet entered the state of rebellion against all authority, or have got through it to the other side, you know that there is more to any good rule than the power of the strong over the weak. Every rule, even a school rule, also always implies a view of the meaning of things.

Our school uniform rules, for example, imply the belief that the growth of your inner life is of greater meaning than the impressiveness of your external image. Whether you prefer to exhibit more of your colorful boxers than of your Black Watch plaid, whether you prefer to wear your belt around your knees or around your armpits, the uniform says that it is who and what you are inside that really counts. Similarly, detentions for tardiness assert that what begins in the classroom when class starts is or ought to be valuable and important. Even the rule about not walking on the quad before noon exists not only to protect the grass but to protect our common appreciation for the beauty of our campus and the labor of our gardeners [see "Cutting Corners on the Quad" in Other Writings].

The three rules I want to discuss now are not particular to our school but universal, and whether we know it or not, all of us have been following one or more of them all our lives. I'll call them the iron, the silver, and the golden rules. Iron, I remind you, is hard, dull, and worthless as currency, and wherever humans can live, iron will rust. Silver is softer, shinier, and more valuable as currency, though it will tarnish with time and the human touch. Gold is the softest of the three, the brightest, and the most precious. Hidden or visible, it is always incorruptible, in earth, water, air, and fire.

Each of the three universal rules I want to discuss, the iron, the silver, and the golden, not only sets a standard for human behavior but also implies something about the meaning of life. Specifically, each asserts something about the maker of the rule, something about the nature of human relationships, and something about the nature of the world.

The first, the iron rule, can be expressed in many ways: "Look out for number one," "I have my rights," "It's not my problem," "Follow your bliss," "Who are you to tell me what to do?"

Who is the maker of this rule? What relationships can we expect to prevail under it? And what is the nature of the world in which it intends to operate? Clearly, the maker of the rule "Look out for number one" is number one, the self. According to this rule, whatever my own self wants is right. If I want something, I *should* have it. As for relationships, they too exist for the sake of my self. There are other selves out there that think I exist for the sake of their selves, but that is irrelevant to me. So far as the iron rule is concerned, they exist merely as means to my self's ends.

Under this iron rule, relationships of trust, loyalty, or justice are impossible because the desires of the self may overrule all other commitments at any moment. If my rule is "look out for number one," then betraying number two or three or twelve will be okay if number one stands to benefit. Hence the world implied by the iron rule is that of Hobbes's state of nature—the war (or at least the competition) of all against all. Meaning lies only in my grades, my college acceptance, my career, my feelings, my pleasures, my rights, my goals, my life, the key word being *my*.

You've all seen the iron rule in practice. It is the rule I am following when I take someone's book from his locker or backpack because I need it, and the rule someone else is following when my book is the one taken. It is the rule I follow when a dented fender in the parking lot is only my business if it is my fender that has been dented. My self's desires being paramount, how can I be faulted for ditching my date at the prom when between invitation and prom night I've fallen in love with someone else? That teachers and fellow students would feel betrayed if they knew I had plagiarized my term paper is too bad for them. My priority is to get my self ahead. That's what life is about—looking out for number one.

To graduate from the iron rule to the silver rule is to take a significant moral step. The silver rule may be expressed by the now popular sentence "What goes around comes around." Its author is the structure of the universe itself, whether called necessity or fate or the laws of nature.

Relationships under the silver rule will be characterized by calculation and fear and occasionally relief. And the world implied by it is a mechanism, one that enacts an unpredictable but inexorable justice. So-and-so took my book from the terrace and didn't give it back in time for me to take it to class. Oh well, eventually he'll be paid back: What goes around comes around. Last month So-and-so dented someone's car and didn't admit it; today someone dented her car: See? What goes around comes around.

The silver rule is not really one we choose to follow, though we can choose whether or not to admit we've dented someone's car. As the rule implies, it is the universe itself that follows the rule. We follow it not by choice but by necessity. Nonetheless, to live in the universe of the silver rule demands careful calculation. We had best look out for number one by keeping an eye on the other numbers also because injustices are eventually repaid one way or another.

My great teacher, Mary Holmes, often reminded people that we all tend to want mercy for ourselves and justice for our enemies. With the silver rule we get half our desire. There is a kind of justice for everyone. One who takes the silver rule as her guide will be likelier to stick with her prom date for the evening out of fear of being ditched on some future evening by the new boyfriend. The obeyer of the silver rule will be discouraged from plagiarism by fear of potential consequences, whether the teacher finds out or not.

This is a moral advance over the iron rule because it recognizes that something out there sometimes says no even when the self says yes, that what goes around may come around and kick the self's butt. Of course it can be seen more positively as well. If what goes around does come around, then we may hope that if we brought in a can of Alpo for the pet food drive last week, we'll get an A on the Spanish quiz today. Though its underlying principle is still selfishness, the silver rule modifies the iron rule by implying that there will be rewards for good deeds as well as by recognizing that every merely selfish act may become a boomerang.

The third rule, the golden rule, you already know. It is expressed in the Torah by the sentence "Love your neighbor as yourself," and in the New Testament by the sentence "Do unto others as you would have others do unto you." To graduate to this rule is an even greater moral step. The establisher of this rule is neither a limited self nor a mindless process. It is an infallible higher will that creates us precisely for the purpose of caring about more than ourselves.

The relationships promoted by the golden rule are not between subjects and objects but between living souls who are mutually free to be both trusting and trustworthy, free to give of the self without calculating consequences or rewards. And the world is the garden of our freedom to choose between participation and isolation, between harmony and discord, between really connecting with others and being alone even when we are among people. The rule says do unto others what you'd have others do unto you whether doing so looks out for number one or not, whether what comes around goes around or not.

One who lives by the golden rule, as I know many of you strive to do, will refrain from taking someone else's book, even if it would be useful, not because he fears the consequences from discipline committees or fate but because he doesn't want the book's owner to have to do without it any more than he wants to do without it himself. Trying to follow the golden rule, a student will encourage the denter of a fender in the parking lot to admit the fault and repay the debt, or will even report the incident to an authority, for several reasons: because if her car were the one dented she'd want to know who was responsible, because if she had dented someone else's car she'd want to pay for its repair, and because she does not want to live in a community of unrepentant fender-denters and uncaring witnesses.

A prom date who abides by the golden rule would not leave her date unaccompanied because she recognizes in him a soul that is capable of the same pain she herself would feel if she were similarly abandoned. In addition, for the sake of her newer and truer love, would she not want to be the sort of person who does not renege on her promises? Finally, no student who accepts the golden rule as law could bear to plagiarize because he would know that his false pretense turns his grade, his awards, his parents' approval, his college acceptance letters, and his reputation to dust. As he wants to trust in the validity of others' communications with him, so he will not falsify his communications with others.

According to the iron rule, my raw desires are the only ruler, other people are my tools, and the world is a slot machine from which my nickels of selfishness may win jackpots of pleasure. The iron rule makes of me a slave to the hungers of my limited self.

According to the silver rule, the ruler is the invisible laws of necessity or fate, other people are as likely to be my punishment as my pleasure, and the world is a checking account from which I can withdraw no more nor less than what I have deposited. It makes of me either a well-oiled or a sticky cog in a machine over whose operations I have no control.

According to the golden rule, the ruler is a loving will that has created me and all other selves with the desire to be cared about and with the freedom and the duty to care about others. Under this rule every relationship with another person is potentially a relation of love and as such carries absolute value and ultimate meaning. And this rule alone implies that the world is an inheritance of incalculable treasures which I can truly enjoy only if I am willing to share them. To graduate from the iron rule to the silver rule to the golden rule is to move from the perpetual slavery of selfishness through the perpetual constraint of necessity toward the perpetual freedom of love.

My conclusion is this: Whether our school seems to you a garden of caring or a prison of rules, every legitimate rule of this community—of any true community—grows out of an attempt to graduate us all into the embrace of the golden rule. That is the graduation that makes all the others worth celebrating.

What Is Knowledge For?
[Cum Laude Address, April 27, 2001]

Thank you for the honor of being invited to speak on this happy occasion.

I want first to offer my congratulations to the new members of the Cum Laude Society for their manifold academic achievements and to wish all the members of the Class of 2001 a lifetime of joy in learning. I would also like to take this opportunity to express publicly my deep personal gratitude for being an ongoing beneficiary of the learning of my colleagues at school, and in particular of the extraordinary moral and intellectual integrity of Mr. Richard Kirk and Mr. David Morgan.

Mr. Headmaster, Deans, Colleagues, Students, and Guests: By way of celebrating excellence in the pursuit of knowledge, I thought we should challenge ourselves today with the following question: What is knowledge for?

Some audiences would think this question too easy. To them it is obvious that knowledge is for getting grades, and thereby for pleasing parents, deans of college admissions, and future employers. This illustrious audience, however, will wisely desire a few moments to come up with a better answer. While you are doing so, I want to talk about dogs.

My teacher, the artist Mary Holmes, observes that, besides man, the dog is the only creature with a conscience. Of all the animals, only a dog can be trained by its master's approval or disapproval implied in the use of phrases like "good dog!" and "bad dog!" By contrast, just try saying "bad horse!" or "bad parrot!" or "bad kitty!" and see how far you get.

Mary Holmes has mythically depicted the origin of the canine conscience in a painting of Adam and Eve. The painting records her conviction that "after Adam and Eve ate the apple, they threw its core on the ground, and the dog checked it out, as dogs always do, and ate the core. And so all dogs recognize good and evil." It is perhaps upon this kinship in the knowledge of good and evil that all the loving relation of mutual help, affection, and fidelity between us and dogs is founded.

However, despite the dog's morally supreme place in the animal kingdom by virtue of its unique relation to man, there are some obtuse and cruel human experimenters in cosmetic, cognitive, and biomedical research who every day pay human jobbers to procure for them what they outrageously call "junk dogs." Such potential best friends to man these human beings then subject to hideous tortures for the sake of knowledge. This betrayal of man's calling to husband well the garden of the world raises my question: What is that knowledge for?

Other kinds of scientific experiment raise the same question. The infamous psychology experiments performed by Stanley Milgram at Yale in the early 1960s were constructed to demonstrate whether wholesome Americans, like Germans during the Nazi Holocaust, could be made to inflict murderous torture in obedience to authority. The experimenter set his subjects the following task: They were to give commands to someone in another room and, if the person resisted those commands, they were to prod him with electric shocks whose voltage they controlled. Dressed in a white lab coat, the experimenter did his best to persuade the subjects to increase the voltage of the jolts despite the cries of pain of the supposed victim. The person being electrically prodded was in fact an actor, pretending to disobey, then to suffer agonies, finally to fall silent in response to the punishing shocks. The obtuse Professor Milgram was himself shocked to discover that the majority of his subjects were very easily talked into inflicting what they believed to be lethal doses. Those miserable human guinea pigs had to live the rest of their lives knowing that under the banal conditions of a university psychology experiment, they had, morally speaking, become murderers. Since almost any significant artistic, social, or religious tradition in the world could have informed Professor Milgram that not only Germans and Americans but all men, including Yalies, are capable of evil when deprived of the conditions that foster good in us, of what value was that experiment? What did Milgram think knowledge was for?

What was knowledge for to the Nazi medical experimenters who, among many worse experiments I won't mention, broke the bones of human beings in the same spots over and over to discover how often human bones would knit up again? Needless to say, when the human subjects of those experiments ceased to be useful, they were tossed into gas ovens and thence into incinerators. Surely medical knowledge gained at this cost is infinitely worse than any disease.

Now some of you will falsely imagine that I am attacking scientific experimentation itself. It isn't so. Why would I take so absurd a position, when my life and others as dear to me as mine would before now have been lost without it? It is not experiment that I am opposing but experiment that in the name of knowledge abandons all *other* values.

My question "What is knowledge for?" applies as much to the humanities as to the sciences. In college I knew an English professor who professed that the villains of Shakespeare's *King Lear* were the real heroes of the play and the virtuous characters were boring. He thought he was being clever and original. To him power-hunger was real and virtue was a preachy old platitude. In using his extensive knowledge of Shakespeare and the authority it conferred on him to promote these ideas, he was in fact doing his best to rob his students of their natural and true responses to one of the world's greatest works. What did he think knowledge was for? Was it for producing a society of power-hungry cynics?

In the colleges and universities you will be attending there will be professors—avoid them if you can—whose knowledge in their fields of art, language, literature, history, and government will be marshaled into the service of blindingly narrow political or social agendas: whether the race, class, and gender follies of the left or some vainglorious Social Darwinism of the right—though there are not many right-leaning professors to be found in most colleges these days. There will be others for whom the pursuit of knowledge is merely a disguise for the pursuit of career advancement. You may even come upon a professor who imports all the apparatus of historical and rhetorical knowledge (except honesty) to prove that Abraham Lincoln was the enemy of the slaves or that the Nazi Holocaust never happened. Here bits of knowledge are pressed into the service of big fat lies. I don't mean to sour you on the idea of going to college. There will be true and good pursuers of knowledge teaching there too. But you must seek them out with discernment, and then "Grapple them unto thy soul with hoops of steel."[1]

There are many reasons, historical and moral, that our culture has forgotten to ask what knowledge is for. Even if I were sure I knew them all, I wouldn't have time to go into them today. But I will mention the unquestioned assumption, which we inherit from the Enlightenment, that the progress of human reason is linear, forward, infinite, and inevitable, and that with every bit of knowledge we add to our store and lose nothing. As Wendell Berry describes the situation, "Nobody … is attempting to figure out how much of the progress resulting from this enterprise is *net*. It is as if a whole population has been genetically deprived of the ability

---

1 William Shakespeare, *Hamlet*, I.iii.63.

to subtract."[2] In other words, are we losing more than we are gaining?

We might be corrected about the assumption that knowledge automatically equals progress both by some knowledge of history and by even the slightest attention to the meaning of the Genesis story about the Tree of Knowledge. But having been told by our culture, rather paradoxically, that the facts of history are not relevant and that Bible stories are not historical, we have ignored both. As a result, we have drifted into what Jacques Ellul calls the Age of Technique, in which we are superb at asking *how* something *can* be done but terribly bad at asking whether it *should* be done.[3] How can we send a man to the moon and bring him safely back? That question we have brilliantly answered. But who bothers to explain to us *why* we should do so?

So what is knowledge for? Have you come up with a good answer? Perhaps most of us would start with "to satisfy curiosity" and then add "to better the human condition." But what do we mean by "better"? Have we spent any time and energy on gaining *that* knowledge?

Here is my own answer, subject to correction, of course. Knowledge is for two kinds of purpose: On the one hand, knowledge is for satisfying our natural human curiosity, enjoying intellectual adventure, fulfilling our divine gift of reason, improving practical living conditions for ourselves and others, and appreciating the wonders of creation. On the other hand, knowledge can be used to gratify our lust for wealth, power, and all the forms of self-aggrandizement. These two sets of purposes are usually intermixed, but the difference between them can be discerned. That difference does not lie in the content of the knowledge itself. Both the biochemist and the Shakespeare scholar may be evil or good or both. The difference between the two kinds of purpose lies in the extent to which the pursuit of knowledge comes under the government of principles that are *higher* than knowledge.

In John Milton's *Paradise Lost*, the angel Raphael tells the yet unfallen Adam that

> ...knowledge is as food, and needs no less
> Her temperance over appetite, to know
> In measure what the mind may well contain.[4]

---

2 Wendell Berry, *Life Is a Miracle: An Essay against Modern Superstition* (Washington D.C.: Counterpoint Press, 2000), page 21.
3 See *The Technological Society*.
4 VII.126–28.

That is, the desire for knowledge, like the desire for food, must be governed by the virtue of temperance. As it is possible to go astray by not caring to know anything, so it is possible to go astray by trying to know too much or to know things forbidden or to know things not worth the cost of the knowing. Shall we intellectualize and experiment in order to gain knowledge about the future, or love, or God? Well, yes, up to a point. But beyond that point we will be trying to reduce to mere knowledge what can give meaning to our lives only by being *more* than knowledge. That which is greater than we can comprehend only retreats further away when we try to grasp it as knowledge. Consider the knowledge Masters and Johnson gained about sexuality by attaching electrodes to body parts. Was it worth what was lost in such experiments? What is knowledge about sexuality for when we banish intimacy, modesty, and love in order to get it?

I challenge you to ask what knowledge is for because if you don't, you will be tempted either to abandon all pursuit of knowledge or to sacrifice for it what is more valuable than knowledge: You will be tempted to sacrifice virtue. But, as Dr. Otto Mower reminded us not long ago in this building, nothing—not even knowledge—is equal to virtue. Knowledge is profoundly worth having where it is gained in accordance with justice, patience, courage, fidelity, temperance, kindness (including kindness to animals), and all the kinds of love (including love of truth). These qualities are what make knowledge itself valuable. It is for their pursuit of knowledge in accordance with virtue that we honor our new Cum Laude members today. And the more knowledge promises personal pleasure, money (including government or corporate grants), professional advancement, power, or fame, the more we must ask not only "*How* can I gain this knowledge?" but "What is this knowledge for?" And we must ask "Am I pursuing this knowledge in accordance with virtue?" even when what we seek is that vague distant good, "the betterment of the human condition." It is good that we should strive to better the human condition, but not at the cost of making particular human beings worse.

Knowledge is precious. But it is *not* for setting up as an idol to be worshipped for its own sake. If to gain a piece of knowledge you must pretend that dogs or even rats are junk, if for the sake of knowledge you treat human beings as merely means to your ends and not as neighbors whom we are to love as we love ourselves, if your pursuit of knowledge corrupts your loyalty to goodness or to that greater truth of which knowledge is only a part, then the pursuit of knowledge has become evil. Far better to drop out and be the witless beggar of your worst nightmares of failure than to succeed by gaining such knowledge at such a price.

Now, if I may paraphrase the Book of Proverbs: May the Giver of all knowledge cause wisdom to enter our hearts and knowledge to be pleasant to our souls, discretion to watch over us and discernment to guard us, to deliver us from the way of evil, that we may walk in the way of the good and keep the paths of the righteous.[5]

Thank you.

---

5 See Proverbs 2:6–20.

Tikkun Olam—Cheating
[April 22, 2004]

There has been some cheating on campus this year. Apart from the taking of others' books, and sometimes money, without permission, and of trying to win unearned popularity with the display of clothes and skin, there have also been collusion on homework, illicit sharing of test questions, open-book work on closed-book quizzes, shortcut downloading from SparkNotes, and the plagiarizing of others' ideas and words.

Cheating at school is the result of three causes: The first is lack of integrity in the cheater. The second is the pressure of adult expectations. And the third is the cheating that students see around them, and not only by other students. Let's look first at this cheating by others.

In addition to the several forms of student cheating, the school itself sometimes engages in a kind of cheating by sending double messages to you without admitting it: We say we value learning and nail you with grades; we establish limits on the amount of homework we can assign and neglect to monitor how much time our assignments actually take; we complain that you don't sleep but demand that you work harder and do more; we praise sportsmanship but accept the water polo custom of ignoring underwater fouls. Some parents inappropriately revise homework, rewrite essays, lie to the attendance office, or meddle with coaches.

Cheating is even more common outside the school: You hear of adults who cheat in business, on their taxes, on their spouses. Highly paid athletes take illegal steroids to win for teams whose owners have made careers of cheating others out of money; city governments cook their books to hide deficits resulting from previous cheating; entertainment media cheat youth of their innocence and idealism by pandering to their lowest instincts; sound bite journalism substitutes slanted impressions for balanced reporting; and political factions, demonizing their opponents, cheat us all out of instructive discourse on subjects about which good people might disagree with civility.

In American cities teenage gangs, cheated of better goals, cheat others of their youth and often their lives; in the Sudan, adult gangs cheat women and children of their humanity by rape and murder; the free, democratic state of Israel, which would live in peace with its neighbors if it possibly could, is cheated of a fair reputation by a vicious propaganda machine built on manufactured hatred; and millions of Muslims around the world are cheated out of true divine service by the lies of some of the greatest villains of our time, who cynically proclaim that God rewards the killing of innocents and that to die in murdering your neighbors is better than to live in peace with them.

Well, this is a depressing litany. But what can we do about it besides complain? We could give up. One student informed me the other day, as if the news were not as old as the world, that many people succeed by cheating. My response is, yes, but succeed at *what*? We could succumb to the pressure to think only of getting higher grades, winning more games, making more money, and killing more real or imaginary enemies. It is a possible choice, and many make it. But does measuring our success in quantities rather than qualities lead to meaning or to happiness?

The chaplain has asked me to speak about *tikkun olam*, the repair or perfecting of the world. The daily *Aleinu* prayer in Judaism speaks of "the perfecting of the world under the kingship of God." The Hasidim, the sect of religious Jews, followers of Rabbi Israel Baal Shem Tov (Master of the Good Name), apply the concept of repair of the world to the individual. They teach that a human being is capable every moment of contributing to the repair of the world. In every situation, in every choice we make—so the Hasidim teach—we are free to choose between good and evil, between serving our lower impulses only and raising up our impulses to serve our whole selves, our neighbors, and God. Each good choice releases from bondage the spark of divinity that was hidden in the shell of the moment as a potential. When released, it joins with all other sparks of divinity that have been released to help enlighten, uplift, and heal the world and its inhabitants.

But how do we make these spark-redeeming, world-repairing choices?

Think of the kind of movie in which, at the last instant, the underdog we identify with wins the playoff game against the bigger, stronger, nasty opponent. Why are we moved? Would we be as pleased if the underdog had cheated in order to win, had become like the opponent of whom we disapprove? I don't think so. Whether we are aware of it or not, we get the thrill of victory because the hero has won *with integrity*, because the good guy has won by being better, not by becoming another bad guy.

But wait a minute. Such movies are often themselves a cheat. If they make us think that the good guy, the one with integrity, will always win the game in the end, they're lying to us. In reality the good guy often loses the worldly game, and movies that promise otherwise set us up for disappointment. If we assume that such movies depict reality, and then look from them to the real world, we are tempted to despair, to think of integrity itself as a cheat. And this despair is only deepened by those corrupting movies in which villains are killed by a worse villain with a bigger gun.

There are, however, better movies and books, which show that people with integrity must sometimes sacrifice worldly success to achieve something of greater value. One of the worst parts about the cheating that our culture engages in is that it cheats young people—you—out of better movies and books and paintings, out of actual experiences of the value and meaning of integrity. For example, when you download the plot summary of *A Tale of Two Cities* because you find the book hard to understand and you're under time pressure and want to impress the teacher to get a top grade to get into a top college to get a top job, what you are being cheated of is the meaning of what the character Sydney Carton does at the end of Dickens' novel. From SparkNotes you'll find out *what* Carton does, but you won't *get* it. On you will go, thinking you know the story, never realizing what Carton's act of sublime integrity might really mean to you.

Among other things, a true education offers you experiences that confirm and reinforce your inner longing to believe that the soul's integrity is superior to worldly success, that in the things that really count, integrity *is* success. When you concentrate enough on a Harry Potter novel to notice at its heart the moral integrity Harry achieves, when you actually do the work necessary to appreciating the meaning of integrity in Tolkien's *Lord of the Rings* or Virgil's *Aeneid* or Shakespeare's *Hamlet*, when you read history carefully enough to comprehend what the integrity of Socrates or Abraham Lincoln accomplished, then you are experiencing education that is not a cheat.

It is our obligation as a school to provide you with such experiences, and where we fail to do so with integrity, we must strive to do better. It is your obligation as students to do the work necessary to *receiving* those experiences.

When we say, in the cliché phrase I've heard more than one of you quote sarcastically, that in cheating you cheat yourself, what we mean is that you have substituted the momentary illusion of success for the real thing, the quick fix of quantity for the lasting satisfaction of quality. Can you feel good about a high grade on a quiz you've cheated on? Or about a teacher's praise for words you have plagiarized? Would you feel comfortable at your top college knowing that you had cheated to get in? Would the jeans you buy with stolen money feel like yours? If you've had to betray a friend to get into the popular clique, could you really feel that you belong even with yourself, let alone with the group?

In his little book called *The Way of Man According to the Teaching of Hasidism*,[1] Martin Buber says,

> The origin of all conflict between me and my fellow-men is that I do not say what I mean, and that I do not do what I say... By our contradiction, our lie, we foster conflict-situations and give them power over us until they enslave us. From here, there is no way out but by the crucial realization: Everything depends on myself, and the crucial decision: I will straighten myself out. (page 29)

But *how* do we straighten ourselves out? We straighten ourselves out by turning our attention from fear of immediate consequences toward unifying our souls, toward integrity. Buber retells the following story:

> A hasid of the Rabbi of Lublin once fasted from one Sabbath to the next. On Friday afternoon he began to suffer such cruel thirst that he thought he would die. He saw a well, went up to it, and prepared to drink. But instantly he realized that because of the one brief hour he had still to endure, he was about to destroy the work of the entire week. He did not drink and went away from the well. Then he was touched by a feeling of pride for having passed this difficult test. When he became aware of it, he said to himself, "Better I go and drink than let my heart fall prey to pride." He went back to the well, but just as he was going to bend down to draw water, he noticed that his thirst had disappeared. When the Sabbath had begun, he entered his teacher's house. 'Patchwork!' the rabbi called to him, as he crossed the threshold. (page 21)

Buber asks why the rabbi was so harsh to the hasid, who was obviously

---

1   Martin Buber, *The Way of Man According to the Teaching of Hasidism* (New York: Citadel, 1990).

doing his best to rise to a higher spiritual level. The answer is that the master is warning the disciple against his "wavering, shilly-shallying" way of proceeding, like resolving to study and then spending all afternoon on the drums, or opening a book to read a chapter and then repeatedly counting how many pages are left, or enrolling in our school for a good education and then copying someone else's homework.

> The opposite of 'patchwork' [says Buber] is work 'all of a piece.' Now how does one achieve work 'all of a piece'? Only with a united soul. (page 22)

The rabbi's criticism implies that

> a man can unify his soul. The man with the divided, complicated, contradictory soul is not helpless: the core of his soul, the divine force in its depths, is capable of … binding the conflicting forces together … is capable of unifying it. (page 23)

Of course, adds Buber, unity of soul is not achieved once and for all. It has to be won again and again out of each particular situation. But, he says, "Any work that I do with a united soul reacts upon my soul, acts in the direction of new and greater unification" (page 24), until eventually one is able to rely on one's soul, to overcome its inner contradictions with relative ease.

Buber then retells a tale that hints at *how* to unify our souls:

> On one of the days of the Hanukkah feast, Rabbi Nahum, the son of the rabbi of Rishyn, entered the House of Study at a time when he was not expected, and found his disciples playing checkers, as was the custom on those days. When they saw the zaddik, they were embarrassed and stopped playing. But he gave them a kindly nod and asked: "Do you know the rules of the game of checkers?" And when they did not reply for shyness, he himself gave the answer: "I shall tell you the rules of the game of checkers. The first is that one must not make two moves at once. The second is that one may only move forward and not backward. And the third is that when one has reached the last row, one may move wherever one likes." (pages 24–25)

Receiving an education, like providing one, is a big job, especially at a pressure-cooker school like ours. It requires spiritual, intellectual, emotional, and physical integrity. To make your education not patchwork but all of a piece, you must strive to unify your soul by following the rules of checkers:

First, do not make two moves at once: that is, don't focus on the semester grade when you should be learning the content of the chapter; don't focus on how popular your friends are when you should be striving to be a worthy friend. Second, move only forward and not backward: that is, grapple with what is new and hard to understand instead of retreating to infantile reductions of it on SparkNotes or to the kindergarten task of copying what others have written; challenge the school to live up to its stated standards instead of compromising your own integrity with excuses; ask for help instead of childishly pretending that you know what you don't; think of the people whom you admire for their integrity and choose to hang out with them a little more. Third, when you arrive at the end, you can move wherever you like: Having learned to unify your soul—spirit, mind, heart, and body—your education will have become all of a piece, you will graduate with integrity, and whatever your past scores or future income, you will be ready for the tasks that turn out to be yours.

Proms of Innocence and Experience
[May 16, 2005]

Proms of Innocence

She A: The prom has to be perfect. Perfection means being asked by the cutest boy in the class above me, spending weeks getting ready for the best night of my life so that every girl in the room will envy my dress and my luck in having such a gorgeous date. But it won't be luck, really, but the reward of all my hopes and dreams, and if it all goes the way I want it to, he will dance me to the stars, and—who knows?—maybe it will lead to our being lovers forever. I can't wait for the prom!

He A: The prom has to be perfect. Perfection means asking the cutest girl in the class below me, spending a fortune getting ready for the best night of my life so that every guy in the room will envy my suavity and my luck in having such a gorgeous date. But it won't be luck, really, but the reward of all my expenses and planning, and if it all goes the way I want it to, she will let me French-kiss her, and—who knows?—maybe it will lead to our making love that night. I can't wait for the prom!

She B: I hope we have fun at the prom. He's not the cutest boy in my class, but I like him. I hope he likes my dress. He's sort of shy underneath. If I can just get him to laugh early in the evening, we'll both relax and have a better time. I have to remember not to be disappointed if we don't dance to the swing numbers; he thinks he's not good at swing. I hope he did well on that exam yesterday. I won't bring it up unless he does. But he doesn't seem to hold onto stuff like that, so maybe it doesn't matter. I can't wait to see him in his tux!

He B: I hope we have fun at the prom. She's the nicest girl in my class, and she makes me laugh. I hope she likes the corsage. She's so easy to be with. I hope we can get through the first dance without my stepping on her toe or something. Where will I put my hands in the slow dances so she doesn't think I'm being fresh? I hope she did well on that exam yesterday. I won't bring it up unless she does. But I don't think she really gets upset about stuff like that, so maybe I can ask her. I can't wait to see her all dressed up!

Proms of Experience

She A: What a horrible night. That noisy band and that repulsive food. I never want to see him again, or that—I'm not even going to say her name. How dare he agree to dance with her when he's supposed to be with me? And how dare she tell him what happened *over three weeks ago* with—I don't want to think about it. What a baboon to close my dress in the car door. And those stupid jokes of his. What were all his jock friends laughing at? How dare he think I was the kind of girl who would—why didn't I say no when he asked me to the prom; I might have been asked by—what an awful prom.

He A: What a horrible night. That clueless band and the waiter taking my plate away before I was even done eating. I will never go out with her again. That friend of hers is ten times better looking, and obviously liked me. How can I get her number? Imagine saying she'd go to prom with me when only three weeks ago—oh who cares what she did with him. She didn't even get my jokes. What were all her stupid friends giggling about? Who does she think she is, hanging on me all night and then not even letting me kiss her? Instead of her I should have asked—what an awful prom.

She B: What a great prom! The band was okay and the food was good. He looked so gorgeous in that tux, and his laugh is really infectious. I wish I hadn't let the corner of my dress get stuck in the car door; he was so apologetic, I felt bad for him. And how stupid I was not to get his joke about—but at least he didn't rub it in. Anyway, it was fun. Watching him dance that one dance with—what a good dancer he is. He is such a gentleman too, and so are his friends. The way he looked at me when he came back to the table—I think he really liked my dress. I hope he calls me tomorrow. I can't wait to thank him for a wonderful evening.

He B: What a great prom! The band was okay and there was a lot of food. She was so gorgeous I couldn't stop looking at her, and she's so funny too. What a dork I was to catch the corner of her dress in the car door, but she was so nice about it and didn't seem to care at all. And why did I have to tell that stupid joke about—I hope she didn't think I was trying to show off. Anyway, it was fun. She is so lively and relaxed at the same time. I like her friends too. The way she looked at me when I came back after having to dance with—I think she meant it about how good I looked in my tux. I'm going to call her tomorrow to thank her for a wonderful evening. Maybe she'll want to go to a movie next week.

Commentary

Like commencement, the ceremony celebrating graduation from childhood learning into adult learning, the prom is a ceremonial graduation too, from childhood social relations into adult, where male and female, united to one another as individuals, also take their place in that larger society composed of couples.

Formal dress, courteous behavior, traditional gestures—the corsage, the opening and closing of doors, the dinner, the dancing, the feminine whispers and male bonhomie during temporary separations, the attentiveness and good humor in rejoining—all these are the forms in which two unions are practiced as a kind of initiation into the life of marriage in society:

One union is the ceremonially acknowledged joining of a young man and a young woman on a personal date that (however remotely) prefigures wedding. The other is the ceremonially acknowledged joining of each couple with all other couples in a collective date that (however remotely) represents society's foundation upon marriage. Courtesy toward one's date ceremonially represents the personal love upon which marriage is built. Prom traditions ceremonially represent the courtesy of couples upon which society is built.

Eros underlies and energizes both these kinds of union without in itself compromising their meaning. The prom, like marriage, like society, is in part a harnessing and channeling of eros in the name of civilization. Nor does it matter whether the prom date eventually becomes the spouse. (And none of this disparages those individuals who, for whatever reasons, do not or cannot participate in the ceremony.)

The point here is that the prom's ceremonial civilization of eros is corrupted when the envisioning of it is hijacked by sentimentality, whether of the romantic (She A) or the erotic (He A) kind, which turns it into a mere wish fulfillment fantasy. No evening can possibly live up to such expectations—and a good thing too, considering how socially and spiritually impoverished are the people imagined in and imagining it.

Eros is active in both couples. But Couple A is doomed to disappointment, in the prom and in life, until they graduate from self-centeredness to civilized human kindness. It is for Couple B that the prom may both be a true pleasure and become a joyful memory. Upon them, as upon a solid foundation, society may rightly hope to build its future.

Cum Laude Address
[March 18, 2009]

I want to thank the Members of the Cum Laude Society for the honor of being invited to speak on this occasion.

I congratulate the newest members of the Cum Laude Society for their achievement of academic excellence. In honor of that achievement, I aim to achieve two things today: One is to help banish a certain rhetorical question from serious conversations at school. The academic life is built on asking and trying to answer questions, but this question is deadly to the pursuit of truth. It is the question "Who is to say?"

My second aim is to help restore an unfashionable concept to respectability, a concept without which the meaning of the Cum Laude society and of education itself would cease to exist. That concept is absolute values.

These two aims are related because we are all apt to react to the word "absolute" with the question "Who is to say?" Bred for individual liberty, we Americans fear that absolutes lead to oppression and tyranny, and we sense danger. Overreacting, we retreat for safety into what Pope Benedict has called "the dictatorship of relativism." "Who is to say?" really means "since everything is relative, no one has a right to judge me." Whew! Safe. So we are tempted to think, or rather to feel without thinking.

But consider the illogic: To deny that any values are absolute is to make an absolute of relativism. And without faith in an absolute value like justice, a secondary value like individual liberty loses all meaning. If justice is relative, on what grounds can we argue that oppression and tyranny are bad?

Of course it is not easy to apply an absolute like justice to particular situations. What one calls joking another might call bullying. And often the absolutes themselves seem to conflict. Like the Duke in Shakespeare's *Measure for Measure*, our own Ethics Committee must regularly balance the two absolute values of justice and mercy, and tempering the one with the other in any particular case is hard. However, the difficulty is not removed but only increased when we pretend that justice and mercy are not absolutes. The function of human intelligence is not to deny those absolutes but to do the hard work of approaching them as nearly as we can.

Certainly, absolute values do not apply to matters of mere taste. If you say "I like chocolate ice cream," no one is going to say, "You're wrong; I like vanilla." But when it comes to good and evil, right and wrong, truth and error, meaning and nonsense, beauty and ugliness—the most important subjects of human thought—replacing absolute values with relativism leads only to intellectual confusion.

A few weeks ago I said to one of my classes, "There is such a thing as beauty." You should have heard the outrage. You would have thought I was advocating the torture of puppies and kittens. "Beauty is in the eye of the beholder," they shouted with passionate intensity, as if I must never have heard that cliché before. "Who are you to say what beauty is?"

It is true that the experience of beauty is always a relation between the viewer and the object. Something beautiful will not appear beautiful to one who is blind. Discerning people may find elements of beauty in something otherwise ugly. And there are many gradations of twilight between the high noon of beauty and the midnight of ugliness. But discerning those gradations is part of the challenge and the joy of life: making and comparing judgments is what human beings like to do, and *will* do no matter what. To renounce judgment by pretending that all beauty is relative—that there is no essential difference between the beautiful and the ugly—is to bury human discernment alive in a coffin made of error.

If a picture is worth 10,000 words, I'm going to save myself 40,000. Here are two faces and two vases:

credit: Metropolitan Museum, public domain

Relativists may kick and scream, but their empathic responses to these images tell the truth: one of the faces is ugly (as Quentin Matsys, following Leonardo,[1] meant it to be), and one is beautiful. And the same with the vases. You yourself may be more or less beautiful than your neighbor. Beauty is not and should not be a requirement for invitation to the Cum Laude Society. But like it or not, true beauty—like true academic excellence—is real, and it is the farthest thing from ugliness.

The same is true for the other absolute values by whose light all human judgments are made: justice, love, truth (and we could add *arete*, *dike*, and *time*—*dike* is justice—the motto of the Cum Laude Society). To deny their reality leads, as I said, only to confusion.

One form of confusion is the self-contradiction I mentioned earlier: Relativists who deny absolutes make an absolute of relativism.

A second form of confusion is the abolishment of the grounds for moral judgment. I think you will agree with me that scientists should not falsify their data, that your friend should not date your girlfriend or boyfriend behind your back, that cutting in the lunch line is wrong, that the strong should not tyrannize over the weak. But who are we to say so unless we agree that the values of truth, loyalty, and justice are absolute? We might not *like* others to fake their data, betray our friendship, or push

---

1 The painting is by Quentin Matsys, made after a drawing attributed to Francesco Melzi, itself the copy of a lost original by Melzi's master, Leonardo da Vinci (c. 1490). The sculpted head is a fifth-century Greek kuros.

us around. But without faith in absolutes we cannot reasonably claim it is *wrong* for them to do so. Similarly, when relativism dissolves our faith in honesty, the rule of law, and the brotherhood of man, how can we assert that it is bad for CEOs to embezzle, politicians to lie, mobs to lynch, or terrorists to blow up buses full of children?

The study of other cultures and civilizations is essential to education. But the relativism that goes by the fashionable name of "multiculturalism" leads to a third kind of confusion when it preaches that all cultures are created equal. For example, when we say that the principles of freedom, equality, and the rule of law are merely "Eurocentric," on what grounds can we condemn other cultures who practice autocracy and persecution?

In fact, the very idea that we should treat other cultures justly and without prejudice is derived from no other culture but the one into which we have all been born or transported: the English-speaking West. Several thousand years of Jewish and Christian teaching that all men are the children of God, a thousand years of English Common Law, and two centuries of American Enlightenment doctrine that all men are created equal and are endowed with fundamental rights—these are the only grounds we have for asserting that we should respect our neighbor's cultural differences.

Which brings me to the hugely complex matter of whether, when, and how we should thrust our own values upon others. Responding to these questions requires even deeper loyalty to the absolutes of justice, love, and truth and a careful study of history, language, culture, and politics. I am not foolish enough to claim that in such matters wisdom comes easily. In the history of the British rule in India, for example, it is safe to say that there was plenty of good and evil behavior on all sides. But consider what the theologian George Weigel writes about General Sir Charles Napier:

> As one point in his pacification of [the province of Sindh, now part of Pakistan], Sir Charles confronted the long-entrenched and religious-ly-warranted practice of "suttee," according to which a widow was thrown onto the funeral pyre of her dead husband. Napier invited the local leaders to a meeting and said, "You say that it is your custom to burn widows. Very well. We also have a custom. When men burn a woman alive, we tie a rope around their necks and we hang them. Build your funeral pyre; beside it, my carpenters will build a gallows. You may follow your custom. And then we shall follow ours."

Underlying Napier's declaration was the conviction that the sacredness of human life, including female human life, is an absolute. After pointing out that in the wake of Napier's decision, suttee was soon abolished in India, Weigel asks whether India would have been better off if Napier had said "Who am I to impose my values on you?"[2]

Only in light of absolute values can we avoid the moral confusion of cultural relativism, which justifies the abuse of women, the toleration of the violently intolerant, and the greater outrage over Abu Ghraib than over the genocidal brutalities of the Janjaweed in Darfur, the Chinese Communists in Tibet, and radical Islamist jihadis everywhere.

The question "Who is to say?" really means "No one is to say": There is no authority over me; there are no such absolutes as beauty, justice, love, or truth to which I am answerable. Under the dictatorship of this relativism there can be no meaningful discourse about values at all. To see this, all you have to do is consider what answer to the question "Who is to say?" *would* persuade you. "Who are you to say?" "Well, I'm a doctor of philosophy in English and American Literature." *Ffft.* "I'm a Harvard nuclear physicist who plays a Stradivarius violin, has won three Super Bowls as quarterback, written two novels, directed a hit movie, served with Mother Theresa, and been elected Secretary-General of the United Nations." *Ffft.* I am Moses, Socrates, Buddha, Confucius, Jesus. The relativist response is still *Ffft.*

When we ask "Who's to say what is right or wrong?" because we recognize no absolute authority, it doesn't mean there is no such thing as evil. It means we are allowing evil to conquer. If we continue to dissolve absolute values in the corrosive bath of this all-purpose question, soon we will ask "Who are you to tell me what to do?" and the only answer will be "I'm the one with the gun, that's who."

But the universal absolute values really do exist, and we must be faithful to them. Who is to say so? *We* are, every one of us. Whether we prefer it in a Chinese vase or a teen magazine, we know that there is beauty, even though getting it to appear in an essay we're writing is not easy. Whether or not it is possible for anyone to be perfectly good, we know that justice is always better than injustice, even though it is hard to figure out how much weight to give mitigating circumstances in any particular case of plagiarism. We know that love is more than sex, even

---

2   On the website of the Ethics and Public Policy Center, https://eppc.org/publication/robust-interreligious-dialogue/ [May 2006].

though plenty of pseudo-Freudians and TV episodes would have us think otherwise. We know that truth exists, even though no one person can know all truth and a lifetime is not long enough to know very much for absolutely certain.

We can all perfectly well see for ourselves the value of absolutes if only we stop asking the fake question "Who is to say?" and recognize that unexamined relativism is a form of prejudice. Teachers and school and Cum Laude societies are not here to dictate that you must like vanilla more than chocolate. They are here to help you to become excellent at making sound judgments based on the absolute principles of goodness and truth. And precisely because that goal is not easy to achieve, we celebrate today the induction of new members into the Cum Laude Society. May it inspire all of us in the pursuit of excellence.

Commencement Address
[June 1, 2012]

I am very grateful for the honor of being invited to speak on this festive occasion, on which we confer diplomas and celebrate the accomplishments they signify. We also mark the transition of the Class of 2012 from our protective care to greater academic and personal liberty, with which comes greater intellectual responsibility.

Considering this new responsibility, I want to address the intellectual challenge of false dichotomies. I mean those "either/or" alternatives, arising from mental laziness, that cloud rather than clarify our thinking—like "pro-life or pro-choice?" (which usually evokes from me a lecture on sex and human responsibility); or "screen addict or Luddite?" (surely not my only two options). Today I want to focus on the three false dichotomies I think most important for new college freshmen to beware of: science or religion, Western Civilization or Multiculturalism, and injustice or utopia.

In college you will find friends and teachers who think that science and religion cannot both be true. I hope you have learned here to reason better, to understand that science and religion relate us to different aspects of reality. Science looks at what things materially are and how they physically work; religion involves us in purpose and meaning. In Aristotle's terms, science considers material and efficient causes, religion final causes. To achieve the valuable ends of science, we become detached observers and make all things, including people, our objects. By contrast, religion draws us into communion and humbles us before ends beyond our own. Science determines whether the brain of an intensive care patient is functioning; religion articulates the sacredness of that patient's life. To imagine that science disproves religion is to be intellectually confused.

Some of you have told me you are atheists. To me this means that you don't believe in the existence of what you imagine God to be. In this the atheist is in surprising agreement with the greatest spiritual thinkers in all traditions, who say that in reality God, being infinite and all-containing, is ineffable, beyond anything that a human being can imagine. As Wendell

Berry writes, "we can't comprehend what comprehends us."[1]

Yet to believe that nothing exists beyond what we can see or touch or measure, or that everything is random chance, is to make an act of faith as great as that of any believer in God. Leaving aside Shakespeare and Rembrandt and Mozart, if you have ever laughed at a joke, cheered for your team, or loved a friend, you know that things of the spirit are as real as things of the body—Plato would say more real—and, to most people, more important. Moreover, science could not exist if it were not built on a foundation of faith—faith in the universality of physical laws, faith in the logic of mathematical axioms, faith in the trustworthiness of measurements. You have to believe that a ruler is a foot long before you can measure anything with it.

Since science can improve our lives but cannot exist without faith or account for things of the spirit, I conclude that both science and religion are valid human enterprises. So in college, don't fall for the unreasonable argument that religion and science have mutually exclusive claims on reality. Using the scientific method to refute the creation story in Genesis is like using a steak knife to cut up your soup. Genesis was never meant to be science but to evoke the right relation to the Creator, and science cannot tell us how to be good, or why we should be.

A second false dichotomy is Western Civilization or Multiculturalism. As you know, I believe strongly in the value of studying Western Civilization. That conviction is rooted in my own experience of college in the mid-1960s. All freshmen in my college studied Western Civ for a year in five classes per week of history, literature, and art. The course was deeply enriching then and has served as an excellent foundation since. But my advocating the study of Western Civ implies no demeaning of other cultures. As sophomores we also studied the history, literature, and art of India, China, Japan, and the Arab world. This invaluable two-year curriculum was an expression of my teachers' esteem for Western Civilization at its best, for it is the West which, since Herodotus, has taught the value of learning about the cultures of others.

There is, however, a terrible price for the inability properly to value one's own culture. American academic multiculturalists who value all cultures except the West are busily sawing off the branch on which they sit. Out of a superficial notion of fairness, they condemn the civilization that brought us not only Greek philosophy, medieval cathedrals, the rule

---

1 Wendall Berry, *Life Is a Miracle* (Washington, D.C: Counterpoint, 2000), page 34.

of law, Shakespeare, Rembrandt, and Mozart, the idea of equality, and modern science, but the value of fairness itself.

It is true that the West, like the East, has had to overcome evils like the subjugation based on race that you have read about in Frederick Douglass and Joseph Conrad. Western Civilization does not magically make men good, any more than nature does. But it has also produced and honored the dream of Martin Luther King, Jr., who wished his children to be judged not "by the color of their skin but by the content of their character."

We are all the beneficiaries of that dream. One of the best things I have observed about students here is a genuine affection that crosses the boundaries of diversity: gender, race, ethnicity, religion, language, sexual orientation, wealth, intellectual ability, artistic bent, athletic prowess, and looks. But you will find that the present fashion of many university academics is to condemn the very civilization whose founders are the source of Dr. King's ideals: Moses, Socrates, and Jesus. The word "university" comes from the Latin for "entire" or "whole": When the *uni*versity is demoted to the *di*versity, emphasizing the secondary elements that divide us rather than the universals that unite all men, the result is not education but bitterness and conflict. So in college, don't let anyone persuade you that the flaws of the West justify sneering at its ideals and accomplishments. One of its best products is your own affection for the people of different backgrounds sitting around you at this moment.

A third false dichotomy is unjust past or utopian future. "Utopia," comes from the Greek *u topos*, no place. Every utopia is an imaginary place that cannot exist in reality. But modern age utopians have believed that it is possible for government to do away with the evils of the past—as if man's sins were not perennial—and to establish an ideal world. The corollary is that any government not attempting to bring about utopia now is oppressive and unjust. Utopians want government to make sure that all human beings have not merely equal rights and liberty under the law but equal incomes, pension plans, schooling, health benefits, and nutritional balance. Of course I am for government safety nets, and all people of good will would like everyone to be healthy, wealthy, educated, and well-fed. But you all know the difference between community service done freely and that done under coercion. The effort to enforce a utopian ideal requires that government trample on the equality of rights and liberty for some in order to provide a phantom equality of outcome for others.

Every utopian movement that has come to power in modern times has engaged in extreme violence against people and human rights in the name of its ideal future: the French Revolution; the Nazis in Germany; Communism in Russia, China, Cambodia, Vietnam, and Cuba; the radical Islamism of the Muslim Brotherhood, of Iran, of Al Qaeda, Hezbollah, Hamas, and the Taliban, under whose rule, don't forget, women not only could not vote but were regularly mutilated and murdered for crimes like appearing in public or speaking to a stranger.

By contrast, the oldest wisdom traditions in the world teach us to focus less on where we are going than on how we are getting there. In China, before the Communist revolution, the ideal society was thought of as being far in the past. In Judaism, the ideal messianic age may come any day in the future. But about how to live, the wisdom of both China and the Jews uses similar language: The *Tao* in Chinese means the way or the path, both the right path for human beings to follow and the way the universe goes. To follow the Tao is to be in harmony with reality. The word *Halacha* in Hebrew also means the way to walk, the way one may best fulfill God's commandments. In both traditions a better future can be attained only by living rightly now, and ideal ends cannot justify evil means. When I urge people who care about justice to stand up for Israel, it is not because I am pro-Israeli instead of pro-Arab—another false dichotomy—but because disputes over legitimate claims to land should be settled by negotiation not violence, and because I am for justice, liberty, equality, and peace and against the use of delegitimizing propaganda and terrorism to achieve genocidal ends. I remind you that in no country in the Middle East but Israel can Muslim and Christian Arabs vote their conscience, women marry as they please, and same-sex couples (including Palestinian Arab couples) dance in public without fear of persecution.

In college, whenever anyone tries to convince you that because the world is not perfect, we must compromise virtue in order to move forward, I hope you will remember the words of Rabbi Tarfon, who in the *Ethics of the Fathers* says, "It is not up to you to complete the work; neither are you at liberty to abandon it." We all want a better world and must not despair or tire in working for it. But an imaginary perfect future must never be used to justify actual evil in the present.

To recap: Science and religion are not mutually exclusive; Western Civilization is the source, not the enemy, of our ideals of universal justice and equality; and utopian ends do not justify evil means.

I will close with a few specific suggestions. Rabbi Yehoshua ben Perachyah says, also in the *Ethics of the Fathers*, "Get yourself a teacher, take yourself a friend, and judge every man by the scale of merit." In college, find yourself a great teacher—not necessarily an easy or popular one, but one that upper classmen will tell you is honest, illuminating, and wise. There will not be many, wherever you are, but there will be one or two. Find those teachers, no matter what they teach, and make use of their office hours. Then, make at least one good friend. That will probably not happen before Christmas break, but along about March you may realize that it has happened already. Even if you're having a tough year, unless you're on the point of total collapse, don't transfer before June. You might just miss a future BFF. And continue to judge others, especially in election years, not by race or religion, coolness or wealth, but by merit. Finally, I remind you that knowledge is more than information, wisdom is more than knowledge, and virtue is above all. Be brave, ask for help when you need it, and once in a while, instead of texting, call home. We are all very proud of your accomplishments, and more of your character. Congratulations.

Reviews

C. S. Lewis, *Till We Have Faces*
[1989]

I received a letter from Philip Thompson, c. 1976–77, in which he wrote:

> Urgent! Have you read C. S. Lewis's *Till We Have Faces*? (Oh, that
> title! Hot water! It sounds like those Russian loudspeakers "Are We
> All Right," "Our Daily Bread," "The Things We Have Seen," etc.)
> Anyway, read it immediately and you will meet yet another Lewis,
> a great artist (not the inventor of tricks with space and light, strange
> vegetation, and phantoms wise, foolish and wicked), for this mythic
> novel (Cupid and Psyche story) certainly ranks with Mann's *Holy
> Sinner* and Joseph books. The mysterium tremendum at its heart
> emerges from a visionary sequence that is unlike anything else in
> words, and after one reading I have no words for it yet (except words
> like power, beauty, truth, reality, form, body, soul, etc.). When it was
> published (1956) it seems to have been ignored, reviewers saying
> things like "another pleasant little tale by…" or "a well-earned
> holiday for Mr. L. from the strenuous job of converting the world to
> his persuasion," and so it went no further than one printing, at least
> in the U.S. You never know what masterpieces lurk behind familiar
> faces. Urgent!

In response, I read the novel, and was deeply moved by it. Over ten years
later, having reread the novel several times, I wrote the following:

In *Till We Have Faces*, C. S. Lewis's version of the Cupid and Psyche
myth, Cupid is a god and an image of Christ as God. Psyche is a soul
and the soul. Orual is everyman (or-you-all) and also the fallen, fallible,
temporal self for whom life is the business of learning surrender to the
divine. In the visionary sequence at the end of the book (mythically
universal and at the same time particular and personal) Orual is brought
to knowledge that her interior complaint against the gods has been the
whining of a "craver," one whose love for her sister was more selfish
possessiveness than self-sacrifice. The revelation bestowed by the god,
that "You too are Psyche"—i.e., beloved by Love/God/Cupid—a

revelation that Orual can receive only once she has emptied herself of herself and surrendered *her* idea of love to love itself—prepares for the final recognition that the god gives no answers because he *is* the answer. Lewis is able to dramatize the essential Christian definition of man—namely that we are souls separated from the divine more by our self-concern than by flesh and mortality, and that the divine grants us the means of reunion with it through the suffering that breaks our self-will and compels our surrender to that which in fact we truly desire, namely love—love as it is loved absolutely by God and not fallibly by men.

The triumph of this book that retells the story of the relation of the soul (Psyche) to the god of love (Cupid) is that it makes palpable in Orual, and hence believable and real to us, the experience that meaningful suffering, divine revelation, and truth are all one, subsumed in the word and the experience of love.

Dead Poets and Living Clichés[1]
[1990]

"You'll like *Dead Poets Society,*" some of my students said. "It's about a great English teacher. He's sort of like you." A flattering recommendation, I thought—until I saw the movie.

The story is certainly compelling, as is the acting. And visually the film is almost irresistible. But if that teacher is sort of like me, God help me. *Dead Poets Society* angered me. Though it pretends to inspire idealistic rebellion against the evils of society, in reality it is a melodramatic indoctrination in the Romantic clichés that have brought our society to the brink of dissolution.

The film's obvious manipulation of the audience did not in itself offend. When the English teacher, John Keating (earnestly played by Robin Williams), has a student in his poetry class read aloud from the introduction to their textbook, I enjoyed the parody. (The author proposes a system for measuring the greatness of any poem by plotting its qualities on a graph.) And I was perfectly content to be manipulated into merriment when Mr. Keating said to his students, "Tear that page out of the book. Go ahead. Tear it out!" But tear it out in the name of what? What does Mr. Keating substitute for the graph model of poetry appreciation?

He substitutes the standard modern vulgarization of nineteenth-century Romantic literary theory: A poem, his teaching implies, is the expression of personal emotion. It has little to do with the music of words, still less with truth or beauty or any other reality that may lie outside the poet's emotions. It owes nothing to imagination or to the inspiration of the muse. Above all, it has nothing to do with thought, form, readers, or literary tradition. Poetry, according to this teacher, is purely a matter of inner feeling, impulse, and self-expression, just those things the adult society in the film is in the business of stifling.

How do we know that this is Mr. Keating's idea of poetry? In one class session, he calls a repressed and tongue-tied youth to the front of the room,

1   Published in The Reporter section of *Independent School*, Volume 49, Number 2 (Winter 1990), page 11.

spins him around, and orders him to verbalize whatever images come to his mind. The result is a gush of words that express the boy's feeling of confinement and his desire for freedom. According to the teacher, however, that gush is not merely the raw material of poetry. It is a poem. There is no follow-up scene in which the boy is taught to arrange his words to be moving to others. (They certainly are not moving yet, though the scene itself is fraught with emotion.) Mr. Keating gives no hint that the poem might be a way of *sharing* experience. The poem has accomplished all a poem needs to in the world of this film. It has testified to the absolute value of the self in rebellion against society.

Indeed, the film is not concerned with actual poems at all. It uses the *idea* of poetry solely as a metaphor for the individual's relation to society. And its image of that relation turns out to be a composite of the threadbare platitudes of Rousseauist Romanticism: The individual self and its emotions are basically good; society's attempts to train the one or temper the other corrupt them; the instruments of that corruption are tradition, discipline, and schools; the only worthy authorities are those poets and teachers who tell us to follow our own impulses (ignoring even them); and so on. In short, the film presents the specious axioms of the popular culture masquerading as high idealism.

Another class session shows the absurdity of these axioms, though the scene is intended to reinforce them. Having taken his students out of the classroom and into a courtyard, Mr. Keating asks three of them to walk around while the others watch. The three begin moving uncertainly but soon fall into a march. The rest of the students start to clap in time. Before long, military marching ditties are shouted, the clapping becomes syncopated, and all are caught up in a crescendo of excitement and fun.

Suddenly Mr. Keating brings everything to a halt with a withering accusation: You have been herded into uniformity by social pressure. You have sold your birthright of individuality for a mess of conformist pottage—three of you by marching in step, the rest by clapping in time. The students are chagrined. Mr. Keating then asks them all to walk around the courtyard again. Only this time each is to move at his own pace and in his own unique way. They do, and we are supposed to believe that they have been freed to be themselves. The lesson? Nothing a group can offer is more important than one's individuality.

But what the scene cannot help revealing, in spite of its intentions, is that in marching and clapping the boys had become joyfully united in the exalting communion of play. By contrast, when they walk around trying to be different, each is self-consciously isolated within the limits of his own imagination, and, significantly, every one of them looks like a fool. Yet we are expected to believe that they are now better off. (The one boy who refuses to participate in this communal exercise in individualism is praised for his choice to be even more individual than the rest.)

What is so offensive in all this propaganda is that it offers a corrupt idea of education to the very audience that is most in need of a valid one, namely adolescents. Of course at times it is right to rebel against mere conformity for conformity's sake. And of course students need to be challenged to think for themselves. But the differences between excellence and shoddiness, truth and error, good and evil, are crucial, and the essential task of the teacher is to help students see them. The non-conformist is no better off than the conformist if he is being different merely for the sake of being different. Murderers, rapists, and suicides are non-conformists too.

Which brings me to the film's most damnable participation in the swindle of Rousseauist Romanticism. One of the boys, under Mr. Keating's new dispensation of self-expression, decides to pursue his love of acting. His tyrannical father, who is determined that his son will be a doctor like himself, forbids it. When the boy disobeys the paternal orders by playing Puck in a local production of *A Midsummer Night's Dream*, the father announces he is sending the boy to military school. After he has glowered his son into silence and despair, there is a prolonged scene of visual schmaltz—moonlight, open window, snowy woods, half-naked boy ever so slowly donning Puck's wreath of twigs, which now doubles as a crown of thorns. Then the boy kills himself with his father's pistol.

Everyone is shocked and saddened. The boy has obviously been driven to the only gesture of self-expression left him by the conformist society that his father represents. But the school administrators, in order to protect the school's reputation from tarnish, blame the suicide on Mr. Keating's unorthodox teaching and fire him. This arouses our righteous indignation because it is clearly the father who is guilty of the boy's death, or so we are made to feel. But having martyred the liberated actor, relentless society will now make a scapegoat of the teacher who liberated him. It is typical adolescent paranoid fantasy—so unfair, so sad, so beautiful.

But it is also pernicious. For all its sadness, the suicide is portrayed as an inevitable response to adult society's oppression. No one hints that it might have been an error on the boy's part, perhaps forgivable, but wrong. No one remarks that his action exhibits a failure of imagination. (He could have run away, after all.) No one suggests that maybe the boy was cowardly, or revengeful toward his father, or cruel toward his mother and toward himself. Mr. Keating's response is only to cry a bit. Thus, all we can conclude about suicide from *Dead Poets Society* is that it is a reasonable, meaningful, perhaps extreme, but touching last resort.

Of course there are excellent reasons for not killing oneself, but the dead poets in whose work such reasons might be found are not heard from in the film. Except for a few lines from a sonnet by Shakespeare—quoted only for purposes of seduction—Mr. Keating and his protégés confine themselves to the Romantics. They worship "at the altar of Whitman, Byron, Keats," as film critic Duncan Shepherd points out, but "you don't catch them reciting Herbert or Pope." Nor do you catch them experiencing even one complete poem, Romantic or otherwise. They are too busy quoting poetical snippets that urge them to be true to their impulses and seize the day.

"Seize the day" is the essence of Mr. Keating's doctrine. Standing before a display of photographs of the uniformed "old boys" who had been killed in World War I, he asks his students to lean in close and listen to what the ghosts of the dead are whispering to the living. What they are whispering, says the teacher, is "*Carpe diem.*" (The phrase comes from Horace: *Carpe diem, quam minimum credula postero*—seize the present day, trusting as little as possible to the next.) Eat, drink, and be merry, they say. Go for it. For tomorrow you die. Such is the spiritual legacy of the dead, according to Mr. Keating. Reject tradition, discipline, allegiance, and honor, which lead only to disillusionments like that of World War I. Do your own thing while you can.

To be fair, there is one moment when the doctrine is modified slightly. One of the students, in a fit of desperate resentment after the suicide, has disrupted an assembly, mocked the powers that be, and nearly gotten himself expelled. Mr. Keating urges him not to follow his impulses so stupidly in future. "Suck the marrow out of life, but don't choke on the bones." Seize the day in such a way that you will be around to seize the next day too. But for all its seeming practicality, Mr. Keating's advice proves useless—not only because it comes too late, but because it is shallow. If *carpe diem* is your only guide, why not choke on the bones when there seems to be no more marrow?

In spite of Mr. Keating's enthusiasm for it, *carpe diem* is a doctrine of despair. It eliminates hope for the future because it renounces faith in what is eternal. In reality, of course, no one who writes off the future and busies himself with seizing the day would bother teaching anything to anyone. But this flaw in characterization is less significant than the film's moral flaw. It is clear from the exaggerated evil of his enemies that Mr. Keating is meant to embody the good. But the good he embodies is a sham. For if there were no values outside the impulses of the self, the sensualist, the autocrat, and the suicide would be as admirable as anyone else. Yet about being true to reason or conscience or law or any other value beyond seizing the day neither Mr. Keating nor the film has anything good to say.

The film implies that following our impulses unhindered by society is good. So Rousseau says. But the truth is that to be good we must distinguish among our impulses and choose to follow the better ones. And how can we distinguish the good from the bad without principles to guide us? In the final scene, when the boys disobediently stand on their desks in a symbolic gesture of solidarity with their fired mentor, we are moved by their action. But we are moved not because they have followed their impulses. They also have an impulse to sit still and let the moment safely pass. Nor are we moved because they are rejecting conformity. They are acting in perfect conformity with one another. We are moved because they stand on those desks to uphold principles that we still believe in despite films like this one that strive to debunk them—justice, loyalty, selflessness, and truth. The boys have behaved rightly, though nothing taught by Mr. Keating has prepared them to do so.

The seemingly revolutionary doctrines that he *has* taught have been banalities of our culture for nearly two centuries. Mr. Keating is not rebelling against the norms of society but voicing them. Morally speaking, *he* is the establishment. Hence his ideas are even more subversive than those of Miss Jean Brodie. The evil in her teaching was eventually unmasked because fascism became an external enemy. In John Keating too we have met the enemy. Only we have failed to recognize him because, as Pogo says, he is us.

Dead Poets Society is the enemy of education because it proclaims that dead poets live insofar as they legitimize our self-indulgence. But the great poet in fact lives by virtue of his power to carry us *out* of ourselves—the meaning of education. The great teacher does the same. Both provide access to truths and freedoms that cannot be reached in a lifetime of seizing the day.

Lenore Tolegian Hughes,
Faces of Change[1]
[1995]

We die with the dying:
See, they depart, and we go with them.
We are born with the dead:
See, they return, and bring us with them.
　　　　　　　　—T. S. Eliot, "Little Gidding"

"Art exists to make the invisible visible," says Professor of Art Mary Holmes, a truth compellingly illustrated by "Faces of Change," a collection of watercolors by Lenore Tolegian Hughes displayed in the David Zapf Gallery in San Diego last October.

What Hughes' paintings make visible is the invisible legacy of the persecution and slaughter of the Armenians by the Turks during World War I. Hughes' images speak eloquently of the weight of an unfathomable horror on the memories and imaginations of four generations of Armenians. They also speak of the spiritual transformation possible to those who have confronted the awesome mystery of that horror and demanded of it a blessing, as Jacob demanded a blessing of the Angel of God. "We will not let thee go," say these paintings to the past, "except thou bless us." In saying so, they testify that our imaginative participation in the lives of our ancestors, like the painter's imaginative participation in the psyches of her subjects, can heal as well as hurt. Baptized in the living watercolors of a loving imagination, the remembered and inherited pain, though undiminished, emerges saturated with the promise of redemption.

As befits the medium, Hughes paints her "Faces of Change" moved by the heart, quickly, with deft conviction and few *pentimenti*. Within her abstracted human faces the fervent souls of particular Armenian survivors and their offspring flicker into visibility. In the instant and lasting impressions they make, anguish is transformed into testaments—to the irreducible value hidden in every fleeting moment of our lives.

---

1 Published in *Ararat*, Volume 37, Number 1 (Winter 1996), page 10.

Stepping into the Zapf Gallery, one is met first by the burning dark eyes of the "Chairman of the Board," Hughes' depiction of the Catholicos of the Armenian Orthodox Church, who presides over the exhibit. The triangular *varigour* on his head, bearing an embossed Armenian cross and reflecting the triangle of the chain around his neck from which hangs a golden Armenian cross, drives the eye upward through a background of cloudy spiritual substance toward — toward what? Toward that invisible reality which alone can give meaning to the blackness of his ceremonial garments, of his eyes, of his suffering and of our own.

Eighteen real and burning votive candles surround each of the four paintings called "Generations," turning into icons of the meaning of suffering the living and dead of whom they are portraits. The spellbinding faces, one a death mask of the artist's grandmother, another a psychological self-portrait, are condensed and clarified by the abstract technique until we seem to be communing with souls made visible. And as our sympathy for their burden deepens, we begin to acknowledge the generations of suffering that we too inherit.

"Regenerations" is another series of abstract portraits, these seen through the grid of barbed wire that hems them in. One of them, "Crosses," is the portrait of an Armenian actress whom Hughes knew as a child, a tough, old, wiry-throated self-dramatizer. Her earrings are golden crosses, her eyes blue-green worlds into which it is impossible to gaze without both sympathy and awe, for in them is to be seen the indomitable vitality of every woman survivor in history, freighted with the past, afraid of the future, yet determined to make life yield its meaning by playing the hell out of her part.

Another, "Cigarette," depicts a storyteller whose beautiful, ancient, deadpan clown's face reveals (by hiding it) what dare not be spoken. His tales of the old country slowly transform his listeners from innocents into inheritors of their people's tragic history, even as his cigarette was slowly transformed into the growing ash that mesmerized the children watching for when and where it would fall.

Turning to the winged faces of angelic, transcendent souls forming the monoprint series called "Someone to Watch over Me," we see images of the occasional intuition that makes human history bearable, the intuition of an immortality that not merely escapes but redeems the paralyzing horror that is the apparent boundlessness of human cruelty. Cruelty *is* bounded, in fact, if only by death. And death, so these souls whisper, is not only what the living remember with anguish but what the dead expiate with a loving and compassionate sorrow.

Most symbolic are the works Hughes calls "Heirloomed." They are large rectangular watercolors, broader than tall, in whose centers appear golden-winged faces in spiritualized grief. The faces, sometimes two, sometimes four, facing outward in opposite directions, float in a sky of deepest blue dotted with golden stars. Borders of significant decoration surround them: an iron chain, linking them to their inescapable past; a row of sheep, tying them to nature and to the earth of Armenia; the blues, golds, and maroons of the Armenian Orthodox churches of Hughes' youth. The paintings have the look of Armenian carpets, and they are meant to. For enshrined in the center of these imitation carpets, the faces have themselves become "heirloomed," that is, translated into the inherited valuables of the Armenian people.

Why carpets? Because for the Armenians, the finest carpet connoisseurs in the world, carpets represent survival. Carpets are moveable, as houses and land and the graves of ancestors are not. More than any tangible thing, carpets have sustained the Armenians in their exile by embodying their past. A guest in any Armenian home in America will be shown the carpets first and told in what place they were made, how long they have been in the family, how they were brought to America.

In her versions of those carpets, Hughes has revealed the Armenian catastrophe to be itself an heirloom. She has woven the memories of the slaughtered and the faces of those who cannot forget them into images that make visible the value of what invisibly remains: the memories themselves, the haunted love, and the holy and mysterious pattern of suffering and redemption that is sometimes revealed to the survivors and heirs of the twentieth century's unprecedented terrors.

Roberto Benigni, *Life Is Beautiful*[1]
[1997]

Let no one forget that art is powerful: Masaccio's natural background and *Uncle Tom's Cabin* changed the world. It is powerful because seeing is believing, and art makes the invisible visible, makes both true and false imaginations seem real.

As with all kinds of power, art can be used for good or for ill. "Goodness without knowledge is weak," says the motto of Phillips Exeter Academy, "and knowledge without goodness is dangerous." Being one of the major vehicles of our knowledge of the world, art too without goodness is dangerous.

For fifty years, since the revelation of the horrors of the concentration camps, the Holocaust has commanded our most serious attention. The name Hitler has stood for evil in its most complete believable incarnation, and the concentration camps have stood for the greatest depravity of which man is capable. They force us to confront the most serious questions human consciousness ever must address: Is there justice? If so, why do the innocent suffer? What is the nature of evil? Does God exist? Since this can happen, what—really—are we?

Now along comes Roberto Benigni with a sweet little movie about a father's imaginative and self-sacrificial love for his son. So great is that love, says the film, that it can save his son from the Holocaust—not only from actual death, but even from the taint of the horrors of suffering and evil. The boy can grow up grateful to his father for having preserved him from pain. The trouble is that it also preserves us from reality. No need to ask why man is capable of such evil. *What* evil? No need to ask why the innocent must sometimes undergo such terrible suffering. *What* suffering?

The true objection to the film is not that it is not powerful. It certainly is. Not that life is not beautiful. It certainly is, at least if you do not find yourself in a concentration camp, or perhaps, if you are a tzaddik or a

---

1 A version of this review was published as "A Dangerous Lie: Roberto Benigni's *Life Is Beautiful*," *Epoch Times*, October 3, 2022.

saint, even if you do. The real objection to the film is that it lies about the concentration camps in order to justify its fantasy about life, that it softens and distances real suffering in order to reinforce the dubious idea that love—self-sacrificial, inventive, persistent love—can save the innocent from the taint of suffering and evil. Well, love is good. Inventive, self-sacrificial love is good. Trying to save your son from evil and suffering is good. And because of goodness, even ugly aspects of life can be transfigured into beauty. But the film is a big, sweet, juicy lie. In reality, the reality of Hitler's real concentration camps, that boy could not possibly have been saved from suffering and evil as the film depicts him being saved. In reality, that boy would have died in a matter of days.

The film's parable would not be so offensive, or so misleading, if what tested the father's love were as symbolic or allegorical as the fantasy means he uses to pass the test. Instead, the director has combined two incompatible forms of art—a true historical horror in which no amount of love or sacrifice could in fact have guaranteed the preservation of either innocence or survival—and a fairytale happy ending. I do not object to either form of art, realism or fable. But their combination in this film is a corruption of both. The film uses the pseudo-realistic concentration camp as a generic background of danger and stupidity against which to depict the fantasy triumph of love and self-sacrifice. In reducing that background to a mere cipher in its parable, the film compromises the horror of what, in real life, love sometimes has to overcome. As such, the film becomes a great lie masquerading as a bittersweet truth.

In an interview, the filmmaker reveals the true sentimentality of his motives and his vision: Speaking of the audience's responses to seeing his film, Benigni says, "When they embrace me, you feel the tears. For me it's wonderful, it is a new emotion." Benigni himself calls the film a fable, and adds, "You can't laugh free. You suffer. When you are laughing you are suffering. This is the summit. There is nothing higher than this. Even though laughing and crying is the same emotion, really." Well, there you have it: there is nothing higher than this—that is, than the combination of two contrary emotions. Laughing and crying are the same thing. Now what does it mean to say there is nothing higher than this combination of emotions? To feel that the "new emotion" of evoking tears is so wonderful? What does it mean to call laughing and crying the same thing? It means that it is emotion itself—*any* emotion— that is the greatest thing in life, the only thing worth aiming for in making a movie. This valuing of emotion for its own sake and not as an appropriate (or inappropriate) response to some reality, defines the word "sentimentality." This cultivation of emotion for its own sake is the last stage in the long decay of Romanticism.

Why is such a film so successful? Why did so many love it? You will not like what I have to say in answer, but I hope you will consider whether it is true.

In his book *Simple Words*, Adin Steinsaltz has called Hollywood a kind of religion, concerned with "intention, sentiment, and emotion." The hero is defined not by his deeds but by his good intentions.

> The Hollywood religion is also a great believer in the happy ending … Hollywood conveys the message that the world is like a fairy tale: somehow, it will all work out well in the end.

> Even when the happy ending is not built into the story—some stories just cannot have a happy end, the source material does not contain one—the Hollywood version will end happily, because otherwise it would be sacrilegious.

> The main tenet of Hollywoodism can be summed up in one word: happiness … [and] Hollywood's definition of happiness is comfort… The motivation behind every Hollywood story is the pursuit of happiness—which is, of course, attained at the happy end.

> Hollywood depicts an amusement park world.

> [It is] an advertisement for a dream, a very shallow dream—a dream about a simplified Heaven, about life that is supposed to be reality, but is not.

> Even in those few movies that leave us unhappy, we somehow think that this unhappiness is incidental, it is not that important. We believe that the misery will somehow be resolved by itself, by a hero, or by good luck, and that it will surely pass. People know that those are dreams, but they believe that they can somehow become real. In that sense, the Hollywood religion is the 'opiate of the masses.'

Steinsaltz was obviously writing about *Life Is Beautiful*, though he may not have known it.

Life Is Beautiful is a falsification of reality, not because life isn't beautiful, but because seeing its beauty from inside a Nazi concentration camp is a lot more difficult than the film suggests. And the reason so many people have been grateful to Mr. Benigni for making the film is that the film has finally succeeded in giving people what they have wanted for fifty years, a way to give the Holocaust a happy ending, a way to harmonize it with their modern religion of happiness.

The director should have listened more closely to his own doubts. "I was afraid people would not want to see it," says Benigni, whose idea for the film came in the form of wanting to place his clown character "in the most extreme situation imaginable." Why?

> I was very moved by this. I love the simplicity of the idea, a father protecting his son... It's an oxymoron to think about a gag in a concentration camp. It's impossible. The body refuses to move. But I tried to put my body as a clown in the extreme situation 'par excellence.' And the goal is to reach some sort of poetry, or beauty.

Notice, poetry or beauty do not arise out of the truth of the situation. They are goals. The situation is constructed to produce them. This is, again, simply the definition of sentimentality. Yet people who would sneer at the manipulative tear-jerking of a weeping, big-eyed young child painted on black velvet hail as a triumph this far more extreme example of the same vice.

"Most meaningful to Benigni," says his interviewer, "have been the thousands of letters he's received from children, thanking him for introducing them to a subject they knew little about, in a way they could comprehend." This sentence sends ice down my spine. A way they could comprehend? Of course. Reduce the concentration camp to a sentimental backdrop for a fantasy triumph of love over adversity and anyone can understand it, and will be thankful for it! Why not just feed them opium?

About his research into the Holocaust for the movie, Benigni says, "The details are unbearable... I had to stop." Unbearable, presumably, because he saw no way to join laughter to the tears evoked by the facts? So his solution was to remake the facts to fit his desired goal: Beauty. We will say life in a concentration camp can be made beautiful whether it can or not.

Nicoletta Braschi, the co-star and the filmmaker's wife, says, "The father not only saves [his son] physically, but he also saves his soul."

He doesn't have the shock, the trauma that otherwise he would have forever. All of this ridiculousness helps him in each moment, even through the worst.

Well, yes. How beautiful to have the boy so happily helped through the worst—if only we can believe it. We want to believe it. Our Hollywoodism commands us to believe it. And through the persuasiveness of the film image, many, it seems, do believe it. All those children who now have a way to "comprehend the subject." All those adults who enjoy the movie because it allows them to drag even the Holocaust into their religion of happiness. And they are so grateful to Mr. Benigni for giving them a way to see the Holocaust as okay after all. Here is a way out of it, past it (certainly not through it). We don't have to confront evil anymore; we can just imagine loving our children enough to protect them from it and they will be protected. What a relief!

The truth no one seems to want to address is that, whether we know it or not, and whether we settle comfortably into enjoying and praising such sentimentality or not, what we really crave is a faith that can transcend the Holocaust through addressing it, not a fantasy that escapes the Holocaust by avoiding it. Such a faith, in an age like ours, is perhaps impossible to come by through the medium of Hollywood and its offshoots. But let's not pretend anymore that Hollywood is a suitable substitute for it. If we cannot find a way to see the beauty of life in the face of the sacred and terrifying truths of life, in the face of the Holocaust, at least let us not settle so easily into the false comfort of the ersatz beauty of sentimentality.

The greatest sin of the film, which it commits not willfully, of course, but in probably invincible ignorance, is to have obliterated with its false image of heroism in the concentration camp the true images of those who, in reality and usually at the cost of their lives, found ways to make life beautiful and good despite their very real suffering and the very real depravity around them. Turning to *Life Is Beautiful* for an image of heroism in the camps is like seeking in the fast and easy frozen food section for Bubbe's chicken soup, or turning in to a brothel to find love. We can pretend all we want. No one is going to stop us. But what we really want we will not find there, and pretending we have found it will only prevent our seeking further.

Richard Dawkins, *The Blind Watchmaker*
[1998]

Having now had the unpleasant experience of reading Richard Dawkins' *The Blind Watchmaker* cover to cover in order to earn permission to speak without being accused of speaking in ignorance, I find my initial response to the first chapter to have been perfectly justified. The book is an example of the impressive power of the rational-scientific mind to generate elaborate and plausible conjecture. Some (but not most) of its facts were new to me and some of its theories were interesting. However, the book has completely failed to persuade me of the truth of its essential thesis, for reasons which I will try to express. I group the points of my critique under the headings logic, rhetoric, aesthetic, ethic, and practic.

Logic

1.   Dawkins repeatedly and disingenuously presents conjecture as fact, though he often pretends to be distinguishing between them. He repeatedly slides between evidence and hypothetical evidence with great and therefore misleading fluidity, built upon phrases like "it is nearly impossible not to believe that…"

2.   A superstructure of conjecture built upon the foundation of the assumption of the absolute and exclusive truth of material causation cannot prove the theory of material causation. The central argument of the book—that there is a material, and *only* a material, foundation to the development of all living things—is essentially question begging. The conclusion is only possible if it is held from the start as a premise.

3.   Even if one were to accept entirely the plausibility of the theory of cumulative selection as an explanation for complex life-forms, the nonexistence of a non-random, non-accidental cause for apparently random micromutations and for the very order of a universe to which

such explanations might apply cannot be proven. Its existence or non-existence can only be a matter of a priori assumption. Mechanisms and processes, even if we accept Dawkins' descriptions of particular ones, cannot be shown to comprise all causation. Efficient and material causes are not first or final causes.

4. The weight of the argument is carried by calculations of probability, all of them based on hypothetical assumptions. But no process of argument based on probabilities can prove causes. The resort to arguments based on probability in matters so far remote from empirical experience may be useful for imagining possibilities, but it is, at the same time, a confession of ignorance, evidence that knowledge about causes is inaccessible.

5. The requirement that we abandon the realm of common sense and empirical experience for the realm of pure abstraction (vast quantities in time, infinitesimal quantities in space), while essential to the kinds of explanations conjectured, necessitates that we enter, at the same time, the realm of unprovability. Mathematics and probability may theorize and predict; they cannot prove without evidence accessible to our sense experience, of which Dawkins offers none in the matters under dispute. His argument therefore remains purely speculative and his claim that Darwinian theory has earned exclusive right to the solution of the mystery of how life arose is false because no particular conjecture has been proven. I don't see how most of them ever could be proven, barring the discovery of apparently lost or inaccessible fossil records. Explanation of the reason for the absence of fossil record (for example, the lack of fossilized ancestors of the "Cambrian explosion") can be no more than hypothesis. It may be plausible, but it cannot be proven. Again, conjecture is not knowledge. And nowhere does Dawkins demonstrate that there has been sufficient geological time for all the micromutations and the resultant effects of cumulative selection to have arrived at the complexity he sets out to explain. He *assumes* there has been enough time, and under that assumption, proceeds to argue that with sufficient time all complexity can be explained by mutation and natural selection. Perhaps he is right. But he has not proven that he is or must be right. He can be believed to be right only by those who have already embraced an unquestioning belief in

material explanations of everything and in the power of the human mind to solve all mysteries.

6. Dawkins' argument against Paley—the watch is evidence of a watchmaker—is a straw man argument, as are his arguments against religious points of view generally. In his pompously displayed ignorance of what believers actually believe, Dawkins becomes guilty of precisely the kind of intellectual mistreatment that he complains of (from the press and other scientists) in relation to Darwinism. All theistic beliefs about the creation of life are inaccurately and unfairly lumped together with a particular nineteenth-century version of theistic creationism which almost any theist today would agree to be discredited in its particular claims. All beliefs in God are reduced to caricature far more egregious than the caricatures of Darwinism Dawkins complains of. That one believes in God in Dawkins' mind is ipso facto evidence of ignorant fundamentalist obscurantism.

7. Just as the actual randomness of an event apparently random to us cannot be proven, so the existence, intention, and methods of causation of a will that might exist outside of time and space cannot be proven or disproven by any time- and space-bound forms of explanation. If Occam's razor is invoked, it may be asked whether hypothetical conceptions of vast quantities of time and accident do not constitute a greater multiplication of unknowns than the more immediately accessible (to some) and (to some) empirically experienced existence of a divine will. The answer will be influenced by the degree to which one has already made a commitment to belief in materialism or theism. Therefore, proof in the matter remains inaccessible. Either faith in pure materialism will seem to make God an "unnecessary hypothesis," or faith in God will seem to make the doctrine of pure materialism a false idol. In either case, proof is inaccessible. If one believes that faith in a divine will is not incompatible with reason, one will think differently from the way one will think if one believes that reason is identical to positivistic science. But this difference is a difference of faith, not of correct or incorrect reasoning, and therefore it can be argued but never finally resolved by reason.

8. The underlying presumption of the book is that human rational explanation of all things is the highest human purpose, and that

by comparison with the act of scientific explanation (in this case, scientific conjecture based on faith in materialism and on extremely loosely calculated probabilities) all other human forms of relating to the fundamental experiences of existing in a complex world are negligible. This is yet another a priori assumption presented as self-evident when it is far more self-evident that Dawkins' own experience of the complexity and variety of life is severely limited, one might say impoverished, indeed benighted, by virtue of his apparent total lack of any spiritual insight whatsoever and his unquestioned faith in the absolute authority of the reasoning powers of his own mind.

9. Dawkins is simply stupid about what people mean by "God."

> To explain the origin of the DNA/protein machine [see below under "aesthetic"] by invoking a supernatural Designer is to explain precisely nothing, for it leaves unexplained the origin of the Designer. You have to say something like 'God was always there,' and if you allow yourself that kind of lazy way out, you might as well just say 'DNA was always there,' or 'Life was always there,' and be done with it (page 141).

> There are people in the world who desperately want not to have to believe in Darwinism. They seem to fall into three main classes. First, there are those who, for religious reasons, want evolution itself to be untrue (page 250).

> If we want to postulate a deity capable of engineering all the organized complexity in the world … that deity must already have been vastly complex in the first place. If we are going to allow ourselves the luxury of postulating organized complexity without offering an explanation, we might as well make a job of it and simply postulate the existence of life as we know it! (page 316).

This utter ignorance about what people mean by God, along with the presumption that no one who does believe in God is or can be a rational being who has rational reasons for opposing Dawkins' theory rather than being the victim of an irrational desire not to believe, puts all his arguments against religious ways of thinking about evolution out of court. If I have been required to comprehend the arguments for evolution before judging the truth of the theory, why is Dawkins not required to comprehend what intelligent believers mean by "God" before engaging in this kind of summary rejection? Once again, the unquestioned faith in materialist explanations takes religious faith and comprehension to be only another form of materialist rational explanation in disguise and then rejects it as simply a stupider form. Dawkins is an intelligent theoretician, but he is as far from providing us an avenue to the fullness of truth as the weatherman. He defines reality so narrowly that he misses most of it.

10. Darwinist materialism, like Platonism, Kabbalism, Talmudism, Scholasticism, and other teachings, demonstrates the almost limitless capacity of the human mind to generate explanations based upon fundamental assumptions that are themselves taken on faith. Whether these ways of looking at reality are true or not, in an absolute sense, cannot be finally determined by human reason from within them. They are therefore, from the human viewpoint, rightly seen as matters dependent on and informed by faith. Only from the divine viewpoint can they be known as ultimately true or not. From the human viewpoint they may be compared as to their persuasiveness, their fruitfulness, their apparent comprehensiveness, their self-consistency and logic, their aesthetic integrity, and their correspondence to experience. This fact ought to humble us rather than make us proud of having "solved the mystery of the complexity of life." In the case of Dawkins' Darwinism, there is only self-consistency to support it, and only that self-consistency which eliminates from consideration all human experiences except the abstract intellectual. On grounds of persuasiveness, fruitfulness, comprehensiveness, aesthetic integrity, and correspondence to experience, the theory is a dismal failure.

Hence: Even if Darwinian mutation-plus-cumulative selection is a true description of what happens, its effort to eliminate the "hypothesis" of a divine creator fails, a) because the divine creator is not a hypothesis in the scientific sense, is neither provable nor disprovable within materialist science, b) because it can provide no explanation of the causation of the physical laws underlying it, c) because its own foundational assumptions have eliminated the divine from the start, d) because the "hypothesis God" is a straw man that does not correspond to what any intelligent person arguing against Dawkins really believes, and e) because it denies its own basis in an equal and equally undemonstrable act of faith (i.e., in materialist explanations), and to that extent departs from the realm of science to become a thinly disguised form of special pleading for a view of the world that can be taken only on faith.

Rhetoric

1. The argument of the book is extremely and exasperatingly repetitive.

2. The particular parts of the argument are labored and tiresomely hammered.

3. The tone is condescending and glib.

4. The various instances of the author's claim to a high level of literary ability are themselves significant evidence of his deficiency in that quality.

Aesthetic

If the elegance and beauty of a mathematical or scientific proof are evidence of its truth, Dawkins' argument fails on aesthetic grounds. Apart from the rhetorical ugliness mentioned above, his use of metaphors reveals an intellect itself at war with the aesthetic responses of vast numbers of his intended readers.

1. Even if one grants Dawkins a personal love of the machine so intense that any mechanistic image is in itself satisfying, he ought to know that such is not the case for the very readers he is presumably trying to influence. His assertion that there is no essential difference between a computer and a human brain, between organic and inorganic processes, apart from being false to the whole empirical experience of being human and of distinguishing between living and non-living, man-made and natural, living being and machine, reveals a complete ignorance of what will be persuasive to the very readers whose minds he seeks to change. To him, but not to most men, to say the brain is a computer is to flatter the brain. This is because he

begins with an aesthetic rooted in mechanism. To him the physical and mechanical are the only beauty. This is certainly a possible aesthetic, but we may ask whether it is not an impoverishingly ugly and therefore (by the beauty-is-truth standard) falsifying one.

2. The arms race metaphor of Chapter 8 is similarly distasteful to any who experience life as in part a longing for harmony. (The same argument, for what it is worth, may be made against Darwin himself.) The image of nature as a battlefield divided every moment between the dead-end dead and the future-bearing survivors is not an image whose beauty is calculated to inspire us with the truth of an elegant simplicity. It is in fact rooted in a form of depression and despair, to which Darwin himself was more and more prone as his life went on, and which is all too familiar to us. It is our curse that we cannot believe that images of harmony are truer about the universe than images of war. (This is why the good characters in Shakespeare are so often debunked and reconceived while the evil ones are taken on their own terms.) Dawkins is blithe about this and tries to make a virtue of necessity. Or perhaps images of war really make him happy. But there have been better images of the universe than his, and nothing he says demonstrates that they have been less true in essence, even when incorrect in particulars.

Ethic

1. After quoting Fleeming Jenkin, Dawkins remarks,

> Don't be distracted by the racist assumptions of white superiority. These were as unquestioned in the time of Jenkin and Darwin as our speciesist assumptions of *human* rights, *human* dignity, and the sacredness of *human* life are unquestioned today (page 114, his italics).

The implication of Dawkins' statement is patently clear. He rejects and expects the reader to reject (without argument, as if the argument of the book were argument enough) any notion of the rights of human beings as distinct from the rights of animals (or indeed of plants, of machines, of carbon molecules) and any notion of the sacredness or unique value of human life. If any particular human being is to be seen by any other particular human being as merely a machine for conveying genetic information from the past into the future (as he argues explicitly), then there can be no significant grounds for that being's choosing to do good instead of evil. In fact, there are no good and evil. There is only the propagation of genetic information or its failure to be propagated. Even if the concept goodness were nothing but a tool for survival of that genetic information, there can be no reason, in Dawkins' line of reasoning, to suppose an obligation to help it survive. What survives survives, and what doesn't doesn't. There is nothing that *should* survive. All *shoulds* are eliminated from consideration except as an accidental characteristic that may or may not promote survival itself. Whether even some genetic information ought or ought not to survive is a non-question. Hence, to adopt Dawkins' view of life with any thoroughness is to abandon all obligation to moral behavior. Any one being bears no moral responsibility at all, whether for his own survival or for any other purpose. He will do what he will do and the process of which he is an infinitesimal mechanical part will continue, perhaps altered, but unimpaired by any act of his. Particular lives are meaningless; only evolution (and of course the *understanding* of evolution by Richard Dawkins) is true. One might ask whether anyone, however scientific-minded, actually would wish to live in a world thoroughly converted to this doctrine of evolution and to its implications.

2.   In addition to being an ignorant writer (ignorant about religion and faith, about the Middle Ages—"I am heartily thankful that we have escaped from the small-mindedness of the medieval church" [page 143]—and the history of philosophy, ignorant about the relation between his beliefs and a significant portion of his own mind, feelings, and life), Dawkins is a nasty writer. His use of epithets like "redneck" to characterize beliefs that have nothing to do with Southern Protestant fundamentalism (even if the term were admitted to be appropriate there) and his apparently intentional effort to insult all Christian and Jewish believers by asserting that the Genesis creation story has no more special status than the belief of a particular West African tribe that the world was created from the excrement of ants— these are simply signs of nastiness. He has fallen into the trap of using his own sense of victimization and the perceived victimization of his beliefs to justify sheer malice. And of course the malice undermines

his argument. If the Genesis story really did have no more status than he says, he would not have to go out of his way to insult it.

Practic

The practical implications of Darwinian materialism as espoused by Dawkins, even if it could be shown to be true rather than merely potentially plausible from a materialist perspective, are irrelevance, fruitlessness, and meaninglessness. In return for the momentary thrill of apparently having understood the true nature of life, of having "solved" its "mystery," what would we gain? The feeling of conquest, of comprehension, of mastery in terms of knowledge, perhaps. What else? How would this knowledge (were it proven to *be* knowledge and not simply a kind of faith in matter) affect our daily lives, our relations to others, our behavior, thoughts, feelings, "reproductive choices," moods? In one of two ways: either it is thoroughly and wholeheartedly embraced, in which case every subsequent gesture is rendered meaningless, nugatory, the mere epiphenomenal fluff surrounding the selfish gene's march to the future, the only possible honest response to which would be depression and despair; or it is willfully ignored, retreated from in a desperate act of intentional cognitive dissonance or a blind leap of faith in the name of making life bearable. In other words, the truth, as Dawkins imagines it to be, though he certainly has not carried his reasoning to its logical conclusions, must lead either to meaninglessness and despair or to the very kind of truth-falsifying self-delusion he hates most. In his world, meaning, hope, and the significance of human life for anything beyond the survival of genetic information are inescapably rooted in falsehood. The greatest triumph of the human mind — the solution of the mystery of existence — would turn out to mean the rendering ultimately and inescapably insignificant that discovering and solving intellect. Darwinian materialism has always been and must always be a dragon eating itself up from the tail. The apparently meaningful task of finding a material basis for all things ends by finding a material basis for itself, and the finder reasons himself out of any but a material and therefore empty existence. Dawkins' own joy in having "solved the mystery of life" is but an accidental event in his own selfish genes' march toward the future. And if so, why should he be either so proud of himself or so pleased?

Of course, as C. S. Lewis points out in *The Abolition of Man* (a book which successfully refuted Dawkins' worldview before Dawkins ever embraced it), it may be that the truth turns out to be such that if we embrace it, we die. Do we not still have an obligation to seek the truth? Well, not according to Dawkins. If we are merely the carriers of genetic information and our particular lives and choices have no other ultimate meaning or purpose than that, then there can be no reason for embracing such "humanly sacred" illusions as loyalty to truth. Nothing Dawkins tells us provides any reason for not abandoning his "truth" in the name of any "redneck" belief that might make us happier. This is the profound stupidity of all materialist worldviews. He is angered that believers in God refuse to adopt his self-evident truths. But why should he be angry? On what grounds that Dawkins believes in should truth matter to anyone? His righteous indignation is justified only by a worldview he has rejected (the view according to which love of truth has an absolute and non-material value). In short, he is trying to eat his cake and have it too, living off the income from an account whose capital he doesn't believe in. Dawkins is a wonderful hypothesizer about physical processes. As a would-be authority on "the mystery of life," he is a moron.

Luckily, of course, in reality we are not faced with having to make the choice between despairing truth and blind faith in falsehood. We are perfectly safe from the meaningless conclusion of meaninglessness, a) because (like Dawkins) few people tend to follow the logic of their belief out to its conclusions, and b) because one of the gifts we have been given, in addition to the gifts of life, a hospitable world to live in, and the reason with which to appreciate it, is that Dawkins' materialist ideas about what is true can never be proven to be true. We will never have to be called on to choose between truth and despair on one hand or happy self-delusion on the other. Dawkins gives us a vision, an image, an elaborate, probabilistic fantasy. We may choose to believe in it or not, but we are choosing belief over belief, not knowledge over blind faith. Therefore, we can always live in meaningful hope, the hope that the inescapable mystery of things hides what to those who live in faith it also sometimes reveals—the love of the Creator for his creatures.

James Atlas, *Bellow: A Biography*[1]
[2000]

In the late 1970s, when I was a graduate student in English at Brandeis University, Saul Bellow came to speak. His most memorable sentence was a response to the question, "Why did you become a writer?" He said, "It was *plus fort que moi*"—stronger than me. The sentence was not original, but at the time it seemed radical.

Until a few years earlier, Philip Rahv (Bellow's friend, *Partisan Review* editor, Brandeis professor, and dominating critical voice of the previous generation) was still asserting that great novels were about "how to live and what to do." Now Rahv was dead. The protests and relativism of the 1960s had swept through the academy, and in their wake we were left awhirl in the dust devils of theory. Literature was not speech but text, not meaning but structure. Pursuit of truth was an old wives' tale; pursuit of promotion was all.

Yet here was the famous Bellow, asserting that there was something stronger than the self whose commandment must be obeyed. At the time, I didn't see the irony in Bellow's being the one to say so. I found the statement refreshing, uplifting.

In the years since, I have approached any Bellow book with excitement and been rewarded by superb writing, the famous Bellow exuberance, and intelligence enhanced by wide reading in history and philosophy. When Bellow touches on deep questions in his deepest books (*Henderson the Rain King, Herzog, Mr. Sammler's Planet*) it is still refreshing, even moving.

But once a Bellow book is digested, there is always disappointment. Bellow has approached the deep questions but somehow not responded to them. Profundity of vision just isn't there. This observation is tersely expressed in a quatrain (responding to Bellow's 1983 interview in *The New York Times Magazine*) from an unpublished alphabet of authors by the late poet Philip Thompson:

---

1 Published in the Books section, *San Diego Union-Tribune*, October 22, 2000, page 1.

B is for Bellow,
A planet (he thinks),
Who remembers old Paris
For sex and for drinks.

Thompson noted that the author had gone to Paris not "to see and feel the city and to learn from it [but] to get a better sense of the planet Saul Bellow (whose essential mission is simply to declare its detachment from real cities)."

The writer's incapacity to turn from "the planet Saul Bellow" and engage any other part of the cosmos is implied and thoroughly documented but never properly addressed in James Atlas's monumental *Bellow: A Biography*.

The great virtue of this biography is that Atlas is able to map the planet Bellow with so much authority. Besides the ten years he spent researching and interviewing Bellow's friends and relatives, wives and lovers, colleagues and rivals, Atlas has Bellow's own books to go on. And all of them, his research confirms, are about Bellow and the people he knew. Wilhelm (in *Seize the Day*), Augie March, Henderson (inwardly), Herzog, Sammler, Citrine (in *Humboldt's Gift*), and Chick (in *Ravelstein*) are all versions of the author. Thanks to this wealth of sources, we get a thorough chronicle of Bellow's life, along with anecdotes, letters, quips, and identifications of the models for characters who *aren't* Bellow.

This biographical thoroughness contributes invaluably to our understanding that Bellow's life too, like his art, evades Rahv's "how to live and what to do" with "Here's how *I* live, what *I* do—what I *think*." Atlas paints Bellow as a brilliant and determined artist who earns his glory but also as an egocentric who is perpetually abandoning home, marrying and philandering, justifying himself, forever avoiding deep human connection.

In places, Atlas's psychological analysis of Bellow's self-exaltation is tonic. Defending himself in a letter to a friend for retelling a real-life escapade in *Humboldt's Gift* when he had "given his word" he wouldn't, Bellow writes, "I should think it would touch you that I ... wanted to remember you as I took off for the moon." Atlas nails him: "Bellow's letter ... offers a glimpse of the soaring valuation he placed upon his own work ... and his total lack of empathy for [the friend], whom he dismissed with withering condescension."

The drawback to Atlas's approach is that his biography sometimes turns tediously into psychography. Too often are we reminded that Bellow is always competing with his successful older brothers, that he has insufficiently grieved over the death of his mother, that he is forever trying to impress his father. Though these Freudian observations may be true, Atlas's overemphasis of them obscures more important matters.

For example, Atlas quotes from Bellow's 1976 Nobel Prize acceptance speech, in which Bellow articulates our modern plight: "an immense, painful longing for a ... more coherent, more comprehensive account of what we human beings are ... and what this life is for" in a time when "humankind struggles with collective powers for its freedom" and "the individual struggles with dehumanization for the possession of his soul." Thereupon the psychographer brings the soaring down to the pedestrian with a thud. The theme of Bellow's speech, he writes, "inevitably evoked memories, conscious or not, of his family's resistance to his vocation."

This psychologizing, along with Atlas's political bias (which plops Bellow into the "neo-conservative" category with no discussion of the intellectual grounds for his political opinions), results in the book's most significant flaw: Atlas fails to take his subject seriously as a man of thought. Bellow's greatest gift, his exhilarating eagerness to question life's meaning, is to Atlas a merely psychological phenomenon. As a result, the biography reveals but fails to grapple with Bellow's deepest limitation.

What this limitation is and the biographer's failure to identify it are pointedly illustrated in Atlas's dissection of a letter Bellow wrote to another Jewish writer, Cynthia Ozick, after a reviewer had criticized her for not "dealing directly with the Holocaust" in her novel *The Messiah of Stockholm*. Noting that he had brooded about the Holocaust since the late 1940s, Bellow confessed that he couldn't "even begin to say what responsibility any one of us may bear ... in a crime so vast that it brings all Being into judgment. To assess and assign responsibility as [the reviewer] seems to do (as if he were referring to an understandable phenomenon) is a mistake, to say the least... [R]evelation is something you can't send away for."

Although he observes that Bellow was haunted "that he may have failed to comprehend the fathomless depths of human evil," Atlas emphasizes the "more personal motif," Bellow's "deep sense of personal failure." In other words, Bellow may think he is discussing universal human problems, but he's only really talking about his own psyche.

Here Freudianism distracts Atlas—and us—from acknowledging the real issue: whether Bellow is *justified* in edging away from the admittedly terrifying question of responsibility, whether he speaks authentically not only for himself but for his time and place. If Atlas were not out of his depth here, he might have dropped the psychoanalyzing for a moment to take Bellow at his (eloquent) word. Only then would he have observed that, when it came to offering (instead of just longing for) an "account of what we human beings are … and what this life is for," Bellow was out of *his* depth, not only in his letter to Ozick, but in all his fictional brooding on the great questions of life.

Responding with authenticity to the overwhelming terror and mystery of the Holocaust, of life itself, requires discerning one's participation in a cosmos larger than oneself, facing the terrifying existential and spiritual fact and addressing it *nonetheless*. That is the mark of the truly great and responsible writers of the time, such as I. B. Singer (whom Bellow dismisses as a "stage manager, supplied with props from the *shtetl*"), William Golding, and Elias Canetti.

Bellow is quite right that you can't send away for revelation. But his saying so reminds one of the old joke about Goldberg's fervently praying every day to win the lottery, until a voice boomed from heaven in exasperation, "Goldberg! Do me a favor. Meet me halfway. Buy a ticket!" Inability to get beyond himself to meet revelation halfway characterizes both Bellow's masterful art and his now well-chronicled life. In this sense, at least, Bellow *does* speak for the age, gravitationally bound to the planet of the self.

Philip Roth, *The Human Stain*[1]
[2000]

"Wait. He's black? I thought he was Jewish!" Thus the reader wonders about the main character two chapters into Philip Roth's novel *The Human Stain*. "Roth mixed together the manuscripts of two novels by mistake?" Nope. Keep reading. "Aha, Alzheimer's? He forgot his main character was the son of a Jewish saloon owner and now makes him the son of an African-American Pullman porter?" Wrong again. Read on. In the past decade Roth has won four major awards, including a National Book Award and a Pulitzer. He knows what he's doing.

Coleman Silk, Roth's protagonist, is a vital, willful, and successful professor of classics and former Dean of the Faculty at Athena College in the Berkshire Mountains of western Massachusetts. As the book begins, he has resigned in a rage from his tenured teaching position. After five weeks of taking roll one semester, he had asked about two students who had never appeared, "Do they exist or are they spooks?" The missing students turn out to be black. Given the political climate on American campuses in the 1990s, "spook" is interpreted to be a derogatory racial epithet, and Professor Silk becomes an instant pariah. When his wife dies at the height of the scandal, he calls his colleagues murderers.

The action of the novel consists of what happens after Silk's resignation: his rage-generated book, the problems with his children, an anonymous letter, and, most fatefully, his affair with a younger cleaning woman. The significance of these events is deepened, layer by layer, through the recounting of Silk's past and that of several other characters. Slowly we come to realize the existence and the deeply ironic significance of Silk's secret.

The whole is compellingly narrated by Nathan Zuckerman, the fictional authorial persona of several of Roth's novels. He has been brought "back into life" by his brief friendship with Silk and finds "the proper presentation of his secret my problem to solve." *The Human Stain* is that presentation. Thus Roth turns the novel we are reading into one of

---

1 Published in the Books section, *San Diego Union-Tribune*, April 30, 2000, page 8.

its own subjects. But the unfolding of Silk's secret becomes more than a narrative problem.

As its main character challenges all who know him, the novel itself challenges us to be (in Eliot's words) less "assured of certain certainties." Is Silk an African-American or a Jew? Libertarian hero, libertine, or Uncle Tom? Is his abused and battered love a hopeless illiterate, a divine "Voluptas," or a tragic prophetess? Is her former husband villain, victim, or nemesis? Can the self-invented "I" escape the conventional "we"? Tragedy or ritual purification? Free will or fate?

As always, Roth uses explicit language to war against social (especially sexual) taboos. ("Enough already!" say we. "Oh yeah?" says he, "read the press on the President!") At the same time, it is a pleasure to watch him pillory the hype artists of political correctness that have polluted the intellectual atmosphere of academe. In addition we get intelligent commentaries on the Clinton affair, the press, the decline of education, the Vietnam War, black-white relations, feminism, and lessons on milking, boxing, ice fishing, and the secret life of crows.

But the novel's meditations add up to more than table talk. In this study of the inner life of a fascinating man, Roth's goal is to achieve something like the far-reaching vision of the classical tragedies that his character taught for a living. "How accidentally a destiny is made," he (Silk? Zuckerman? Roth?) observes, and "on the other hand, how accidental fate may seem when things can never turn out other than they do"—an observation the author strives to embody in the plot.

By the end, having thoroughly unfolded Silk's secret, Roth pronounces the "human stain" inescapable, no matter how successfully we make ourselves what we want to be. Even to talk of redemption is to miss the point of life. That point, so the book suggests, lies in a vaguely Thoreauvian, vaguely Buddhistic acceptance of the here and now, the embrace of both the beautiful *this* and the tragic *that*.

Yet eloquent, engaging, and even moral as the novel is, it fails to reach the true tragic height. An essential measure of spiritual vision is missing. One feels Roth himself to be enclosed within his own anti-conventional conventions: sexual liberation, individual freedom, the beautiful, meaningless processes of nature. Aeschylus and Sophocles articulated the presence of the divine in the tragedy of man. For Roth, character plus nature equals fate: man is but nature aware of itself, and irredeemably stained.

Edward Albee, *The Goat*[1]
[2004]

In a review of the San Diego Rep's remarkable production of Edward Albee's play *The Goat, or Who Is Sylvia?* one drama critic rightly finds some moments in the play to be gripping and properly observes that it *should* disturb. But his assertion that the essential thing the play does is to question "the limits of tolerance" ignores (or fails to see) the real issues Albee raises. To avoid really addressing them, the critic distances himself by complaining about dramatic flaws in the play ("Albee's penchant for switching from the rational to the irrational, the comic to the tragic") and the production ("acting's too over-the-top to be believable").

The production on the night I saw it was nearly flawless. The set was perfectly realized, the directing was crisp and compelling, the acting of all four cast members was riveting, the spoken language was crystalline, and the overall effect was thrilling—no dramatic flaw in sight. And Albee's technique of joining the comic to the elegiac to the tragic, of breaking the tension at just the right moments to keep us coming back for more deep implication, puts him, so far as dramaturgy goes, at the top of the A-list of modern American playwrights.

And yet the play is an outrage. Albee, profoundly, is guilty of the same blindness to the moral and spiritual implications of being human as the critic is shallowly.

The play is not merely a "controversial" questioning of the limits of tolerance. It is an assertion that the most powerful reality of human life is passion—whether of eros or of jealousy—and that there are no higher, no more fundamental, grounds for human behavior.

That the character Martin Gray is in love with a goat and thereby evokes the jealousy of his loving and beloved wife and the disapproval of their conventional friend is not just an allegory in which the goat might signify *any* adulterous affair—with another woman, with a man, with a youth or a child or a grandmother. The realism of Martin's profound erotic passion for the goat lures us into identifying with that passion: He *really*

---

1 Adapted from a letter to the editor, *San Diego Reader*, November 7, 2004.

loves that goat, and why can't we all just be free to love whomever we want? The friend, Ross, is objectionable to us *not* because the actor doesn't do a splendid job of characterizing him, but because Ross represents the oppressive social conventionality that the play, like the critic, questions. It is not the acting that rings false but the character, as he is meant to do.

But the real flaw of this play is its refusal to recognize any higher authority in addressing the matter of erotic passion than passion itself. In persuading us of the authenticity of this man's erotic passion, the play blurs the distinction between woman and goat, between human being and animal. It claims no higher calling for mankind than suffering the conflict between individual passion and social taboo.

Evidence? There is not a single moment of moral conscience, spiritual insight, rational judgment, or religious outrage in the play. The wife's long and brilliantly acted response to the revelation of her husband's infidelity climaxes in an act not of sacrificial redemption but of violent revenge. All the marginal sexual responses in the play (to animal, to infant, to father) unfold in a context of no higher calling for humanity than the magical impulses of eros and their tragic conflict with intolerant society. It is the old Romanticist Rousseau's pseudo-tragic holy war between the individual man's natural impulses and their enemy, the conventions of the group.

The outrage lies in the complete absence of any authority *besides* mere social convention for the suppression or redirection of degrading human impulses. If tragedy defines the real, then Albee's play shows that the reality of man is that he is no different from a goat.

But though the play fails to show it, we *are* different from goats. For one thing, we write plays about men in love with goats in order to discover what we are. That itself puts us beyond the goat level. For another thing, in every culture of the world there are sacred taboos that call human beings to distinguish themselves from animals, and from the animal in themselves—in every culture, that is, except the modern culture of pseudo-Freudian, Darwinian, Existentialist anti-religion that tells us that there *is* no nature of man to be distinguished from the nature of anything else, that we are nothing *but* nature, that we are whatever we do and are not meant to be anything more.

One problem with this culture is that in the end it will leave tolerance too behind. The only reason for human beings to be tolerant of others' differences is that we are called to be so by the conviction that it is right to do so, that in doing so we fulfill our nature as human, not merely animal, beings. But to push tolerance beyond the traditional standards of human culture and religion toward the acceptance of any behavior whatever, so long as it comes from a deep natural impulse or a pseudo-divine revelation, is to push tolerance itself out of the human world. Why be tolerant if impulse is the only authority and the deepest impulse in me is *not* to be tolerant? If we say we are nothing but nature, then we surrender all grounds for arguing that we *should* be natural, *should* be unconventional, *should* withhold judgment upon others' strangeness.

Albee, like the critic, wants to have reality both ways: The critic wants the play to be disturbing, but claims no right to judge what it depicts as depraved: the emotion of disturbance is natural, and hence good, but the passing of judgment upon what disturbs us is bad. Albee wants us to be tolerant because intolerance turns the mystery of erotic attraction to tragedy, and so to entertaining theater. But to be tolerant of a decent man's betrayal of his good wife for another woman, or for a man, or for a goat, is to undermine the very source of the value of tolerance: the conviction that to be human is to be called to rise above merely animal nature toward the *super*-natural ideals that require the making of distinctions—justice, kindness, and truth—ideals of which tolerance is but a poor, wraithlike reflection.

In making a man's sexual affair with a goat the stuff of a tragedy unmixed with psychological sickness, immoral infidelity, or spiritual blindness—in worshipping impulse unilluminated by reason or religion—Albee is embracing a controversial attitude very old and very disturbing indeed: it is called idolatry. But here the idol is not the goat. It is the goatishness of man.

The Flying Karamazov Brothers,
Don Quixote
[2007]

Last night I went to see the San Diego Repertory Theatre's *Don Quixote* at
the Lyceum in downtown San Diego. The show is not a dramatization of
Cervantes' picaresque novel. It is a show: an extravaganza of costumes,
stylized acting, poetic evocations of medieval Spain, and juggling. It also
conveys a worldview and an implied political agenda, and there's the
rub.

The show features The Flying Karamazov Brothers, whose work in
the past I have always loved for its brilliance in combining movement,
timing, beauty, comedy, and meaning. To see the Karamazovs at their
best is to experience perfection in the combination of physical motion and
aesthetic delight. The Karamazovs are led by that master of significant
juggling, Paul Magid, who also wrote the script. Magid (whose name
means "teller" or "teacher" or "preacher") is a remarkable and gifted
clown, juggler, imagist, playwright, and entertainer. He is also a teller, a
teacher, and a preacher, and there again lies the rub.

The cast—actors, movement artists, and musicians—was a superb
band of multitalented performers. Despite the hard-to-lighten content,
they did wonderful and entertaining work. The Rep is known for its
multicultural, multiracial, multiethnic mix of productions and is a mainstay
of peace-making theater in San Diego. And there's that rub again.

In the play the Cervantes character named Benengeli (played by
Magid) is a Muslim Moor of seventeenth-century Spain who holds as his
ideal the way Christians, Muslims, and Jews got along in Andalusia in
the tenth and eleventh centuries. He tries to be the friend of Don Quixote,
who in this play has gone mad not in the name of chivalry, but in the
name of Catholic anti-Moorish jingoism. What he finds is that only in
dying and in death can he and his prejudiced friend just get along.

Well, here's the promised rub: This *Don Quixote*, for all its hilarity and
costume and movement and juggling, is really a work of thinly veiled
political propaganda. Don Quixote is a stand-in for that image of President
George Bush invented and promoted by the anti-war Democratic left: he

rushes in to tilt at enemies who don't really exist and messes everything up. So far as the play is concerned, we all *would* be able to get along if it were not for our own (i.e., America's) irrational and hysterical hatred of the imaginary other—Muslim, Hispanic, or Black.

The implication of the play, repeatedly and heavy-handedly made, would be merely childish and ironic if it were not also dangerously stupid. Please don't misunderstand me. I want us all to get along too. I really do. But I don't think Americans like those sitting in the Lyceum last night or those sitting in the White House or the Pentagon are the main problem.

The play's raison d'être being relevance to current events, the play associates America's war against Muslims in Iraq and the movement opposing illegal immigration with the Catholicism of the Inquisition and the reconquest of Spain. President Bush, for whom Don Quixote is the fairly obvious stand-in, is presumably the bad guy on both modern counts (though many who wish he were more aggressive in securing the borders would put him on the other side): One would have to be as mad as "DQ" (so this Sancho Panza calls him) to justify the war in Iraq or to want America's borders secured.

The irony is that America, more than any other country in the world at any time in history, *is* the Andalusia of the Magid Benengeli's dream. Only those brought up from the cradle (by the likes of Maureen Dowd, say, or Noam Chomsky) to believe the world would be Eden were it not for America and capitalism could possibly think otherwise. Of course we are not an ideal society. But where else in space or in time, since America fought to abolish slavery, have so many people of such different races, backgrounds, cultures, ethnicities, languages, opinions, and customs gotten along so well with one another for so long and fought so consistently against racial and ethnic and religious persecution at home and abroad?

Is it right to judge others by different standards from those to which we hold ourselves, the universal standards of kindness and love that the play embraces? Or is America to be judged a hideous failure against the impossible standards of the Garden of Eden before the fall—or rather the Marxist utopian future—while other peoples are given a pass for not rising above the world's norm of conquest, hatred, corruption, violence, and injustice? Are we or are we not the least nasty society the world has ever seen?

And from which culture came the ideas that have caused it to be so? It is only because of the biblical doctrine of the brotherhood of man and a thousand years of Christian government that the Western world has come to value so highly the ideal of getting along with others. Yes, Western Christianity produced the Inquisition. But it also produced the American Revolution and the abolition of slavery and Martin Luther King, Jr.

Ironically, it is not the imaginary Moor Benengeli who holds the ideal of love-despite-differences. It is the American Jew Magid and his play's American Christian director. Without two millennia of the Western religious tradition, where could they possibly find grounds for the shared belief in loving their neighbors as themselves?

Ask the Benengelis of Iraq, grateful for our help in setting up a government of laws in a country racked by sectarian religious violence, who is better represented by the Spanish Inquisition: the American army or the Shiite death squads? If the author and director really want to be relevant to the present moment, it is not Don Quixote's Catholicism that they should be indicting for inquisitorial cruelties but the likes of the Taliban and the Wahhabists and Hezbollah and Ahmadinejad. [Update: Add the Chinese Communist Party and their useful leftist idiots promoting cancel culture. Add Hamas.]

When has George Bush ever called for the expulsion from anywhere of anyone but terrorists and murderers? And yet every day we hear calls for the destruction of Israel and the Jews and the Christian "crusaders" and the West from the real live present-day inquisitors that the play and the media and the entertainment left pretend would just get along if only America would let them.

Sitting in the theater last night, approving by their responses, was an audience that could only sit there approving of such upside-down "relevance" because the play depicts the opposite of the truth. Where would they be if they clapped at a play put on in Tehran or Damascus or Gaza or Riyadh that made Muslims into the cruel and unjust persecutors of Jews and Christians? Oh, wait. Clapping there would be okay; if you *didn't* clap at the cruelty and injustice against Jews, Christians, and secular Westerners you'd be beaten up or killed. "Let's all just get along" would probably not be that play's theme, though.

Has the artistic/aesthetic/entertainment community gone completely mad? Say what you want about the errors and follies of our war in Iraq. But please spare us the superior moralizing that refuses to acknowledge the most obvious facts of history and current events.

In reality, the medieval Christian and Muslim rulers of Spain were almost perpetually at war, and the Jews were persecuted from both sides. The century of relative harmony enjoyed by Christians, Muslims, and Jews in Andalusia under the Ommiad caliphs was ended when the country was overrun, not by Jews, but by the Almoravids in the eleventh century and the Almohads in the twelfth, medieval North-African versions of the Wahhabis and the Taliban respectively. Not all those who were expelled in the Reconquista were decent folk like Magid's Benengeli and Jews like Magid.

Why are the Crusades and the Inquisition and the Reconquista the icons of evil in this play and not the Taliban, Hezbollah, Hamas, and Al Qaeda? Cruelty and unjust violence are evil whoever perpetrates them, aren't they? It is not the Christians or the Jews or the American capitalists who are fighting today out of race hatred or religious fanaticism. To pretend that one is in favor of everyone's getting along while refusing to recognize where tyranny really lies is not only quixotic. It is suicidal.

Summer Paradox
[2007]

My teacher Mary Holmes used to call Los Angeles the "last gasp of Western Civilization." She might have expanded her geography to include San Diego had she known about this little poem that my friend found scrawled on the Mission Beach seawall several years ago:

> Surf, dooby, chow,
> Party, helmet, sleep.

Say it over a few times. It has many virtues: simplicity, clarity, rhythm, honesty. It has become one of my favorites. Not only because in it one may, in the words of the poet Philip Thompson, "Behold the darkness of one long good time." The poem is an instance of a profound paradox. Its being says more than its words.

Why did the anonymous poet, whose words proclaim that he lives in the body, of the body, for the body, bother to compose this ditty, to write it on a wall? From whence sprung his affection for metaphor ("helmet"), his embrace of rhythm (trochaic trimeter catalectic), his fidelity to chronology, his generalizing of an ideal day? Why not just live it? What is the impulse also to say it?

The Mission Beach poet is a pagan, of course, worshipping nature and sensation. Or so he thinks. Yet is there a more devoted worshipper of the invisible in our time than such a surfer? He rises from sleep to surf, desiring to ride the perfect wave perfectly, to find his way into harmony with the mysterious nature of the land-longing waves, the sea itself, rhythm, beauty.

As in surfing, so in verse, something in him craves more than physical sensation. The poem exists because the poet craves to embody meaning in an artifact, to convey it to his fellow human beings. He may know nothing of the forms of Plato or the *logos* of John or the *ordo amoris* of Augustine, but being human like them, he cannot live without more meaning than the merely physical world can provide. And so he writes a poem, worshipping the invisible whether he knows it or not.

My teacher would not have been surprised by the poem's paradoxical nature. In *Mary Holmes: Paintings and Ideas,* she calls paradox "the natural condition of the world. It is both the working principle and the mystery of life... We are always surrounded by paradox because all of creation is the union of opposites. All energy comes from the union of opposites."

By mysterious paradox the Mission Beach poet consoles me. Even as his words depict Western Civilization's dying away into mere sensation, his poem cannot help revealing that there is more spirit to our life in the body than our body can contain.

Philip Pullman, *His Dark Materials*
[2008]

The Golden Compass (so-called in America; in England it is called *Northern Lights*), *The Subtle Knife*, and *The Amber Spyglass*, by Philip Pullman, form a trilogy called *His Dark Materials*. The trilogy title is based on a phrase from Milton's *Paradise Lost*, by which epic poem Pullman claims to be influenced. If so, he is influenced as William Blake was influenced by Milton: that is, to turn Milton's vision on its head. Pullman is also influenced by Blake, of whose worst qualities he is a shallow but loyal devotee, for he too takes his own Romantic fancies to be a true imagination of reality. But whereas Blake made up for that fault with genius and poetry, Pullman has no such aces up his sleeve. I grant that he went to a lot of work to think up all the things he thought up for these books: lots of invented places and beings, a complex plot, and a consistent purpose. But their effect on me was that of occasional sparks of hope being relentlessly doused by an inescapable spiritless drudgery.

It is not necessary to get too excited that these novels are not only anti-Catholic Church but explicitly anti-Christian, anti-Jewish, anti-Muslim, anti- any theistic religion you care to think of. No less are they anti-philosophical: none of Alfred North Whitehead's "footnotes to Plato" here. Because these novels ignorantly or maliciously reduce the Christian religion to nothing more than a doctrine of tyrannical war against the body, nature, pleasure, love, and sex, their atheism poses no real threat to religion. Like many polemical atheists, Pullman is fighting a war against an enemy about which he seems to know very little outside of stereotypical clichés. (Pullman is an Honorary Associate of the National Secular Society in Great Britain and a supporter of the British Humanist Association, both of which promote atheist and anti-supernatural agendas.) There are, of course, significant Gnostic and Manichean influences within Christianity, as within Judaism and Islam, that do preach the evils of the material world, thereby in part bringing upon themselves Pullman's popular kind of reaction against religious asceticism. But to tar the whole Christian religion with that one brush is dismally shallow.

The real frustration is that as a fantasy-fiction writer, Pullman reveals an impoverished and utterly derivative imagination. Though the trilogy is obviously meant to be the anti-C. S. Lewis and anti-J. R. R. Tolkien chronicles, it depends not at all on a persuasively invented mythical world like Narnia or Middle Earth. The drabness of Pullman's inventions—colorless pseudo-spirituality, repetitive plot structure, awkwardly executed melodrama—in fact only confirms the contrasting greatness of Lewis, Tolkien, and J. K. Rowling as fantasy writers of depth and vision.

Absent real invention, Pullman's moments of dramatic intensity depend instead on parceled-out knee-jerk reversals of one after another fundamental element of the Christian religion—contrarianism in place of drama. The Fall of Man was really a liberation, intentionally repackaged as sin by the body-hating Church, which is synonymous with the Inquisition. The fallen angels are heroic rebels against Blake's tyrannical Ancient of Days, a worn-out old-man angel who is relieved to be dissipated into his constituent molecules in the presence of his savior, the brave little flesh-and-blood girl. Death is not heaven, hell, or purgatory but either shadow lands (like the ancients' Hades), or absolute nothingness, or molecular dissolution and absorption back into the natural world, where one's constituent elements happily though unconsciously mix with the molecules of former loved ones. Consciousness itself is a function not of the God-given soul but of particles of conscious dust—or rather the dust is a function of consciousness—or something. It's never explained. Underworld harpies turn from nasty to nice by being loved and appreciated. The Kingdom of Heaven is evil; the Republic of Heaven is the noble goal.

The redemption of all universes comes when the young heroine gets laid (in both senses) under a tree, or, if you prefer, when she and the young hero—we're talking ten minutes into puberty here—fall into profound love and unite their bodies and their souls, without benefit of clergy, which is evil, in a perfect apotheosis of modestly undescribed sexual intercourse on non-prickly greenery amongst the flowers of a pleasant garden-world. Meantime, the Church's hyperbolical killer-priest, Gomez—who observes that the use of wheels by the innocent rational denizens of this Eden is "abominable and Satanic, and contrary to the will of God" (*The Amber Spyglass*, page 464)—is sent to kill the heroine in order to prevent her from saving the world for natural happiness by falling into erotic love. Before he can do any damage, Gomez fortunately dies by slipping on a rock and having his face held underwater by a weak but determined homosexual rebel angel, whereupon a big harmless lizard eats his body.

The serpent that makes the redemptive tryst possible is a woman scientist who has told the children the story of how an erotic affair converted her to atheism from being a nun.

Apart from a few individual exceptions, the good guys are gypsies, witches, elves, harpies, rebel angels, lone inventors, children (except those perverted by specters, the by-products of the Church's efforts to destroy the heroine), and, of course, animals. The bad guys are God, non-rebel angels, the Church and its institutions, priests, institutional scientists, professors, society, and adults generally. (At least we have been spared anti-Semitism, there being not a Jew in the whole work; Pullman's bitter prejudice is reserved for the Catholic Church.) Okay, fine. Go ahead and invert the main stream of Western Civilization to make your point. But at least make the goodness of the good guys and the badness of the bad believable.

Good writers give us imagined people with characteristics. This writer gives us merely ciphers constructed to carry the characteristics he needs carried. We don't get to know them or care about them except as hooks upon which the anti-theology is hung. His method of psychological elucidation is to invent for each character a daemon who, in the form of a physically palpable, intimate, and conversable animal, expresses by its actions and gestures what is going on in the soul of the human character. The result is an endlessly repeated reduction of psychology to cliché gestures. Person X is afraid of and about to be overborne by Person Y? No need to go to the trouble of describing human experience. Just show Daemon X in the form of a cowering rabbit succumbing to Daemon Y in the form of a hissing ferret, and voila, your work is done.

In rapid succession, skipping transitions with which we might empathize, the characters experience only those feelings that the manipulation of the plot demands. For example, Lyra, our heroine, who has been fighting an exhausting battle for days and is just about at the end of her physical rope, suddenly has to go on some trek for many miles and then fight a whole new set of battles, during which she begins to tire anew. Nothing remains of the previous days of exhaustion. She is infinitely tireable, and therefore infinitely tiring. There are a few hours of rest for her now and then, but none for the reader. Some of Lyra's bruises are treated by someone whom the plot requires for a piece of information; other bruises disappear as soon as a quick change of circumstance makes them irrelevant. At several points the injured hand of Will, the young hero, has bled so much that he's almost dead—that is, until he has to fight some new foe, whereupon he fights, in the midst of which battle he may start (all over again) to feel tired. This lack of verisimilitude can go on for days and weeks at a time. "Well," you will say, "but his name is 'Will'—it's a metaphor." If so, never was metaphor so unimaginatively predictable.

At the same time, characters' entire moral and spiritual orientation may shift for the convenience of the plotting author. Pullman's equivalent to Gollum's last gesture at the edge of the abyss in Tolkien's *Return of the King* is Mrs. Coulter's sudden renunciation of a life of selfishness, deceit, malice, and betrayal in a fit of selfless mother-love for a daughter whom, given the story, she does not really know. Where Gollum saved the day by being true to his nature, Coulter contributes to saving the day by changing internally in a way for which the book does not prepare us and which cannot be reasonably explained according to any known human psychology. The Romantic fantasist's idea of nature can explain it of course. In these universes, a mother's love, once it becomes useful to the plot, knows no obstruction, though a son's love for his mother can be heroically (and efficiently) suppressed until all missions are accomplished. At work in Tolkien's and Lewis's climactic moments was grace, which redeems facts by revealing the larger context in which they exist. Pullman achieves his climactic moments by brazen manipulation. Not grace but only the author is at work, visibly adjusting worlds, people, daemons, and special effects to promote his doctrine.

The characters being mere constructs, no real character development can take place, though a lot of learning does. But that learning is never qualitative, only quantitative. Every breakthrough is merely an added piece of information, rather than an insight, and it comes right on time. One could accuse the Harry Potter books too of timeliness of breakthroughs, except that there each turn in the story is effected by three-dimensional characters we have come to know as people, characters with real motives caught in believable moral crises. Here, by contrast, each turn feels like the result of clockwork. Reading this trilogy is not at all like losing oneself in a strange new world like Narnia or Malacandra or Middle Earth or Hogwarts. It is like listening to a sales pitch: The car salesman creates in your mind the need for a way to defrost the rear windshield, and voila, right on time, there he is pointing to the apparently magic button that does just that. And then he does it again. And again. And nothing is achieved but weariness: what the truth-telling alethiometer will not tell, the subtle knife will cut through, or the amber spyglass reveal—facts, facts, and more facts.

One of the silliest signs of Pullman's agenda-driven invention is the book's modish gender-bending. The heroine is a tomboy who begins the book running around on rooftops and fighting rock wars with village boys. The brave young hero gets to know the heroine by teaching her how to cook an omelet. With a little shove, Mrs. Coulter knocks the powerful Lord Asriel out of the driver's seat of his own helicopter-like secret weapon. Two male angels form a gay-cliché couple, butch and fem, the latter heartbroken when the former sacrifices his life (or what passes for it among the angels) for the pro-sex, anti-Church cause. I am not making this up; Pullman is.

Theme there is aplenty, but it is one and the same throughout. Rather than developing depth, it simply accretes instances. The Church is the bad guy at the start and at the end. Nature is good and God is a hoax from start to finish. First we find it out this way, then that, then another, but the only true meaning always lies in the same place: Nature, matter, the body, and the worship of them are good; the only unredeemable evil is the life-censoring Church.

Such single-minded polemics might be bearable if the unimaginative worlds Pullman creates to carry them at least had some logic to them. But their illogic is persistent and annoying. Take angels, for example. They long for flesh and blood bodies but don't have them. They are bright vaguenesses in the air. And yet regent-angel Metatron, who longs for the flesh of Marisa Coulter, can have the breath squeezed out of him by the strong physical arms of Lord Asriel. What breath? Angels suddenly have lungs? Apparently. And they can also die. Okay, fine. Go ahead and abandon thousands of years of tradition to redefine the term "angels," bringing them down to an earthly level in order to prove that the Church's doctrines are nonsense. Let the body be the only reality. Have the angels breathing in a physically refined, Miltonic sort of way. But then why are they not satisfied with other angel bodies? Why this lust for human physicality when they have their own? For no logical reason but to show that where the physical is concerned, more is better.

Or take the diamond-shaped beings in one of the multiple worlds Pullman gives us. All its creatures have one fore leg, one hind leg, and two side legs (or wings) rather than a central spine with two sets of side-by-side legs. We're told it's because their world evolved without the principle of the spine. Okay, fine. But what keeps those four appendages at the four points of their diamond shapes? From whence (in a book that keeps promoting the knowledge of physics) the integrity of their physical shape? What is Pullman's alternative to the spine? Not given. No need to think it up. Doesn't matter. They're just different, that's all. Like it or lump it.

Or take the land of the dead. Until the great saving gesture of the heroine Lyra, the dead are mere ghosts of themselves stuck in the dead lands. But there are two other deaths: one even the ghosts don't want; the other they do. One is falling into a black hole of nothingness, not otherwise explained. The other is breaking out into one of the natural worlds, whereupon the ghosts dissipate into the multiple realms of nature—air, water, earth, plants, people. It is the book's consummation devoutly to be wished. But wait. Ghosts are made of molecules? If so, how can they be annihilated by falling into the abyss? If not, how can they be redeemed from their temporary death by dissipating into the molecular world of nature? Why is one death better than the other? And even if it were, why weren't they content to dissipate into the molecular world of underground rocks and harpies? Why this arbitrary superiority of the molecules making up air and clouds and flora and fauna?

Or take the tiny space between the laminated universes—thin interstices made of the ultimate abyss of nothingness—through which the hero unwittingly cuts into other worlds with the "subtle knife." Why didn't someone—there's always someone appearing out of nowhere to give timely advice—tell the hero to put Lyra's hair there so that the explosion meant to kill her—oh never mind. It isn't worth trying to explain.

Finally, there is the ineptness of the descriptions of battles, landscapes, and movement. Pullman will pretend to be telling us what we need to know: the sea is that way, the mountain this; good guys are here, bad guys there. But if you try actually to imagine the scene, you find you can't really figure out where anything is. Distances increase or decrease, extreme temperatures are felt or ignored, speeds are varied, people move unnoticed—and I don't mean just the witches, who know how to make themselves invisible—regardless of physics. All relations in time and space are exactly what the author needs them to be for purposes of plot and polemic, whether they make sense in the mind's eye or not—usually not. His attempts to describe with verisimilitude even the physical world he worships are a hoax.

This being a story of multiple universes, characters move from world to world. But as they do, landscapes appear out of no necessity but the author's convenience. There needs to be a shady grove with a spring and a stream so the hero and heroine can rest a bit? Voila, there one is. There needs to be a place where one can cut through the rock of the dead lands into another world? Voila, a character suddenly reports she knows where that place is. It's hard to get to? Okay, fine. Exactly three paragraphs are given us to show how hard it is to get to, and then voila, we are there and the pain of the journey is forgotten because now there are new adventures to meet on the other side. We have to put an end to the cutting through to new worlds? Voila, yet another character appears to tell us yet another fact: every cut increases the number of specters. It is the fantasist's imagination on steroids—a myriad situations with no development or insight or vision we can even temporarily believe in, let alone care about.

There are instances of heroism and kindness and self-sacrifice, of course, as there must be in any fantasy tale with the faintest hope of being read. They are not any more believable than the nonsense, but here at least Pullman rises above his own polemics to indicate in spite of himself that such values are truly valuable. Such instances lead Kurt Bruner and Jim Ware, in a book called *Shedding Light on His Dark Materials*, to claim, as their publisher puts it, that "though Pullman intended to do just the opposite, he has created a cosmos that seems to confirm the existence of a loving God—one where truth wins out over deception, grace trumps the virtue of self-reliance, and relationship is prized above independence." Perhaps. My impression is that they are giving Pullman's inadvertence too much benefit of what should be a greater doubt.

Pullman's own explanation for why things happen as they do boils down to one word. On page 491 of *The Amber Spyglass*, the female angel Xaphania utters the following ultimate profundity: "there are fates that even the most powerful have to submit to." Wow! We've come through 1,168 pages of plot, not to mention 2,500 years of Western Civilization, in order to reach this pinnacle of wisdom: Everything is controlled by fates. How illuminating! What or who are fates? Forget it. Just live in the now, enjoy the air and water and sky and your body, and oh yes, probably you should try to be a nice person, but don't ask why. Nothing in this trilogy even attempts to address that question.

"Immature poets imitate; mature poets steal," writes T. S. Eliot. Philip Pullman demonstrates that primitive writers cannibalize. Pullman's only ideas are pagan negations of the ideas he reductively takes to be Christianity. His is a characteristically modern brew—one part Enlightenment worship of reason, one part Romantic worship of nature, and one or more parts impoverished imagination—producing a pseudo-philosophy of consummate vulgarity.

John Keats, in a letter to his brothers, famously wrote

> it struck me, what quality went to form a Man of Achievement
> especially in Literature & which Shakespeare possessed so
> enormously—I mean *Negative Capability*, that is when man is
> capable of being in uncertainties, Mysteries, doubt, without any
> irritable reaching after fact & reason...

On page 458 of *The Amber Spyglass* Pullman has Lyra use Keats's phrase—
when she could possibly have read and understood the letters of Keats is
never explained—to describe how one reads the alethiometer (the truth
machine) and how one cuts through worlds with the "subtle knife." That
is, you put your rational intellect to sleep and let your impulses and
intuitions do the work.

Okay, fine. It being a Romantic fantasy, let the heroine think she
possesses what Keats observed to be the essential quality of the "Man
of Achievement." Even if we stretch the truth to grant that Lyra means
what Keats meant by "negative capability," Pullman himself lacks it. *His
Dark Materials* instead reveals an incapable negativity. Its only content is
negation of religion, its form an interminable bore.

Sarah Ruhl, *The Clean House*
[2008]

In the production of Sarah Ruhl's play *The Clean House* at the San Diego Repertory Theatre, the direction was deft, the performances competent, and the set impressive. But I have nothing good to say about the play itself. Despite its author's receipt of a MacArthur "Genius" Fellowship, the play exemplifies precisely what is so profoundly wrong with contemporary theater: namely, the incessant production of plays written in banal and manipulative language that convey absolute and uncritical worship of human emotion as the primary, indeed the only, meaning in life.

Here's what the play does not touch on: virtues or spiritual gifts like heroism, justice, humility, compassion, patience, temperance, faith, and wisdom; the real and problematic powers of traditional values and practices in a world of increasing doubt; the pressing philosophical questions posed by science; the ironies of history; the mystery of the relation between body, heart, and mind, nature and spirit, free will and fate; the difficulty of balancing individual liberty and social responsibility. Instead, the play, which like many another seeks to achieve universal human seriousness by depicting a death, dissolves all human concerns in a bath of bathos, feelings the only reality. The ultimate goal of theater today by implication? Sentimentality.

In *The Clean House* a surgeon betrays marital fidelity with an older woman with whom he has fallen in love when preparing to perform a mastectomy on her and then brings her into the home he has shared with his wife, a successful but repressed medical doctor, for the sake of becoming one big happy non-traditional family. In the meantime, the wife's equally repressed sister is secretly cleaning the doctors' house because the Brazilian maid is busy trying to come up with the perfect joke, defined as that joke at which one will die laughing—literally. In fact, the play shares only one joke with the audience (three, if one understands Portuguese), a joke that I first heard in 1980, here told badly. In the end everyone is healed by the power of sentiment.

The justification for the adultery and for the murder by joke is the "aura" surrounding the older woman (who is dying), her ability to make people feel things like vitality, compassion, enjoyment of the taste of apples, and acceptance of death. It is not an aura the audience can share in perceiving. It is not evidenced by any moral vision, human insight, depth of compassion, or religious, philosophical, or intuitive genius. We are simply told of its existence and expected to believe in it. The production attempts to make up for this gap in meaning and authenticity with deconstructed, post-modern stylization, the only thing that distinguished it from a TV sitcom. It was not distinguished from a sitcom by its supposedly poetic language: The height of its inspiration by the muse was represented by such phrases as "something between an angel and a fart."

My response during the play was ho-hum. Thinking about it afterwards, I was peeved. Feel good about adultery; feel good about love; feel good about breaking out of the repression hidden in order and cleanliness by making a mess of the living room; feel good about dying. Feel good because the dying woman with the aura tells you it's all okay. When St. Francis or the Baal Shem Tov tells us to rejoice, we may rejoice. We see that they have won the dues of rejoicing from a triumphant battle with reality. When Sarah Ruhl tells us, in a play about jokes that is almost never funny, to rejoice because love makes adultery okay and comedy makes euthanasia okay, some may walk out feeling good. I walked out exasperated at the shallowness, the banality, and the waste of opportunity. If this is what passes for genius in the contemporary theater, then we are in bigger trouble than contemporary theater is willing to imagine.

P.S. There is one passage in the play that asserts that according to a law of Judaism, finding one's "bashert"—which the play defines as one's soul mate, the person with whom one is destined to share a perfect mutual love—justifies adultery and abandonment of one's wife. The character admits that this was heard on NPR, which for some is sufficient evidence of its origin in whole cloth. Nevertheless, I feel obliged to say that, so far as I know, there is no such Jewish law. One's "bashert" means the person one is destined to marry. Nowhere in traditional Judaism does falling in love justify adultery.

James Cameron, *Avatar*
[2010]

I found the film *Avatar* entertaining, intellectually offensive, and ironic in the extreme.

The story was engaging—a stock tale of sci-fi adventure in which the hero goes native, defends his new underdog community from his own oppressive kind, and gets the girl. The film was visually compelling, with imaginative computer imaging, effective 3-D, and enjoyable alterations of garb and scale applied to flora and fauna—calla lilies, jellyfish, and trees; horses, wolves, monkeys, elephants, rhinos, and pterosaurs.

There was one authentically moving moment in the human/humanoid events of the movie: Challenged to a duel by his rival for power and for the girl, the protagonist pulls his knife, then throws it away, saying "I am not your enemy." It was a gesture of courage, brief but dramatic and noble. Of course it didn't impress the rival, who is prevented from hurting the hero only by a threatening, tooth-baring hiss from the knife-wielding heroine.

Which brings us to the intellectual offense—the film's outrageous festival of propaganda. Reality is caricatured as a Manichean war between the forces of light—the nature-wise noble savages of the feminine planet Pandora—and the forces of darkness—the pseudo-military, mineral-hungry, macho capitalist invaders from English-speaking Earth. (Pandora means "all gifts" and is the name of the first woman in Greek myth.) Here are some of the pro and contra opinions the movie is trying to make sure we hold:

We are to be in favor of nature; animals, plants, and particularly trees; the heart; science as curiosity; females and feminism; woodcraft, environmentalism, equality, and non-verbal communication; hunting and gathering; indigenous peoples; dreadlocks; tribalism; and paganism.

We are to be opposed to civilization; technology, metallic machines, and particularly war machines; the mind; science as conquest; males (unless they are rogue males with a feminine side who rebel against evil civilization) and machismo; industry, capitalism, hierarchy, and military orders; mineral (read oil) extraction; white (and token non-white)

Americans; uniforms; imperialism; and materialism. (The earth's great religions are not included among the ideas to be opposed. This is only because there is not the least hint that any of them exists.)

Think American marines in Iraq with Saddam Hussein as Sitting Bull, or in Afghanistan with Al Qaeda as basket-weavers and opium poppies as Gaia's intercom.

On Pandora all the trees intercommunicate through their roots, making a vast planetary computer that might be called "mother nature," which can do better anything that science and technology can do (*e.g.,* move a soul from one body to another). The heroine is sufficiently liberated from pre-feminist stereotype to be able to run, fly, fight, and kill. She (or was it her oracle-mother?) observes that "They have destroyed their planet and now want to destroy this one"—i.e., Al Gore was right. She observes about the hero that "Your heart is good, but your mind is very stupid"—i.e., Rousseau was right: gut feelings are to be trusted, rationality is not.

In condescending kindness (which soon blossoms into erotic love despite the androgynous physiology of avatar bodies) she teaches him to become his true and better self. This she does by training him not only properly to run, fly, fight, kill, and generally behave himself on Pandora (*e.g.,* to apologize to a food animal before delivering a coup de grace and to tame one's horse or pterosaur by grokking it via the mutual intertwining of the split ends of the braids shared by all species). Philosophically, he must also learn from her that man is not rational spirit united to nature but merely nature itself in one of its variations.

In short, Pandora is a literal apotheosis of the neo-pagan nature-worship of late Romanticism. Movies touting such Rousseauist propaganda have been with us for a long time, and there is no sign that they will soon be grown out of. This one, however, struck me with a particularly intense irony: *Avatar* could not possibly exist as the nature-worshipping movie it is without the most complex technology of the most machine-loving society in human history. Think of the computers it took to make it, or just read the credits. And the money spent by the billion viewers whom it is teaching to despise capitalist America is going to precisely the kind of mega-corporation the film itself condemns.

How is it possible for this self-contradiction not to be registered by the romantics exiting the theater yearning to be translated into avatar-bodies on Pandora? Can there be a more extreme example of the lack of integrity of the Hollywood enterprise? Argue all you want that this is to treat too seriously what is meant as mere entertainment. Entertaining art has power because it allows us to see what we wish to believe. Does the nature we wish to believe in make us so very mindless that we are blind to such an irony?

As propaganda *Avatar* seeks to deceive others into believing what its computer-wielding makers cannot possibly themselves believe (see pro and contra lists above). Like the soma of Huxley's *Brave New World*, it calculatingly stupefies people into desiring their own dehumanization. Winning our hearts with romance and pyrotechnics, it attempts to clip from our minds Aristotle's concept of the proper function of man—to reason well consistently with virtue. Then its makers take the clippings to the bank.

Caroline Roboh, *Shem*
[2011]

Caroline Roboh's film *Shem* participates in neither the cliché rituals of Hollywood nor the inconclusive, abstract detachment of French cinema. Hence it has been misunderstood by critics who fault it for the apparent incompleteness of its plot. In fact *Shem* yields its riches with a subtler mode of aesthetic interpretation, and this we can find in the fourfold method of interpretation that traditional scholars apply to Jewish and Christian sacred texts and that Dante builds in to his *Divine Comedy*. The four levels in this method of interpretation are *pshat* (simpleness)—the literal meaning; *remez* (hint)—the allegorical meaning; *drash* (homily)—the moral meaning; and *sod* (secret)—the mystical meaning. Understood in these four ways, *Shem* will be seen to offer a deeply touching, haunting, and healing image of man's journey toward the meaning of life.

Pshat—the literal level:

The main character, Daniel, is not particularly likeable at the start but exudes a youthful vitality irresistible to others and to us. (He is played by the attractive Ash Newman in a performance that is fresh, subtle, various, committed, and forceful.) Despairing of his life of hedonism and self-absorption, Daniel responds to his grandmother's challenge to find the grave of her father, a righteous rabbi who, after sending his daughter to England, died in Europe in 1939. Daniel follows clues on a journey from city to city in Western and then Eastern Europe, at last experiencing defeat in his quest. Reunited with his grandmother (played by Hadassah Hungar Diamant), he is told that she has learned in a dream that her father had in fact died in a Nazi extermination camp. The grave Daniel has been seeking never existed.

Remez—the allegorical level:

Hints that there is more than literal significance to the quest for a physical grave include several recurring visual and verbal motifs.

1. Awakening: The film begins with Daniel symbolically opening his eyes from sleep, and we see him being awakened several more times during the film. These images hint that Daniel's hedonism, poly-sexuality, temper, rudeness, and arrogance are a form of sleep from which he is being awakened in the course of his journey to achieve the "one important thing" he has been given to do. He thinks it is to find his great-grandfather's grave. He —and we—awaken to the realization that his true mission is something else.

2. Names: The title of the film means "name" in Hebrew. In each city, when asked his name, Daniel gives a false one. In the museum in Paris, he gives the ancient British name Alfred (after Dreyfus, he says). In Berlin he calls himself Henry, also a non-Jewish name, though we see him secretly typing his real name on a museum computer. When he enters the synagogue in Prague, he calls himself David, the first time he has used a Jewish pseudonym, and one which begins with the same letter as his real name. This is followed by the transforming experience of seeing, on the walls of the otherwise empty synagogue, the names of the Jewish dead killed by the Nazis. In Belgrade Daniel says his name is Paul, and the name's association with Christianity is explicitly discussed. Finally, in Sofia, whose name means "wisdom," Daniel at last gives his real name to the man who will tell him the truth about what his great-grandfather actually did in life. Symbolically, Daniel is both avoiding and seeking himself. Having learned the truth about his great-grandfather, whose name, Theodor Weiss, means "Gift-of-God White," Daniel finally becomes himself.

3. Hiding: In addition to the sleep imagery and the false names, Daniel engages in other forms of disguise, hiding, and avoidance, often related to his eyes. At different times he dresses in drag (with tears from his right eye drawn onto his face), is blindfolded, wears sunglasses in nightclubs, buys dope, pretends to poke himself in the eye with a pool cue, becomes blind drunk. (We see him with a real tear after he leaves the first person in his life who refuses to be seduced by him despite his beginning to fall in love with her.) Another form of hiding is sexual license: "I can have sex with anyone I want whenever I want," he says, and he does.

4. Cities: The journey—to Paris, Berlin, Prague, Budapest, Belgrade, Sofia, and Rome—traces Theodor Weiss through the European capital cities whose Jews disappeared into the Nazi attempt at annihilation, leaving only names and artifacts behind. In each city (until Sofia) the search turns up nothing but a slim reason to go to the next city. In all these places, the Jewish synagogues, museums, and libraries are often just closing and usually nearly empty. Former Jewish buildings and neighborhoods are populated by non-Jews. All the cities bespeak the destruction of European Jewry, the few living Jews constituting a tiny remnant.

5. Yarmulke: At every synagogue Daniel visits looking for information, the man in charge puts a yarmulke (skullcap) on Daniel's head before he admits him to the building. Symbolically the hand of a Jew draws Daniel into participation in his own history. Daniel acquiesces in increasing respect for the places in which Jews have worshipped God and for the Jews expunged from them.

6. Words: Daniel is exposed to one repository after another of words and names—printed in books, written on papers, embossed on walls, carved on gravestones, called up on computer screens, and inscribed on "synagogue scrolls." With no access to the written word that, as he will discover, his great-grandfather spent his life trying to preserve, Daniel learns the truth from living people. Early on, Daniel refuses to say the *Shema* (the Hebrew words of the central Jewish confession of faith in God's unity) at the request of his grandmother. Later, Zara, the young Jewish woman in Berlin who evokes Daniel's incipient love by refusing to sleep with him, persuades him to repeat those words after her by rote, and he does.

7. Dead ends: People from whom Daniel hopes for information have died, recommended repositories of information have changed functions, records are absent, rooms are empty, clues yield no fruit, even physical alleys are blocked. Every lead seems to lead to a dead end.

8. Contemplation of death: After a night of debauchery in Prague, Daniel is taken next morning to the forest of Kuks Castle by a young man interested in Baroque art. Daniel brags about his "Baroque"

affair with a mother and her son "at the same time," whereupon the young man takes him to a group of sculptures called Betlém (Bethlehem), carved by Baroque sculptor Matthias Bernard Braun (1684–1738) in the natural sandstone rocks of the forest. The young man says that what really mattered to Braun was not his sculptures of vice and virtue at the castle nearby, but his meditation on death in sculptures doomed to disappear back into nature. "This is the true spirit of Baroque," he says, "—man and religion bound together by the glorified representation of death."

He takes Daniel to the Braun sculpture of Juan Garinus the Hermit. (Tempted by the devil to kill a maiden, Garinus gave himself the penance of living like a beast, crawling on the ground, never looking up at the heavens, until eventually he was forgiven. The sculpture pictures him crawling out of his cave, pursued by hounds.[1]) There Daniel reclines upon the sculpture and masturbates in his pants as the young man photographs him. Images of him pleasuring himself are intercut with images of religion and death—Bernini's "Ecstasy of St. Theresa" (a hilarious juxtaposition), a crucified Christ, cupids, death's heads. Daniel says, quietly and seductively to the camera (both that of the photographer character and that of the filmmaker), "Now that's what I call Baroque."

Several scenes later, sitting by the Danube in Budapest as the lights on the nearby bridge come on at dusk, Daniel is invited to converse with a young man walking a dog. He declines. The young man clarifies that he does not want a sexual liaison but rather company in his contemplation of death. Daniel declines.

In these two scenes sexual license and death are identified. In the first Daniel succumbs; in the second he does not. It is between these two scenes that the film presents Daniel's spiritual turning points.

Drash—the moral level:

These are Daniel's turning points: In awe he recognizes his responsibility to the dead; in humility he participates in a festive Jewish religious ceremony; in fear and despair he calls for help; in penitence he is rewarded with a divine promise and encouragement.

The first takes place in Prague after the Kuks Forest scene and after

1 http://www.richtera.cz/betlemari/english/newfor/08_en.html.

Daniel has been directed, as part of his apparently fruitless Kafkaesque search, to the grave of Franz Kafka. He comes to a Prague synagogue, which now contains nothing but the names of "all the Czech Jews who perished" in the Nazi Holocaust. Failing to find the name of Theodor Weiss here too, he is nevertheless moved. In his mind, he says to the dead, "I'm not a monument; I'm alive; I owe it to you to be alive." Then, "Every road I travel has your graves beneath it." Here Daniel begins to transcend his quest for a grave and to intuit that the history of the dead is connected with his own. The central theme of the film is suggested: The dead cannot be found unless they live in the living.

But what does it mean to be living? In the next scene Daniel is invited to spend the Sabbath with the synagogue official. At the latter's home Daniel experiences a traditional Sabbath in which the hostess blesses the Sabbath candles and the host blesses the bread and the wine. He does not know the ritual, but for the first time Daniel participates in a Jewish ritual by modestly uttering the word "amen." He has begun to accept who he is.

In Budapest Daniel is chased in panic to a physical dead end, a locked gate. He chooses not to turn back but to go up—several flights up the staircase of an abandoned tenement—until he comes to an empty apartment with empty rooms and there is nowhere left to go, an apparently final dead end. "Help," he says, quietly, as if to God.

We next see him climbing over a locked gate into a cemetery, where he finds the name Theodor Weiss on a memorial stone. But this Weiss died in the nineteenth century—it is not the man whose grave Daniel seeks. Another dead end. In frustration, Daniel falls into despair, whereupon there suddenly appears an angel in the form of an old man with white hair (played by Hungarian-Jewish film director István Szabó).

"I'm sorry," says Daniel.

"Can I help you?" asks the angel.

"It's my fault," says Daniel. "For once in my life I had something important to do, and I failed. I'm a failure. Basically a fake. I'm never going to find his grave."

"You will find what you're looking for," says the angel.

"It's impossible," says Daniel. "I'm sorry. I'm such a stupid fool."

"You are not," says the angel. And then, three times with kindness, "Continue your way."

Then the angel is suddenly gone, and Daniel continues his way.

In these turning points, we find that the moral journey of the film is from death to life—from the living death that is deluded, hedonistic self-regard to the death-conquering life that is human connection. The final breakthrough is prepared for by what Daniel learns in the synagogue of Sofia.

Sod — the mystical level:

One motif not mentioned above takes the form of an apparently unresolved subplot. Through the film we become aware that Daniel is being secretly observed (Paris to Berlin), cared for and reported on (Prague), saved from death (Budapest), again followed (Belgrade), and finally solicited for information (Sofia to Rome) by a group of spies directed by a Christian prelate called only Monsignor. On the train from Sofia to Rome, we discover that the prelate's followers believe Theodor Weiss to have been seeking or hiding the "stones from the Temple," which they believe to have great monetary value. This is perhaps a reference to the *Urim and Thummim*, stones or jewels sewn into the breastplate of the High Priest of the Temple at Jerusalem through which prophetic knowledge was conveyed. In any case, all that we see of the Monsignor is a jeweled ring. The Monsignor's representative suggests that Daniel is being manipulated by others (those who have helped him, given him clues, shown him kindness), that Daniel knows what his great-grandfather was "really" doing, and that he should come to them when he is ready to admit as much and "when you have decided to be a wealthy man."

Because this subplot leads to no just deserts or villainous triumph for the spies, some critics have accused the film of bad editing in leaving this business "unfinished." In fact, the subplot is all it needs to be: a precisely structured externalization of all the temptations that try to deflect Daniel from his spiritual journey. The spies of the Monsignor, like Daniel's hedonism and the preoccupation with death, are a representation of the *yetzer ha-ra*, the evil impulse, which according to Jewish mystical thought is implanted in every human being as an inner drive whose worldly temptations it is man's mission to resist or channel. The evil impulse is necessary to life—because of it we are moved to eat, to reproduce, to build a house. But one whose *yetzer ha-tov* (the good impulse) does not chasten and prevail over his *yetzer ha-ra* lives a life of material self-indulgence and spiritual emptiness.

Specifically, the stone-seekers tempt Daniel to believe that his great-grandfather was not a righteous rabbi at all but a hedonist like Daniel, who secretly sought the "stones from the Temple" for the sake of his own wealth and power. They promise worldly wealth in exchange for Daniel's agreement to interpret the life of Theodor Weiss in their worldly terms. This is Daniel's final temptation by the *yetzer ha-ra*.

By this point in his journey, however, Daniel has discovered the truth. What Daniel learned from an eyewitness in the Sofia synagogue is that Theodor Weiss had gone from city to city in Europe in order to warn Jews to hide the "synagogue scrolls" from the Nazis so that "the next generation can study the Torah." Daniel has found not a grave but a life—in fact, a life lived for others and for God. Rejecting the materialist interpretation of Weiss's life, Daniel remains faithful to its spiritual meaning, reporting the truth to his grandmother, whom he meets again in Rome.

Daniel's feeling of defeat at not finding the grave is challenged at the end by the news that the grave never existed. Was the journey a waste, or has Daniel found something far more valuable? Rejecting the temptation of worldly wealth, Daniel makes of his quest something akin to what Theodor Weiss made of his life. Daniel has chosen solidarity with his great-grandfather, hence participation in the past, present, and future of his people. In doing so, he has risen out of the death that is sensual self-absorption and self-delusion and into living human relationship. Thus he has completed his mission, though the real mission is not what he thought it was. As the mission of Theodor Weiss was to fight the Nazi intention by striving to preserve the Torah "for future generations," Daniel's real mission has been to subdue the *yetzer ha-ra* and to preserve his own Jewish self through meaningful human relations. Hence the film becomes a vision of the survival of Judaism in living Jews despite the destruction of European Jewry and the alienation suffered by its remnants.

The film's final mystical significance is this: Daniel is not only a young Jew alienated from his people, religion, and history. He is also an embodiment of modern man in the grip of physical pleasure, emotional impulse, and intellectual confusion, cut off from both past and future by ignorance of the spiritual context of life and of its challenge to combat rather than embrace death. Daniel's journey is a journey to wholeness, to the meaningful integration of body, heart, and mind in relation to a world of the spirit redeemed from death and despair by small acts of kindness, generosity, and sacrifice, to which, in spite of himself, his spirit is drawn by its own truest hunger.

This is why the film is in places non-realistic, almost dream-like and mystical. Like the purpose of Daniel's quest, the purpose of the film is not what we at first think. It shows us the death that is worldliness in order to lead us to insight about the life that lies in human spiritual connectedness in the present and through time.

The film ends with the grandmother sitting in a public square on a suitcase. She is about to leave this world in which there is no final destination but only the suitcases we sit on temporarily on our journey. It reminded me of the following tale about the great Rabbi Yisrael Meir Kagan, known (from the title of his book) as the Chofetz Chaim ("he who desires life"): An American businessman with an important question traveled to the town of Radun in Belarus to consult the Chofetz Chaim. When he entered the rabbi's room, he saw no furniture but a table, a chair, and books. Surprised that so great a rabbi would live in so sparse a room, he asked, "Where is all your furniture?" The Chofetz Chaim replied, "Where is yours?" "Mine?" said the Jew; "but I'm a traveler; I'm just passing through." "So am I," said the Chofetz Chaim.

Before she leaves, his grandmother shares a drink of soda with Daniel, whom she loves and who loves her. Her toast is *l'chaim*—to life.

Paul Johnson,
Socrates: A Man for Our Times[1]
[2011]

Without leaving a word of his own writing behind, Socrates became the founder of Western Philosophy. He did so by engaging in a line of questioning focused not on comprehending the natural world, as his predecessors tried to do, but on investigating the moral and spiritual life of man: What are virtue, justice, courage, piety? How may men live in harmony with one another, with the divine? Socrates' inquiries were so illuminating that, after his famous trial and execution, his student Plato felt compelled to record and develop them. Because of Plato's dialogues, the impact of Socrates' life and ideas has continued unabated for 2,400 years.

Plato was not only a faithful devotee but a great philosophical thinker and a great dramatic writer. Hence his dialogues are not mere facsimile recordings. They are works of profound art and philosophy in which Plato sought to extend and elaborate on the implications of his teacher's thought. And there's the rub. Where does Socrates end and Plato begin?

Because the best philosophical and historical minds of over two millennia have been unable to resolve this question with certainty, every reader of the Platonic dialogues is left to answer it for himself. On this subject Paul Johnson, in *Socrates: A Man for Our Times*, leaves no doubt about where he stands.

Johnson is an accomplished historian and writer with a fluid, unpretentious style and an honest voice. These gifts, which have made his twelve previous books enjoyable and popular, are no less evident in *Socrates*. It is troublesome, then, that his wealth of knowledge and inspiring insights are here overshadowed by a tendentious mission.

Acknowledging that "anyone who writes on the subject must make up his own mind [about where Socrates ends and Plato begins], as I have done in this account," Johnson categorizes Plato as an "intellectual, by which I mean someone who thinks ideas matter more than people." (In

1 Published in the Washington Independent Review of Books, October 19, 2011.

Intellectuals, Johnson compellingly warned against venerating morally perverse men just because they have had influential ideas.) Then he accuses Plato of killing Socrates a second time by making him "a mere wooden man, a ventriloquist's doll" in "one of the most unscrupulous acts in intellectual history," creating, "like Frankenstein, an artificial monster-philosopher" (page 11).

Having thus made a villain of Plato (likewise unscrupulously), Johnson takes a dualistic axe to Plato's brilliant works of art, splitting them into the parts he believes to be Socrates' own words and the parts he believes to be the words of Plato's "mindless, speaking doll": Johnson's Socrates (good) vs. Plato's (bad).

Who is Johnson's Socrates? Partly the Socrates all readers of Plato know: original thinker, brilliant and methodical conversationalist, questioner of unexamined opinions, lover of Athens, supremely principled man. But also a conjectured composite of Johnson-approved qualities: man of the people, monotheist, rejecter of all received ideas, originator of the attractive ideas in Plato and responsible for none of the unattractive, rewriter of famous tragedies, cataleptic, equivocator about religion, devotee of three wise women, moral influence on the artists, politicians, generals, dramatists, and historians of fifth-century Athens.

His scholarship has earned Johnson the right to these conjectures. The problem is that he offers minimal evidence and no notes that might anchor them in the sources. The only evidence offered is the sense they make to Johnson.

Here is one example: In the *Phaedo* Socrates, with his last breath, requests that his friend Crito sacrifice a cock to Asclepius in gratitude to the god of healing for being "cured" of the pains of life by his death. "Make this offering to him and do not forget," he says. Because this request does not fit Johnson's claim that "Socrates believed in God [and] was a monotheist" (pages 106–7) and that he "was not in the least interested in the outward observance of religion, but in its inner content," Johnson must interpret the last words of Socrates as a wry joke. It is of course possible that Johnson is right. But a good many profoundly difficult matters of interpretation are here dispatched with just that undoubting self-assurance that Johnson praises Socrates for questioning in others.

Johnson follows his bias into unintended ironies. His commitment to his *idea* of Socrates makes ironic his attack on Plato for caring more about ideas than people. His equivocations —"my belief is," "it must have been," "I suspect," "in my view he would undoubtedly," "no doubt," "perhaps," "I surmise," "I think it possible," "it was probably because," etc.—allow Johnson to preserve the pretense of objectivity, but they make ironic his claim, in one place, that "it is fruitless to speculate." And though Johnson accuses ancient authors of "low regard ... for truth" and "lack of impartiality, historicity, [and] common sense" (pages 12–13), he permits himself the very partiality he has criticized. "Common sense" here means agreement with him.

There is also some cavalier abuse of historical comparison. Though rightly claiming that "One of the most difficult things we have to do, in the early twenty-first century, is to transport ourselves back 2,500 years" to ancient Athens (page 157), Johnson at various points makes that city misleadingly analogous to an American small town, to New York City, to a "cultural capital of the civilized world"; seems to ignore what it took for Western Civilization to get from the "profoundly flawed" legal system of ancient Athens to the functions of a modern attorney general (page 155); ascribes to Athens a "competitive spirit" (page 19) without a word about the metaphysical implications of the Greek conviction that life itself is an *agon* or contest. He even invents a hypothetical missing dialogue in which Socrates must have attacked for all time the institution of slavery.

The most serious flaw in the book is the implication that Socrates did not care about ideas: "For Socrates, ideas existed to serve and illuminate people, not the other way around" (page 191). This is to reduce Socrates' lifelong passion for conversation into a mere excuse for talking to folks. If it were so, why would Plato have cared to dramatize those conversations or we to read them? "His object was to ... teach people to think for themselves." In other words, Socrates' mission was not really to find the truth he knew he did not yet possess but merely to illustrate a method for calling received truths into question. But could Socrates possibly have thought irrelevant the conclusions to which people thinking for themselves might come? Johnson has bound his Socrates into an artificial dualism by driving too far the distinction between caring about ideas and caring about people. People, after all, are those creatures who have ideas, and the importance of caring more about people than about ideas is itself an idea.

Socrates is less a history than an extended essay with an anti-intellectual axe to grind.

The university, with its masters and students, its lectures and tutorials, its degrees and libraries and publishing houses, was nothing to do with him... The notion of philosophy existing only in academic isolation from the rest of the world would have horrified him and probably would have produced ribald laughter, too (page 193).

There is extremely good reason to share Johnson's disapproval of the corrupt intellectualism and isolated academic philosophy of our time. But Johnson has conjured up a straw Socrates with which to attack them.

Stephen Greenblatt, *The Swerve: How the World Became Modern* or Swerving toward Limbo
[2011]

In *Inferno* Canto IV Dante meets the souls of virtuous pagans, who suffer no punishment but hopeless sighing. Their placement in limbo allegorizes the eternal condition of those who choose to believe that the human intellect is the sole vehicle of truth and that pleasure is man's highest good. In a note translator Dorothy Sayers writes:

> it is the weakness of Humanism to fall short in the imagination of ecstasy; at its best it is noble, reasonable, and cold, and however optimistic about a balanced happiness in this world, pessimistic about a rapturous eternity.

In *The Swerve* Shakespeare scholar Stephen Greenblatt records that in 1417, Poggio Bracciolini, papal secretary and seeker of manuscripts of lost classical works, discovered in a German monastery the long poem *De Rerum Natura (On the Nature of Things)* by the Roman Epicurean poet Lucretius (c. 96–c. 55 B.C.). Lacing facts (about ancient Rome, Herculaneum, the Renaissance papacy, and manuscript copying) together with conjecture—within one page of text we find "must have known," "perhaps feeling," "evidently," "probably," "seems to have," "would not have known"—Greenblatt argues that Poggio's discovery contributed significantly to Western Civilization's "swerve" from religion to secular pragmatism. He celebrates that "swerve." His purpose is to confirm in the minds of the "circle of those likely to be reading [his] words" the truth of Lucretius' vision of reality: the very atheistic humanism against whose spiritual limitations Dante's limbo was meant to warn us.

In the chapter called "The Way Things Are," Greenblatt culls from Lucretius' long and complex poem the following teachings:

> Everything is made of invisible particles, which are eternal, infinite in number, limited in shape and size, and moving in an infinite void.

The universe has no creator or designer; everything comes into being as a result of an unexplained and minute but presumably natural "swerve" of the particles from the path of mere falling, the swerve being the source of free will.

Nature ceaselessly experiments, but the universe was not created for human beings, who are not unique, whose beginning was not a Golden Age of tranquility and plenty but a primitive battle for survival, and whose souls die without afterlife.

Death is nothing to us.

The highest goal of human life is the enhancement of pleasure and the reduction of pain, achieved by the avoidance of superstitious delusions such as organized religions, which are invariably cruel.

Understanding the nature of things generates deep wonder.

The list is worded to make Lucretius the articulator of precisely the modern secular humanist's vision of life—atheistic, pragmatic, and cocksure.

Everyone is entitled to his opinion about the essential mysteries, but Greenblatt's embrace of Lucretius' vision is exasperating in three particular ways: It is self-contradictory, prejudiced, and condescending.

The contradictions include these:

Greenblatt informs us that Lucretius ends his poem with a hymn to Venus, the source of all things. This worship of a divine underlying reality represented by Venus (or, as Greenblatt calls her, sex) bespeaks a religious belief as faithfully held as the Christian's.

He praises Lucretius for believing ahead of his time (i.e., agreeing with us) that atoms of irreducible matter are the foundation of all things including the human soul. In doing so, he ignores the actual physics of our time, which finds that there are no irreducible particles of matter but rather patterns of energy that invisibly incarnate information for which no material substance can account.

Greenblatt asserts that "all attempts to fashion a life worth living… must start and end with a comprehension of … atoms and the void and nothing else." But to measure the worth of anything is to measure it in relation to something else known to be valuable. If all values are merely "atoms and the void," the phrase "worth living" is nugatory. Similarly, "trial and error" applied to nature's "long, complex process" implies an end aimed at. If all is matter and void, no one end can have more significance than another. "Trial and error" is another nugatory phrase.

Skeptical about the faith of others, Greenblatt, following Lucretius, is not nearly skeptical enough about his own, which flies in the face of the testimony of human beings in all places throughout human history. His certainty that "all organized religions are superstitious delusions" is itself a breathtaking act of faith.

Greenblatt writes, "Humans do not occupy the privileged place in existence they imagine for themselves" for "many of the most intense and poignant experiences of our lives are not exclusive to our species." It is of course true that like plants we grow and like animals we feel pleasure and pain. But who but a human being would write a book to convince other beings to think as he does? Greenblatt's Lucretian principles are paradoxically contradicted by the human nature they discount, for as writer and scholar Greenblatt evidences precisely the human privilege he takes pleasure in denying. To be human is above all to seek meaning in the "nature of things." It is what drives us to write and study poems and histories. Can Greenblatt seriously believe that his own soul's passion for Shakespeare and Lucretius is accounted for by "atoms and the void and nothing else"? Talk about cognitive dissonance!

To reinforce his polemic, Greenblatt prejudicially slants history and literature. To judge from *The Swerve* one would think that the medieval period were an age of nothing but darkness, filth, and self-interest and that Christianity were nothing but a fear-ridden swamp of venality and oppression. Certainly the Catholic Church has much crime to answer for. But Greenblatt seems blind to the historical influence of Christianity in promoting kindness, patience, humility, brotherly love, self-sacrifice, justice, political responsibility, and the value of the individual he implicitly holds dear—he implies Jefferson was nothing but an Epicurean—let alone the art of the great cathedrals, of Rembrandt, and of that monumental *Commedia* our civilization has rightly called "Divine."

On the basis of one use of the word "atomies" and limited reference to the afterlife in *Romeo and Juliet*, Greenblatt gives the impression that Shakespeare too was an Epicurean and no Christian, to believe which requires that we ignore the themes and many speeches of *Henry V, Hamlet, Measure for Measure, Macbeth, Othello, King Lear, The Winter's Tale,* and *The Tempest*. To defend the principle that "Religions are invariably cruel," he imports the biblical story of the binding of Isaac, ignoring the story's establishment of the principle that man is to serve God with a faithful will rather than with the sacrifice of children. To Greenblatt Christianity and Judaism, "Religious cults originating in far-off places like Persia, Syria, and Palestine," do nothing but "arouse wild fears and expectations, particularly among the plebs."

Then there is Greenblatt's tone. Though he would not burn anyone at the stake for misbelief, he sneers as self-righteously as the inquisitors of the Catholic Church at heretical disbelievers in his religion of atheistic atomism. He presumes "ritual" and "conversation about the meaning of life" to be antithetical (preferring, of course, the latter). He identifies himself and his enlightened readers with that ancient Epicurean elite who, being neither "insecure" nor "of a pious disposition," "would have regarded [the prophecies of Christ] as the overheated fantasies of a sect of stiff-necked Jews." (Why disapprove of the enjoyment of piety and overheated fantasy if they too are products of the merely natural swerving of atoms?)

The best thing about *The Swerve* is Greenblatt's honesty about the psychological reason for his being moved by the vision of Lucretius. In an important preface, Greenblatt tells us that he grew up terrorized by his mother's "brooding obsessively on the imminence of her end" as a way "to compel attention and demand love... [M]y dread of her dying had become entwined with a painful perception that she had blighted much of her life—and cast a shadow on my own—in the service of her obsessive fear." When he reads in Lucretius that "to spend your existence in the grip of anxiety about death ... is mere folly," he realizes that "to inflict this anxiety on others is manipulative and cruel."

Following his own method of conjecture, we may reasonably conclude that Greenblatt's denial of any spiritual authenticity to organized religion is a way of breaking the emotional bonds of his mother's obsession. Instead of having to reject his mother, he projects her fear of death and cruel manipulation onto the convenient scapegoat of organized religion and rejects it instead. The greatest value of this book may thus be to raise the question whether the modern world's "swerve" away from God and toward Epicurean pleasure worship is similarly rooted in the longing to escape the fear of death. Whether that fear *can* be escaped by denying the significance of death is another question it raises. The reader will decide which is the more precious antidote: Lucretius to the delusion of religion or Dante's limbo to the delusion of Epicurean humanism.

Finally, arguing that "the gods quite literally could not care less" about human beings, Greenblatt asserts that "the serious issue is that false beliefs and observances inevitably lead to human mischief." This is certainly a true statement. As applied to organized religion, it is now a cliché. But Greenblatt chooses to ignore the human mischief to which his own Epicurean beliefs have led in our enlightened and rational age: the torture and murder of countless millions effected by those who have been sure that there is no God, no divine justice, no afterlife, only atoms and the void. If cruelty and oppression are the measure of a doctrine's value, Greenblatt's has far more to answer for than that of Mother Theresa.

Ian Donaldson, *Ben Jonson: A Life*[1]
[2012]

In *Ben Jonson: A Life*, Ian Donaldson, eminent professor of literature and humanities and one of three General Editors of *The Cambridge Edition* of Jonson's works (2011), has written a biography of the great Renaissance playwright and poet, Shakespeare's most eminent friend and competitor, in which everything is present *but* the life.

The book is an instructive documentary history of Jonson in his social, political, religious, and cultural context. In it we learn about his background, the luminaries who were his friends and colleagues, his inconstant royal patronage, his two religious conversions, his scholarly and intellectual accomplishments, his literary career. Beginning with his bizarre burial in a vertical position and ending with his posthumous reputation, the book mines Jonson's works and nearly four hundred years of scholarship for the relevant facts.

Jonson's character and poetic gifts, however, the book leaves unilluminated. Donaldson's overriding theme is conflict and ambivalence, as if there ever were a human being worth writing about who exhibited neither. But the essential realities of Jonson's inner conflicts are not revealed. In their place Donaldson presents as personal conflicts what are in fact the standard concerns of any writer of Jonson's (or indeed any) time—money problems, religious strife, variable patronage, political shifts, age, disease. About Jonson's unique relation to these complexities of life Donaldson, lacking vision, is reduced to flat-footed conjecture.

Quoting the preacher Thomas Wright as arguing that the passions must "be controlled, or they would trouble the soul as political agitators trouble the state," Donaldson observes absurdly that "Jonson was evidently impressed by this line of thinking." For evidence he cites passages in Jonson's poems and plays in which "our passions rebel" and reason is called "our affections' king"—as if such ideas weren't venerable clichés of Western thought since Plato. A valuable passage in which

---

1 Published in the Snapshots section of the Washington Independent Review of Books, April 6, 2012.

Jonson, who kept up with the intellectual currents of his time, is rightly seen as prophetic about "the syndication of news, the fighting of wars, the conquest of space, the organization of finance," Donaldson concludes with the ponderous banality that Jonson "was part of that new world that he also intermittently satirized." About the historical relevance of a comical character Donaldson offers the insight that, "however 'feigned' or exaggerated," a dramatic character "may often be inspired by everyday experience." Nearly everywhere that Donaldson reaches for insight, our response is "Well, duh."

In this literary shrine, which contributes much to our understanding of the context of Ben Jonson's life, the man himself will not appear.

On "Disruptive Innovation"
[2012]

I was sent a copy of *Disrupting Class: How Disruptive Innovation Will Change the Way the World Learns* by Clayton Christensen, Michael Horn, and Curtis Johnson. I read a third of it and parts of the rest. It was as much as I could take.

I agree with the authors that it is hard to change a system head-on, and that innovation from the bottom often works better. However, the premises of the book are incorrect; therefore its aims are faulty and its conclusions a prescription for a different but equally faulty education establishment.

First of all, of the four "aspirations" for schools on page 1, three are reasonable, and one is more false than true. There are two aspirations not even mentioned.

Aspiration 1 is "maximize human potential." This is a reasonable goal, but it is so vague and non-specific that it is useless. Potential for what? How is "human potential" to be measured? The answers to these questions are crucial, and they could be answered in ways that I agree with and in ways that I would hate. As such, the principle is too vague to be significant in itself. Aspiration 2 is "educate for good citizenship," and of course I agree with it. Aspiration 3 is "educate for prosperity," and there's no reason to argue with that unless their idea of prosperity comes at the expense of virtue, which they never mention.

I object to aspiration 4, which says, "Nurture the understanding that people can see things differently—and that those differences merit respect rather than persecution." Well, of course there are differences in people and learning styles, and persecution should never be fostered. But that's a straw man. The real truth, abolished in this principle, is that by far most people learn in more or less the same ways, that what they are learning must be more or less the same, and that the similarities are far more important than the differences.

This is a huge question and brings up the philosophical question whether men are naturally good and will turn out okay if left to their own devices or whether men are free to choose between good and evil and need the guidance of culture, tradition, and the past's experience to help them choose the good. The authors believe that any student, left to his own devices with the proper technological devices and opportunities, will learn on his own and in his own way what is best for him and for the society. This is a supreme act of faith in a trajectory of individual development that I cannot believe in. They also assume that what is individual in people is more significant than what is universal. This is absurd. Leave every student to discover logic on his own and the vast majority will never make the first step to master logical thinking. Hardly a student in the world will look at an online picture of the Parthenon and realize that this ruin, totally irrelevant to their lives as they would think, is one of the most important structures in the world in a) embodying the ideals of our civilization and b) influencing to some extent every building in which they will find themselves. (This is an example only.)

Then they leave out the two aspirations they should have mentioned. The first is that we must train up the next generation to inherit the content of knowledge, wisdom, and experience of the past, of the civilization in which they find themselves. The alternative is returning to barbarism because students can have no natural inclination or impulse to absorb the fruits of the past on their own, seeing no practical value in them, without the inspiration and aid of a teacher whose vision stretches beyond that of a child. The other aspiration is that schools foster virtue, and do so both through teaching it as content and through living interactions impossible in a so-called "student-centric" learning system.

Students are ignorant, self-indulgent, and impulse-driven, as well as unique individuals. To leave them to their own devices as individual learners is to sell them down the river of impulse and desire and to sacrifice a shared vision of the meaning of their time, place, society, nation, civilization, and species.

The authors have placed the computer at the center of their concept of education, believing unquestioningly in the premise of "student-centric" learning being best. They neglect to realize that this really turns students into "computer-centric" beings. Social and communal learning are sacrificed for the interaction between one undeveloped person and his machine. The result, because the premises about the nature of man are false, will be a profound perversion of education, and thereby of society.

What would I put in place of their sweeping idea of "disruptive innovation" toward a machine-made future? I would argue that *any* innovation must arise out of a vision of the true meaning and purpose of education, and that any innovation arising out of the same old wrong ideas will result in perhaps totally different but equally disastrous results. The schools of our nation are broken indeed. But the fix is not giving the less and less illuminated children the tools to wallow forever in their ignorance. The fix is to redefine what education is for. And to do that, we must re-examine, as Wendell Berry put it, what human beings are for. So long as we refuse to graduate from the adolescence of Romantic ideas of man and society and education, so long will our schools fail. The authors' wishful thinking about the individual and his personal relation to his own learning style and to his own computer will result in no good for the nation, the world, or the children themselves.

We know how to educate children. We have given up on believing in the content of their education. Until we return as a society to a shared valuing of that age-old content—not in place of new knowledge but as its foundation—we will continue drowning in new techniques and technologies and theories that take us nowhere but down the step-by-step path to ignorance, which, in the long run, is also the path to tyranny.

Jacques Barzun, *From Dawn to Decadence*
[2013]

Jacques Barzun once gave the keynote address at one of the Modern Language Association conventions I attended. In it he savaged those members of the Association—their name is legion—who had abandoned the teaching of the fundamental skills and great literature of the Western tradition in favor of the new idols of race, class, and gender, French so-called critical theory, and neo-Marxist political correctness. There was the most minimal possible applause of politeness at the end of his talk, but one person stood in enthusiastic ovation—only one. That person was yours truly, attending the convention in the vain hope of finding a full-time, tenure-track teaching position at some respectable college or university. The hope was vain precisely because I refused to worship the idols of the day. Only later did I fully realize how thoroughly the word "respectable" had already ceased to apply.

In any case, I have been an admirer of Jacques Barzun for a long time. I have taught with his writing manual, tirelessly quoting its mantra: "Be simple and direct." I have read him on a variety of subjects and found it not possible to read his words without learning something valuable.

Recently I finished his long discussion of the culture of the modern West, *From Dawn to Decadence*. It is a remarkable accomplishment. One learns no end of interesting facts and gains a valuable insight on nearly every page. What follows is not a review of the book, however. It is a meditation on the heart of Barzun's worldview as expressed in the book, a view extremely fruitful yet ultimately disappointing.

What Barzun meant by "Dawn" is not the creation of the world or the birth of civilization. For Barzun "Dawn" means the Renaissance, as if the medieval world were mere predawn darkness. (By contrast, the poet Philip Thompson, in whom I have found a more trustworthy guide to reality, calls the Renaissance "on the one hand an enormous art school, and on the other the birthday of the secular beast."[1])

---

1 *Dusk and Dawn: Poems and Prose of Philip Thompson*, edited by Gideon Rappaport (San Diego: One Mind Good Press, 2005), page 208.

Barzun reveals his spiritual limitation in two key places, most importantly on pages 756–57. There he quite rightly indicts existentialism for being puny, but he does so on the assumption that "man and nature are one: nature is conscious of itself in and through man," whose "links with the cosmos that men have celebrated in worship and song" are essentially man's own creation, since nature is a "man-made construct" that sometimes gives "pure mindless joy."

This is essentially the nature-deifying attitude of Wordsworth, who Thompson says "doesn't go far enough: the love of nature and the sense of nature's holiness cannot exist if love and holiness are not the cause of nature's being...."[2]

In short, Barzun is a Romantic who, with an Olympian view, sees all permutations of man as permutations of nature. He is a kind of Lucretius with the wealth of five hundred years of art to contemplate. He praises Dorothy Sayers on Dante and otherwise and then fails to accept her accurate refutation of the cliché that the *Divine Comedy* is just a journalist's attempt to reward friends and punish enemies. On Barzun's page 654 we have the "infinite diversity of human character" and his rules of history, which are pretty good in their anti-dogmatism. Barzun imagines that he is himself nature contemplating itself without prejudice. Except that it is his own prejudice to assume that all spiritual vision is merely one aspect of the diversity of man's nature, i.e., of nature itself. But, as Philip Thompson has said, "if the lower is the source of the higher, then the lower *is* the higher." Apparently even a vision so Olympian as Barzun's is bound by some kind of prejudice. Either man is mere nature or nature is not all there is. That being so, Barzun operates on the former assumption, interpreting all assumptions of the latter kind as mere products of nature being itself in the minds of human beings. That nature might be a creation and man created to contemplate both nature and what is beyond it is for Barzun no possible reality but a mere idea invented by nature contemplating itself in the form of man.

The other place in which Barzun reveals his limitation is his attack on relativism (pages 760–63), which I think is a red herring. Of course he's right about all the areas of life in which his word *relationism* would be a better one. But he makes the mistake that every high school student makes: thinking that because, for example, the laws against killing people are so various in the cultures of the world, therefore there is no absolute

---

2 *Dusk and Dawn*, page 200.

underlying them. "When the anti-relativist deplores the present state of morals he is judging it relatively to a previous state, which he believes was fixed and eternal." This is too true about many people, of course, but it is not the real point.

The true anti-relativist (like Dorothy Sayers and C. S. Lewis, to say nothing of Socrates and Plato, Moses and Maimonides, Jesus and Aquinas) is not measuring present relativism against any specific past but against eternal principles. Barzun asks, ah, but *whose* eternal principles? By which question he merely plops himself back into Lucretian nature, as if C. S. Lewis, in *The Abolition of Man*, had not long since incontrovertibly established the requirement to assume the fundamental universals in order for *any* value judgment to stand.

It turns out that Barzun does have one absolute value. It is tact. Barzun ends the passage with the deification of tact, in art and society, in his determination to attack any "absolute formula." Why tact should show itself incontrovertibly in one work of art and not in another, and how it is recognized as such, remains according to him, I suppose, a mystery of nature. As in history, so in art, formula is his enemy. And of course he is right to a point, since too many people have reduced too much of human experience to formulas too narrow. But his own formula, that there is no absolute but tact that transcends formula, is the blindness of Philip Thompson's Fleet Astronomer, who

> reads the night
> As the honest fracturing eye
> And studious hairs
> Of the fly, cathedral stone.[3]

Barzun's view reminds me of my teacher Mary Holmes' point that some people are given a spiritual gift and others are not. It is as if Barzun never in his long life had an experience of the spirit that he could not reduce to nature.

The rest of the book is brilliant, even when a little off or reductive. He is best on the last hundred years, the late nineteenth century to the end. His ability to connect ideas, works of art, culture, and history and to unpack their underlying themes is little short of astounding, from the Grand Illusion of World War I to the torn jeans of today's fashionistas.

---

3 *Dusk and Dawn*, page 66.

But he makes me want to ask Wendell Berry's question of him: "What are people for?" He would say the question is absurd, like asking what the universe is for. But I would respond by asking why human beings keep asking the question anyway, just as if they were meant to.

Ross Lockridge, Jr., *Raintree County*
[2014]

I've just read the whole of *Raintree County* again, after forty-seven years. It is a remarkable accomplishment—huge in aim and length. But it is impossible not to be disappointed. The book is a failure at the profundity it attempted, and its latter half is a bore.

The beginning was enjoyable, as it was when I and my fellow students first read it in college, because it offers a youthful and idealistic America, a young hero longing for beauty, truth, and the best kind of patriotism rooted in land, home, family, and values. It is effective in conveying the power of eros, the cynicism of materialist scientism, and nostalgia for pre-Civil War American life. But though the novel succeeds at being popular, it fails to fulfill its promise of depth.

Apart from the two main characters, the symbolic mirror images of Johnny and the Perfessor (idealist dreamer and cynical, libidinous debunker), the characters barely rise out of cliché, and even the protagonists are more constructs than persons. The self-important politician on the make, the incipient robber baron, the southern belle, the braggart athlete-soldier all have certain humanizing qualities, but not enough to dig any deeper into American life and mind than the movies.

I found the technique—one long day (in imitation of Joyce's *Ulysses*) punctuated by flashbacks—to be effective enough. But the historical-novel tricks are threadbare. I didn't mind that the Perfessor just happens to show up no matter where Johnny is. But Johnny just happens to be near Grant, later near Sherman, is visited in hospital by Whitman, then by Lincoln, then happens to be at Ford's Theatre the night of the assassination, and so on. Then the attention and suspense devoted to the novel's supposedly shocking denouements are not rewarded with revelations beyond the predictable: Susanna, right out of *Jane Eyre* and *Rebecca*, goes mad because of Freudian repression of her Negro origins and burns down the house—twice; Johnny comes marching home again to find his true love both married to another and dead; the peak of New York City glamour is a room of mirrors; the Bible-thumping preacher slinks out of town having been caught in flagrante delicto; and so on.

Every chapter ends with an uncropped three-to-five-page stream of pseudo-philosophical, symbolist, Romantic verbiage trying to evoke mood without substance. The philosophical passages try to counteract the Perfessor's Darwinian, materialist cynicism with passionate poeticism that attempts to make a reality of Johnny's imagination and to turn the novel of his life into a vehicle of redemption (for character, reader, author, and the nation). They are 90 percent hogwash, offering no serious philosophical, poetic, or moral resolution of the central conflicts between idealism and cynicism, dream and reality, the ideal and the real Republic, capitalism and progressivism, eros and Freudianism, human culture and cosmic swamp that the novel purports to address.

Though the book was a big success, Lockridge fell into a depression (which his son has analyzed in some detail[1]) and committed suicide at the age of thirty-three. He appears to have read a negative review of the book on the day he died. It is hard to believe that his despair did not arise in part from the meeting with reality of his own fragile but deluded dream of the greatness of this work written with monumental effort.

As a writer Lockridge reminds me of Mary Holmes' description of the kind of pianist who labors for half a lifetime to perfect his technique only to discover, when he has succeeded, that he has no musical vision. The book's melodrama of idealism and nostalgia lacks the stamp of the visionary genius that the subject called for and that Lockridge must have believed he had. So great is the book's promise that if it had succeeded in delivering, I would have been able to delight in reaffirming my adolescent assessment that the Great American Novel has been written. As it is, we have in *Raintree County* an impressive disappointment, the second-rate accomplishment of a first-rate goal.

---

1 Larry Lockridge, "Biography and Enigma: The Case of Ross Lockridge, Jr.," in *Biography and Source Studies*, Volume 3 (New York: AMS Press, 1997), http://www.raintreecounty.com/bioenig.html.

John Williams, *Stoner*
[2014]

At the suggestion of several people and of a review in *The New York Times* that claimed "You Should Seriously Read [It] Right Now,"[1] I have "seriously read" *Stoner*, by John Williams, and I have disliked it thoroughly.

The prose is clear and forceful, and the realism is effective. However, the plot and characters are largely clichés, and the novel is an empty vessel—a self-justifying, spiritless, Godless, sentimental emptiness that presents the emotion of love of literature as having absolutely nothing to do with the content of that literature, as if what Shakespeare and Donne were making of their classical and medieval influences were nothing but objects to be studied in the light of those influences, as if the actual subjects of their works were irrelevant to the academic's pleasure in reading and teaching them.

To me the book reads like Samuel Beckett in ivy and tweeds, giving the picture of a man cut off from any possibility of active human kindness by a solipsism as thick and immovable—despite his devotion to teaching and his passionate love affair—as the clay from which he has sprung. The novel's worldview is utterly depressing in its depiction of an ultimately meaningless universe that it pretends to fill with a calling without any caller. The only good thing in the book is the hero's resistance to the lies and injustice of the villain (whose behavior is an allegory of affirmative action and/or feminism at their collegiate work). But the moral stance of the hero cannot make up for the complete absence of any moral or spiritual foundation to sustain it and therefore remains a mere accident of nothingness being busy about its ultimately meaningless business.

If the novel has become a fad, that is because the *New York Review of Books* and *New York Times* set see in it the complete justification of their own spiritually vacuous lives, in which "literature" substitutes for God, teaching it substitutes for faith, and human discourse is a matter of nothing but noticing nature at work in sex and in words, exactly as if the

---

1 http://mobile.nytimes.com/2014/05/11/magazine/you-should-seriously-read-stoner-right-now.html.

real works of Shakespeare, Milton, Austen, Tolstoy, Dostoevsky, Dickens, Buber, C. S. Lewis, and Solzhenitsyn never existed and as if a Samuel Beckett character who should accidentally fall in love had spoken the final word on man.

The author has used his considerable talent to produce a convincing but deluded picture of unilluminated man caught in the hell of a life of self-centered love experienced as sourceless, goalless, purposeless, and powerless to heal. The hell of reading it is that the author imagines that the feckless existential emptiness of his hero might be redeemed by the mere fact of his falling in love with literature while offering no hint of what is in fact lovable about that literature we are told the hero loves. Hence, the novel is an exercise in subtle but exasperating sentimentality.

Daniel Albright, *Panaesthetics*
[2015]

At the suggestion of a former student I have bought and read *Panaesthetics* by Daniel Albright.

Albright, who died this past January, was a professor of literature and music at Harvard. In his obituary he is described by a former student as "the most generous and warmhearted and kind mentor one could ever ask for"; a colleague of his says that where he was present "the room was full of fun and amusement and delight because of his range of literary allusions and music allusions."[1]

I do not for a moment doubt these encomia, nor do I wish to speak ill of the dead. Nonetheless, from his last book I feel an obligation to warn my readers away. Though the book exhibits intelligence and knowledge, both are put into the service of the utterly destructive nonsense that is the most common understanding of art and life in today's academy.

Here is my letter to my former student:

I write to you to beg and plead that you get yourself out of this kind of thinking before it is too late. The author of *Panaesthetics* is an atheistical, self-congratulatory, sentimental, pontificating, postmodernist, existentialist, nihilistic Harvard smarty-pants. Every half-truth is pressed into the service of destruction, every interesting fact soaked in arrogant, willful misrepresentation.

Yes, art depends on the human body. The human being is a body-soul complex, and art must speak to our souls through our bodies. But that art can be about nothing but itself, that our bodies are the only sources of all experience, that all experience is ultimately mean-ingless except as sensation, that the fact of medium is nothing but a porous illusion, etc. etc. make up the ravings of a desperate and despair-justifying ego at play in a hyper-intellectual sandbox with no adults in sight.

---

1 http://www.thecrimson.com/article/2015/1/10/daniel-albright-obituary/.

I quote almost at random:

> [I]nterpretation, like the rest of human life, is vanity. Even the most heavily overt allegory, or the plainest narrative, can sustain itself for only a little while before it sinks back into unmeaning.

So why are you so busy pretending to interpret?

> [T]he situation was exasperating to painters with an ounce of originality.

He worships originality for its own sake, one of the commonest false gods of art.

> [S]eizing control is the default language of all representation since all representation is an attempt to gain power over, or at least not to be the slave of, the thing represented.

All art is a function of a Marxist power struggle or Nietzschean master morality?

> This is perhaps not quite the story that [the author] meant me to think, but it seems as good as any.

Because no story is better than any other, because all stories mean nothing in any case, because artist, intention, meaning, and form are all illusions that exist to be debunked by Harvard professors making a living from using the great art of the past as grist for the mill of nihilism.

> [E]ach member of the audience at a performance of *Tosca* experiences a different opera because the opera exists only as an airy shimmer generated from components each one of which bulges and recedes in a space uniquely defined by, and for, a particular spectator.

Then why are we almost all similarly moved by *Tosca* or *Don Giovanni* and almost all similarly bored and revolted—if we're honest—by Philip Glass and Penderecki?

[W]onder is a little scary, and we need to relieve ourselves of wonder by verbalizing it.

Because wonder is nothing but a human emotion, nothing real being there to be wondered at.

A dentist's drill touching a raw nerve is sublime: it so fills your mind that there's no space left to contemplate your overdue credit-card payment, or yesterday's poor haircut, or Fermat's last theorem.

Thus are we robbed not only of the sublime but of the very word *sublime*.

Art always exasperates ... it will dissipate under my gaze, deconstruct into a cloud of endless cultural self-interrogations ... [or] it will recede before my eyes, clench itself into a tight closed object ... [or] it diffuses into a swarm of mosquitoes ... [or] it becomes an armadillo curling itself into a scaly ball.

Well, yes, under *your* gaze, you Medusa of an art critic!

There is a danger that intermedial exercises will expose the vanity or uselessness of art.

So by all means let us play with "intermedial exercises" because exposing the vanity and uselessness of all art is the only valid art form.

[T]he aesthetic phenomenon is most strongly felt when art is liberated from itself, a condition that can happen only through the act of forcing it, more or less against its will, into an alien medium.

I neglected above to call him the tyrant that he admittedly is being here.

I'm not sure that an artwork can even possess purposiveness.

Because if it did, the Harvard literature professoriate as it is now constituted would be out of a career.

[T]he infinite multiplication of interpretations tends to erode any viable sense of an objective telos.

And infinite multiplication is the only arithmetic that interpretation has at its disposal; hence all hope for a vision of unitary truth must be nugatory.

> Perhaps every artwork is like that: we imagine that it is full of friendly doors through which we gain intimate access, but in fact we are shut out.

Certainly anyone who denies a priori the possibility of meaning is shut out of any meaningful work of art—and well he should be.

> [I]n the *Eroica* finale these clonks undergo a remarkable development that could be called the apotheosis of the stomp.

Beethoven reduced to infinite multiplication of interpretations of the stomp.

> To learn to see with the epigastrium and to hear with the elbows is part of the mission of the artwork.

To paraphrase Chesterton, those who won't believe in God will believe in anything.

Why must I expend energy refuting this nonsense? It is the fruitless spinning of a very intelligent and knowledgeable mind cut loose from all moorings in real experience, all faith in a meaningful reality inhabited by man, all significance. Meaning is reduced to sensation, sensation to the body, and the body to absurdity. And of course in the process we ride over the cleverly sophisticated debunking of Beethoven and Raphael atop the bandwagon of progress through Schoenberg and Kandinsky toward the frisson of John Cage and Malevich, driven by one who calls on us to sail after him "into the abyss," hyperintellectually freewheeling on the highway to hell paved by Nietzsche and French literary theory.

For an antidote I will quote Philip Thompson's delicious satirical poem called "His Semiotic Hyper-Euphoric Semaphoric Sparkler: Roland Barthes Barks in Bliss":

The ecst-
asy
Of text!
To be
A rol-
ypol-
Ymorph-
eate,
An eis-
emplas-
Tic or-
gias-
Tic hem-
idem-
Isem-
iot!

Panaesthetics provides a perfect distillation of the deadly intellectual poison of our age. I pray you, avoid it.

Into the Wild
[2017]

Into the Wild is a beautifully photographed and very compelling film. But its meaning embodies everything that is wrong with modern Romanticism and therefore with Hollywood.

There is a revealing moment about the writer/director Sean Penn when he has the young protagonist Chris look directly at the camera and more or less wink, a post-modern gesture that breaks the empathy with inappropriate psychic distance just to call attention to itself. It is a sign of Penn's service to his own ego, quite in keeping with his idiotic politics of sentimental utopian worship of mass murderers like Fidel Castro. But the movie is not about politics, so we'll let that go.

The whole film is a thorough worship of the deities of Romanticism: the individual self, nature, and emotion, and a rejection of the enemies of Romanticism: reason, society, morality. Reason is explicitly rejected. The only poets and writers quoted, until the very end, are Romantics: Byron, Thoreau, etc. Though Aristotle defined man as "the political animal" (the animal that lives in a polis), i.e., social, adult Chris has to go to suicidal lengths to discover, reading a bit of Tolstoy at the end, that the "only real happiness is shared." Everyone he meets knows that already, and so does the audience. So the quest is a representation not of everyman's journey to enlightenment but of a fool's journey to the obvious. His sister says, in voiceover, that everything he is doing "has to be done"—i.e., is fated. Perhaps, but only because he is a self-absorbed Romantic. Nature is beautiful in the film, and he gets lucky until the moose and the poisoning. And then nature is revealed as no friend of unaccommodated man. But that's fine for the film, because dying is fine—part of nature, coming after enlightenment, never mind the path of misery he leaves behind for those who have loved him: parents, sister, hippy couple, young girl, old man. They are all caught in "shared happiness," but he knows better that he has to leave everything to find himself. Well, does the film show him as finally stupid for throwing away all that happiness in the name of the quest to be himself in the wild? No. It makes his journey into a spiritualized ideal accomplishment. We are to be happy about his final vision. We are to admire him, to envy him, to immolate our imaginary selves on the altar of self-realization, nature, and feeling as he has done.

There is only one moral moment in the life of Chris in the film, though he keeps meeting good people who care about him. That is the moment when he refuses to be seduced by the girl Tracy. It is not clear whether his resistance is a result of a moral choice about her young age or simply a desire not to imitate his father by impregnating a girl and leaving her with a bastard. In any case, the moral seriousness of the choice is undermined in the next moment when we see him telling her to reach out and grab what she wants in life, and she grabs him, and then he leaves. I thought she *was* reaching out and grabbing what she wanted, which was him in her bed. The film shows the stupid platitude (follow your bliss) in this moment as a dead-end street, but it doesn't seem to realize it is doing so.

Then the whole journey is recorded by Chris in his diary and belt and so on. Why? Because he doesn't really want to be alone; he just thinks he does because he has to be alone in order to get away from his awful parents. Fine. But that only shows the folly of his quest in another way. If he were really committed to the "wild," there would be no writing and no trying to make art of his life. He would just have done it, and we wouldn't know about it. But of course then there would be no film, so the film has to compromise and make him self-contradictory as a character in order to give *us* the thrill of *his* getting away from it all.

The film is a typical Hollywood exaltation of the supposed cure to the supposedly meaningless lives we live in society, the cure being the total devotion to the self, its emotions, and nature, conceived of as our rightful (if dangerous) home. As such it spits on all the social and rational accomplishments of man, on morality, righteousness, self-sacrifice, and kindness to others, and promotes self-indulgence, aloneness, and finally suicide so long as before the moment of death intense emotions are experienced.

And what after all is the "shared happiness" of the film? It is his imaginary reunion with the parents that he did everything to prevent from happening in actuality. So "shared happiness" is in fact unshared, happening only in his head, and that makes it all worth it. Absurd.

Richard Linklater, *The Before Trilogy*
[2022]

Richard Linklater's trilogy of films called *Before Sunrise, Before Sunset,* and *Before Midnight* is one of the greatest religious films of our time. Its religion is the worship of the god Eros.

Before Sunrise (1995) is a perfectly beautiful depiction of the perfectly beautiful meeting of two supremely attractive people, an exquisitely beautiful and vitally inventive feminine young woman (played by Julie Delpy), and an exquisitely captivating and vitally inventive masculine young man (played by Ethan Hawke). In one night of their walking around Vienna an erotic attraction is born and consummated and irremovably fixed in the souls of two young lovers.

Starring the same two actors, *Before Sunset* (2004) depicts the reconnection of the lovers and the rekindling of their love after an unintentional nine-year separation. As the first took place all in a single night, so this takes place all in a single day.

Again starring the same two actors, *Before Midnight* (2013) depicts the lovers, not married but living together with their twin girls, now on vacation in Greece. During one day and evening they are shown breaking up and reuniting several times before their predicated midnight re-consummation in bed.

All three films are built on conversations between the lovers with a steady river of erotic desire flowing under the surface of all that they say. As an exercise in slice-of-life realism, with hypernaturalistic acting, the films are unparalleled, even though the scenes are also saturated with ideas, character quirks, and complex emotions. But what is "real" throughout is eros—the mysterious, overwhelmingly powerful, ever-rekindling invisible force of the mutual erotic attraction of two attractive people. It is an unsurpassed testament to the object of worship of almost all romance moviemaking since the birth of the medium—namely the god of love.

Since we are all romantics in this sense, worshipping in our hearts the unquestioned meaningfulness of erotic love as the fulfillment of all dreams and the healer of all wounds, we find these three films irresistible, compelling, vital, satisfying. Jesse's speech of commitment in the next to last scene of the third film and his inventive way of rekindling the romance in the last scene after an almost final fight we celebrate as we would a wedding or a recommitment ceremony.

And yet—at the same time, as moving and beautiful and compelling and realistically frustrating and re-healing as the films are, they also reveal something else about our time, something that in our pagan worship of eros we forget at our peril. They reveal the limits of the religion of erotic love, its incapacity to satisfy our deepest hunger for meaning when it exists in no greater context than itself. The back-and-forth tensions and attractions between the two lovers, the pulls of the past (the divorced wife, the absent husband), of the children (the semi-abandoned son, the younger twin daughters), of careers (her desire to save the planet and his to sell his books)—all are countered—not overcome, but absorbed— by the centripetal force of the lovers' mutual attraction. Yet behind all this compelling social and personal drama, we cannot help feeling an essential void.

Both members of this ever-separating but inseparable couple are post-Christian, modern, semi-scientific, sexually liberated, practical, emotion-driven, and fantasy-loving. They are fertile in perpetually inventing and then tossing out various notions of time, place, reality, the cosmos, and death, sticking with none of them. They live in the moment and keep discovering that that is the *only* place they live, "just passing through" between one emptiness and another. Probably unintentionally—since he is clearly projecting himself (unmarried), his own condition (twin daughters), and his own notions onto the couple—Linklater cannot help reducing the meaning of the universe to this irresistible but mono-dimensional reality of a couple in love. But though for them the "moment" is always filled with the temporary but ever-rekindled meaningfulness of their mutual love and attraction, we, the audience, cannot help feeling—at the same time that we live in and love them and their love—that the film also reveals the context of this irresistible and ever-renewing love to be a vast spiritual emptiness.

In that empty universe there is no creator of eros, no purpose for its being but its being itself, no metaphysical reality beyond it. There is no human access to the meaning of erotic love as one incarnation among others within a love-created universe. There are no other dimensions of intense and meaningful human life outside of romantic love. There is no hint of the sublimation possible to romantic love through the vehicle of sacramental marriage. The books written by the boy (art) are about his love. The girl's effort to save the world from nature-destroying human villains (politics) is but a shallow backdrop to dramatize her love. The souls of the lovers do not exist except within the passing parade of ideas, feelings, passions, and decisions anchored in their romantic love. There is no exercise of the freedom of the will in any context but the choices to unite with one's beloved, sexually and otherwise, or not to do so. Though there is guilt, there is no ultimate judge of right and wrong. There is only the absolutism of eros itself in all its compelling and exasperating variety.

In the end, we feel that Linklater could go on making more day-in-the-life films about the same two characters until he should depict them on their deathbeds without his ever portraying eros in a context larger than itself. In these films eros *is* the larger context—the only one—for everything else in life.

Thus, in being an irresistible evocation of romantic love, the trilogy becomes, as if against its will, a consummate illustration of the immeasurably influential movie-driven heresy of our age: the worship of erotic love not as one among the divine gifts to man but as the only valid image of the whole. While offering us an experience of the rich, various, overwhelmingly compelling force of eros, at the same time it presents us with an image of the profound spiritual impoverishment of our age.

Mary Holmes, *The Return of Aquarius*
[2020]

Mary Holmes' seven-panel mural of *The Return of Aquarius* hangs in the Mary Holmes Fireside Lounge at Cowell College, University of California at Santa Cruz. It was completed in 1974.

Look at the pictures first, always remembering Holmes' dictum that the greater the work of art, the worse the reproduction. The mural reads from right to left. Then read the commentaries. Then look at the pictures again.

Right-hand panels:

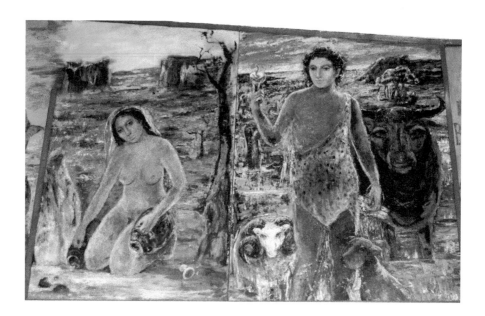

Photographs by Arvey Shier.

Central panels:

Left-hand panels:

When most people read or hear the word *myth*, they think of it as the antithesis of the word *fact*. "The myth is..., but the fact is..." This is so ingrained an idea that we confront any traditional myth from any culture with skepticism. Is it true that Daphne, chased by Apollo, was turned into a tree? That God split the Red Sea for the Children of Israel? That Jesus was resurrected from the dead? That when the sleeping Vishnu breathes out the universe is created and when he breathes in it is destroyed? That Buddha sat under the Bodhi tree for forty-nine days without moving? That George Washington never told a lie? No, we say (unless we are believers)—that's a myth. And we bolster our skepticism with arguments: human beings can't become trees; the Red Sea must have been split, if it was split at all, by some tidal phenomenon; someone probably stole Jesus' body from the tomb; we have no evidence that the universe is the exhalation of a sleeping god; nobody can sit under a tree without moving for that long; nobody gets through life without telling a lie.

I include sacred stories with profane here for two reasons. The first is that we cannot always be sure we know the difference between stories arising from the unaided human imagination and those arising from divine revelation: Can we be certain when the divine is using the human imagination as its vehicle and when not? The second reason is that most modern people are disposed to seeing both sacred and profane myth under the overarching rule of the rational intellect, which attempts to banish from reality the very possibility of divine revelation. By the rational intellect we are permitted only one question: "Is it really true, or is it just a metaphor?" That question itself abolishes the distinction between revelation and folklore. It is prejudicial in itself, and the more so because of the word "just." To paraphrase C. S. Lewis in *The Abolition of Man*,[1] the question does not propose a legitimate philosophical distinction but expresses a hidden assumption, and few in our time are able to resist the implication of that word "just." "Just a metaphor" implies that it isn't really true, because it can't be proven empirically to be factual. Modern people contemplating the splitting of the Red Sea or the resurrection of Jesus or the enlightenment of Gautama Siddhartha are often reduced to asking "Did it really happen?" The implication is that if it did really happen, then we can believe in its meaning. If it didn't then we can't, and the authority of the story dissolves with its authenticity. This approach binds us into the narrowness of the "fact or myth" attitude.

---

1 C. S. Lewis, *The Abolition of Man* (New York: HarperCollins, 2001), p. 5.

But let's look at it another way. First of all, the question whether it really happened or not is unanswerable. It pursues an illusion. Can we go back in time and track on the calendar Buddha's patience under the Bodhi tree? Or observe with our measuring devices the splitting of the Red Sea? Or watch with our eyes as Jesus steps (as in Piero della Francesca's painting) or explodes (as in Grunewald's painting) out of the tomb? (Piero and Grunewald painted it precisely because they could *not* go back to see it for themselves.) Because we can't, we ought not to try. We can have no access to the meaning of those events by trying to discern their material factuality. And since we can't know them in this way, trying to do so leads to a dead end.

But let us suppose that the divine will really did cause these miraculous events to happen. *Why* did it? Not only to bring the Children of Israel out of Egypt and Jesus up into heaven and Buddha out of suffering, but also to cause the events to be written in a book, to be passed down from generation to generation, so that all through time we may re-experience the meaning of those events in the stories of them: namely that God, not man, rules nature and history; that the soul does not die; that suffering can be escaped. These stories exist to dramatize not merely the facts they report but the spiritual reality behind them: the perennial possibility and promise of redemption from the limitations of nature, history, and death.

In modern times, despite the promise of the sacred stories, we tend to think that the only true things are material facts and that in order to live and be well we must embrace material facts and reject as lies the myths of the benighted old past. We are told that myths are the ignorant attempts of people in the past to explain things that we can now explain by science. Get real, we say to the believers in myth, whom we call sentimentalists or fundamentalists or dreamers. We know better. We demand facts, reject myths, are free of delusion, address reality as it is. Evidence for the dethronement of myth is their reduction to silliness in cartoons, films, and advertising, so that the God of the Bible can be played by George Burns (*Oh, God!*) and the life of Christ can be made a Monty Python joke (*Life of Brian*).

But clichés, said Mary Holmes, stick around because they are true. Reductive reference to the clichés derived from myths is also evidence of the myths' staying power. The only way these silly movies can have any meaning is that the myths behind them still matter. We couldn't enjoy the satirical versions if we didn't already know and care about the older ones. It turns out that the idea that myth is the opposite of reality, that myths are discredited attempts to explain what now can be explained by science, is erroneous. For those of us who can receive the myths, their truths are every bit as empirically real as any material fact. For those of us who cannot—or cannot yet—the rejection of the meaning and reality of myth in the name of material fact results in an extreme impoverishment of our intellectual, emotional, and spiritual lives.

What Mary Holmes taught, by contrast, and what she makes explicit in the recorded lecture she gave on these paintings, is that the great myths carry profound truths in a way that the fact/myth or fact/fantasy or fact/lie antithesis does not acknowledge. Myth was never meant to explain phenomena as science means to explain them. Rather, the mythic story is the only way we human beings have to communicate effectively about the realities of the inner life, the life of the emotions, the life of the spirit, which is impossible to communicate in words. Words are too narrow, too particular, to convey the subtleties and complexities of our inner experience. When something significant happens to you—good or bad—and someone asks "How are you feeling about this?" your answer will be something like "Fine," or "Good," or "Unhappy," or "Disappointed," or another word equally limited. Or your response can turn into a great long disquisition that, after many minutes of words, still doesn't come near the reality of what you have just experienced within yourself.

But if you have access to a great myth, to which your questioner also has access, you can say "I feel like Sisyphus," or "like Judas," or "like Odysseus returning to Ithaca," or "like Jacob after wrestling with the angel," and the listener knows more precisely the essence of what you are experiencing in your inner life than any other words could convey. For those who know the story of the myth, its mere mention gives form and reality to the feeling. In fact it reveals to us the *meaning* of the feeling. You can psychoanalyze a person for years and never approach a diagnosis as completely as you can by saying "He is a narcissist." If you know the story of Narcissus, nothing else need be said. And nothing else that can be said would more illuminate the person's psyche than that mythic story. That's why, as Holmes implies, even the would-be scientist Freud had recourse to myth in order to give form to his analysis. *Narcissism* and the *Oedipus complex* are far more illuminating than anything in the scientific vocabulary of psychiatry.

This is why Holmes said in her lecture introducing the paintings that myth is the only way to talk about spiritual and psychological events. Such experience cannot otherwise be articulated in words. Myths do not correct or change or explain reality, she said, but they illuminate it, and they do so because what happens in myth, legend, and story corresponds so completely to reality, as completely as mathematics corresponds to the physical world (so that based on math we can send a man to the moon and back). In this sense — the correspondence of the mythic story to the reality of our inner lives — the myths prove to be not the opposite of facts but deeply true. Of course Holmes was not pretending to be a prophet. As the poet Philip Thompson rightly says (see below), the astrological image in her painting is a "fable." Holmes uses that image, and the images from alchemy and tarot, not to promote an atavistic paganism but to convey her own visionary understanding of redemption, of the way it works in human life. She calls the mythic images into the service of her vision, believing that the imagination illuminated by myth can be a vehicle of truth.

When we look at Holmes' images of a dragon and a unicorn, then, we are likely to believe we have outgrown such childish notions, whether or not we disapprove of the friends who buy images of them in vacation gift shops. Hearing that a set of paintings is called *The Return of Aquarius* will evoke in those who came of age in the 1960s and 1970s the cotton-candy song from the musical *Hair* — "This is the dawning of the age of Aquarius, age of Aquarius…" "Oh wow! Naked people on the Broadway stage! How avant-garde!" In younger people it might evoke nothing at all. But like the story of Cupid and Psyche in the hands of C. S. Lewis (*Till We Have Faces*), or the ancient Irish gods in the hands of James Stephens (*The Crock of Gold*), or the stories of Joseph in the hands of Thomas Mann (*Joseph and His Brothers*), these mythic images in Holmes' hands take on, for those who know or have patience to learn the stories, profound meanings that could not possibly be conveyed in any other way and that offer valuable illumination of our inner life.

With this in mind, let me tell you a little about the mythic stories behind the paintings. If we know them and know the changes Holmes is working upon them, perhaps we will gain access to the profound experience of meaning that Holmes has made available in these paintings to our hearts and minds through our eyes and our empathic response.

Holmes painted *The Return of Aquarius* to address the condition of our time, in which there is almost universal skepticism and despair about the meaning of things, and in which there is a shared expectation of the end of the world. How often are we told, how often do we believe, that the world is coming to an end. When I was in junior high school, nuclear war was going to be the end of us. When I was in college the world was going to freeze, or all human beings were going to die of overpopulation, always twenty or thirty years in the future. (The predictions would be conveniently forgotten by the time they didn't come true.) In 1999 the world was going to grind to a halt because the computers were not programmed to be ready for Y2K (the year 2000). Nowadays we are told that global warming will do us in, or an asteroid, or a virus. Some fear, as Holmes did, that we might run out of fresh water. We all seem to believe that the world cannot go on as it is. Some fantasize that an undefined socialist utopia will arise from the world's ashes. Others may expect that the coming age will be inspired by a new revelation of the nature of God as yet unimaginable. In all these end-of-times scenarios our period is akin to the first century B.C., whose general despair and longing for redemption produced a multiplication of cults—Jewish sects, Gnosticism, Mithraism, Zoroastrianism, and Manicheism, as well as early Christianity.

In addition, Holmes observed that our time is characterized by a tremendous movement toward the dematerialization of the world. Think of all the "realities" we experience every day that have almost nothing to do with material presence, all our techniques of invisibility: We are accustomed to conversing with people who are actually far away; we can listen to dead people singing, like Bing Crosby or Elvis Presley, or watch them making us laugh, like Charlie Chaplin or Groucho Marx. Holmes loved the idea that we can make an electric circuit merely by photographing a circuit. We know that the room we are sitting in is filled with people conversing, playing musical instruments, having political debates, and trying to sell things even when we are alone; all we need in order to hear them is a radio. Holmes lived long enough to be able to add, "and this is nothing compared to the dematerialization going on on those chips!" meaning computer microchips. There is a terrible combination of physical reality and the absence of it, so, she pointed out, there are men who can still fall in love with Greta Garbo—"God forbid they should get a look at her!" she added; Garbo was then age 77. Given these invisibles, does it take much faith to believe that meaningful events are taking place in the air around us even if we don't have a radio handy? To believe that vast quantities of information can be stored on a microchip the size of your thumbnail? Is the dematerialization of our time merely imaginary? Think of AI and Wi-Fi. We have all come to believe in the reality of the invisible.

In response to her observation about our sense of the end of things, our experience of dematerialization detaching us from the natural world, and our longing for transformation and a new energizing vision of meaning, Holmes set herself the task of making the reality of spiritual transformation visible to us so that, seeing it, we could believe in it. Based on her recognition of the power of myth to speak truthfully to the condition of our time, to illuminate the potential for transformation, Holmes drew images from the mythic stories of astrology, alchemy, the Tarot, tales of the Hasidim, and Christianity. But "astrology" to Holmes was not the frivolous bluff of the daily newspaper's horoscope column. "Alchemy" was not just a ruse for nipping other people's gold. The Tarot was not just a card game. For Holmes these ancient mythic languages were great repositories of wisdom that she called upon for images by which to bring healing insight to us all.

For example, the old astrology was not merely a way of predicting the future. It was a way of thinking about the structure of reality. In the old astrological tradition, arising from ancient Persia, the stars participated in the order of creation, corresponding to and influencing the life of man on earth. Holmes said she had read an article explaining that when the three Magi came to King Herod of Jewry, it was not because they were following a star that moved forward in front of them "the way we learned in the hymns." They were following the stars "in the same way that you'd follow a cookbook," she said. In Persian astrology Jupiter represented a king or kingship; Saturn represented the Jews; and Pisces represented the Holy Land. At the time of the birth of Jesus there was a conjunction of the planets Saturn and Jupiter, and the world was leaving the astrological house of Aries and entering the house of Pisces. It was based on this reading of the stars that the three Magi came to the Holy Land to ask King Herod, "Where is the king of the Jews?"

In that astrological tradition, in addition to the cycle of the year during which the sun passes through the twelve houses of the zodiac—so that you know from your birthday that you are a Scorpio or a Sagittarius—the cycle of the great astrological year, twelve periods of two thousand years each, moves backward through the signs of the zodiac—the age of Taurus, followed by that of Aries, then Pisces, then Aquarius—instead of forward as in the solar year. As Jesus lived in the beginning of the age of Pisces, we live at the end of the age of Pisces and the beginning of the age of Aquarius. The painting then ties these astrological ages to historical time: Ancient eras correspond to the ages of Taurus (the bull having been worshipped in India, Egypt, the Mediterranean, and elsewhere) and Aries (the ram having been sacred in ancient France and significant in the Old Testament). The Christian era corresponds with the age of Pisces, the fish, which is both the earliest and the latest symbol of Christ (visible on ancient sarcophagi and on present-day bumper stickers). The Greek word for fish, *Ichthus*, is read as an acrostic of "Iesous Christos, Theou Hyios, Soter" ("Jesus Christ, Son of God, Savior"). Holmes depicts the age now beginning as presided over by the astrological symbol of Aquarius, the Water Bearer, the bringer of spiritual enlightenment.

According to Holmes, the dawning age will also produce, eventually, a new vision of the nature of God as the Holy Spirit, to be revealed in a third testament. This belief arises from Holmes's combining the astrological imagery with the prophecy of the twelfth-century mystic and theologian Abbot Joachim of Flora (Fiore). A devout believer in the Christian concept of the triune (three-in-one) nature of God, Joachim foresaw that the age of the Old Testament devoted to God the Father (the power of God) and that of the New Testament devoted to God the Son (the love of God) would be followed by a third age and a third testament devoted to God the Holy Spirit (the wisdom of God). But whereas Joachim imagined each age lasting a millennium, Holmes expanded the length of each age to two millennia to correspond with the astrological ages of the Great Year and with historical time as we now see it. The Water Bearer fits this trinitarian idea because the Holy Spirit can never be depicted by a visible figure but must always be represented symbolically, and the symbols used have always been water and fire. Thus uniting Christian and astrological prophecies, the paintings depict the spirit in repeated images of water and of fire. We can confidently believe that this third revelation and its testament will appear, said Holmes, because of the accuracy of myth in illuminating reality.

Why are the paintings to be read from right to left? Holmes thought that the transition from one age (Pisces) to the next (Aquarius) would be accompanied by a general reversal of things. Her example was that Hebrew, written in the age of Aries, was succeeded by Latin, written in the age of Pisces. Hebrew is read from right to left, Latin from left to right. Holmes pointed out that writing from left to right prevents the ink from smearing (because most people are right-handed) and then said "but now who's using ink?" (I am writing this on a computer.) All things, she said, like writing, will be curiously reversed.

The inscription flanking the paintings is also read from right to left. It is two stanzas from the hymn *Veni Sancte Spiritus* ("Come Holy Spirit"), dating also from the twelfth century, found in the Roman Catholic liturgy for the mass of Pentecost. It has been ascribed to the Archbishop of Canterbury, Cardinal Stephen Langton (c. 1150–1228), to Pope Innocent III (c. 1160–1216), and to others. (The calligraphy was done by Holmes' friend Bruce Cantz.) It reads:

> *O lux beatissima,*
> *reple cordis intima*
> *tuorum fidelium.*

> *Sine tuo numine*
> *nihil est in homine,*
> *nihil est innoxium.*

> [O most blessed light,
> fill the inmost heart
> of your faithful.

> Without your divine spirit
> nothing is in man,
> nothing is innocent.]

The second of these stanzas asserts that innocence is not an achievement but a gift of grace, and man's duty and joy are to know that. Holmes' painting is an attempt to remind us of it. According to Holmes, the last part of the inscription applies especially to the present time, in which we find it impossible to believe that anything can be innocent—not government, not society, not the founding ideals of the nation, not the founding ideals of the civilization, certainly not the rebels against those ideals, and especially not ourselves. Nothing can be innocent that is not visited by the Holy Spirit and transformed.

Reading the painting from right to left moves us forward in historical time and in stages within the inner life.

The figure in Panel 1 is a shepherd, living, partly by necessity, in close proximity to animals and in harmony with them and with the whole natural world surrounding him. He holds a serpent in a cup, an image of bringing under government our destructive impulses and the destructive potentialities in the world. The image comes from a legend of

St. John, who, given a cup of poisoned wine, blessed it before drinking, whereupon the poison rose out of the cup in the form of a serpent. It also appears in Chapter 47 of *The Golden Ass* of Apuleius, where in a vision the goddess Isis (identified there with Minerva, Venus, Diana, Proserpine, Ceres, Juno, Bellona, Hecate, and Rhamnusia/Nemesis) rises from the sea holding a cup of gold from which an asp lifts up its head. The shepherd, like the bull (Taurus), the ram (Aries), and the fish (Pisces), is a precursor, pointing toward the coming despair at the loss of the world of innocence and to the transformation and redemption that will follow.

When one power begins to lose its potency, and before the next appears, the feeling is despair. Hence in Panel 2 the cup lies overturned, signifying the loss of government over the destructive powers of nature and self. The waters of the spirit are being poured on the ground, indicating the failure to see anything but futility in any other kind of action. The world appears to be emptied of spirit. Nonetheless, there is hope: the sun is rising, and from the seemingly uninhabited house on fire a voice is heard. Holmes took this image from a Hasidic retelling of an exemplum in the midrash (ancient work of scriptural interpretation) called *Genesis Rabbah* (39:1):

> Rabbi Isaac said: It is like one who was passing from place to place and saw a palace in flames. He wondered, "Can this palace have no master?" The lord of the palace looked upon him and said to him, "I am the lord of the palace." Similarly did Abraham our father wonder, "Can this world have no master?" The Holy One Blessed be He looked upon him and said to him, "I am the lord of the world."

Martin Buber concludes his description of the retelling of the tale by Hasidic Rabbi Menachem Mendel of Kotzk by saying that those who heard him say "I am the lord of the castle" "were struck with great reverence, for they all felt: 'the castle is burning, but it has a lord.'" As Philip Thompson puts it below, "The spiritual emptiness of the universe is always an illusion."

But how is the despair to be overcome? Holmes claimed it was only by hitting bottom, like an alcoholic on skid row. Only when there is recognition that one cannot go further down can one somehow bounce back, as if pushing off from that ground below which one cannot fall. This lowest point is symbolized in Panel 3 by the alchemical image of the dragon swallowing the virgin we saw in Panel 2.

Like astrology, alchemy has gotten a bad rap. Because actual alchemists used as a symbol of their efforts the transformation of lead into gold, people came to believe that alchemy was nothing but a con game and that all alchemists were merely out to bilk the trusting of their gold. Eventually, many posed as alchemists to do just that. "Give me a lot of lead and a small bit of gold," they'd say. "The gold will seed the transformation, and all your lead will become gold. The more gold and lead you bring me, the more gold you will have." Then the con men would skip town with the gold, leaving the lead unchanged. But that was only a late decayed development. Holmes pointed out that the original goal of alchemy was not to get wealth but to achieve the philosophers' stone, by which the alchemist could transform the lower in *all* realms to the higher, the transformation of base lead into incorruptible gold being only a symbol of that general purpose. She also found it moving that the true alchemical discipline required not only the symbolic sacrifice of the virgin to the dragon—meaning innocence to the devouring of the time-bound, destructive world—but also the presence of a mutually loving man and woman. It is the only ancient wisdom tradition that required a loving couple to achieve its aim, in this case finding the philosophers' stone and thereby raising us out of our isolation and loneliness and the sufferings of life. (The golden potential of lead, the need for sacrifice, and the union of lovers may also be seen in the symbolic casket test in Shakespeare's *Merchant of Venice*.)

The dragon's devouring of the virgin is also an image of the fate of Saint Margaret of Antioch, patron saint of childbirth, who, according to the legend, was thrown into prison for her faith and swallowed by a dragon. But when she spoke the name of God, the dragon split open and she stepped unharmed from the belly of the beast. In other of Holmes' paintings that miracle becomes an image of the birth of the human child out of its mother's blood and slime and of the human spirit out of the blood and slime of the physical world. Here the dragon devours the virgin, who is holding a cup of flames. As Holmes said, fire is one of the two images (the other being water) by which spirit is depicted in art. Here the virgin holds fire under government as the Shepherd in Panel 1 held the serpent. There what was being contained was destructive power. Here what is being contained is the redemptive power of the spirit. Once the virgin's sacrifice is complete, the dragon regurgitates her. She, the human soul, is now become herself the philosophers' stone, and the dragon tosses her into the air, where she is caught by the unicorn and borne upward toward the heavens.

The virgin with the head of a unicorn in her lap is another common theme in Holmes' paintings. In medieval lore the rare unicorn, whose horn was believed to be a powerful antidote and curative and therefore extremely valuable, was a fierce and unconquerable beast that could not be caught by hunters directly. Only when a pure virgin sat singing in the forest would the unicorn come and lay its head in her lap, whereupon the hunters could surprise, capture, and kill it for its horn. The innocent virgin and powerful unicorn became an image of the incarnation of Christ and of the divine compassion it represented. The unicorn is Christ, who willingly chooses to be borne into the world by a virgin in order that he might be killed and thereby cure mankind of sin and death. Panel 5 depicts a great reversal, the fruition of the sacrifice of Panel 3. The unicorn (an image of the power of the spirit) now catches the virgin and carries her—carries all of us—in ecstatic triumph up to the Water Bearer.

The Water Bearer himself, Aquarius, who presides over this process of transformation, stands on the burned ground of Panel 2, now filling an empty vessel with the waters of the spirit, bearing to mankind the new dispensation of spiritual renewal. The image of Aquarius, obviously influenced by images of Apollo, the god of the sun, and of Christ, is, in his pouring of the waters of the spirit from one vessel to another, merged with the Tarot image of Temperance, who mixes cold and hot, yin and yang, desire and sacrifice, time and eternity, and offers the tempered waters of the spirit to the world thirsty for the harmony of peace, joy, and fulfillment. Holmes said that generally men desire perfection and women desire completeness. The bearer of the waters of the spirit here bestows the harmony of both upon the world.

Once the blessing of spirit is granted, the sacrifice and transformation accomplished, then the waters of the spirit can rise to baptize and fecundate the world. Panel 6 depicts the lushness and fertility of life redeemed from the dryness and despair of Panel 2. The three women are really one woman in her three aspects, another familiar theme in Holmes' work. Holmes refused to countenance the reductive and combative feminism of our time, which she thought did great injury to both women and men. She thought of woman as having three aspects, by which the lives of all creatures in the world, including men, are enriched. Woman is always in a way a young, erotically attractive, flirting, virgin bride; she is always in another way a caring, nourishing, providing mother; and she is always also a prophetess.

Woman's most valuable gift, according to Holmes, is wisdom, the capacity to worship the spirit and to be its vehicle in the life of the world. The three women, who are Woman, stand in water and hold cups of flame. The rising of the waters is an image of the blessing of the spirit upon the physical world, a baptism, contrasting with the image of waters of the spirit fruitlessly poured upon dry ground in Panel 2, where the apparent spiritual emptiness of the physical seems to devour the spirit. The white bird derives from Genesis 1:2 ("And the Spirit of God moved upon the face of the waters"), the dove that brought Noah the olive leaf (sign of the earth's restoration after the flood, Genesis 8:11), the dove that represents the descent of the Holy Spirit in all four New Testament Gospels (Matthew 3:16, Mark 1:10, Luke 3:22, John 1:32), and the doves sacred to Aphrodite/Venus, goddess of love and beauty.

In Panel 7 Holmes depicts the final fruition of the whole transforming process. The original Man and Woman were forced out of the Garden of Eden, the harmonious world of innocence depicted in Panel 1, into the world of labor and pain, despair and death. Now Man and Woman, the new Adam and the new Eve, are at home and at play in the tree of knowledge, which is also the tree of life, and the world begins again, *above* the world. The desires of man for perfection and of woman for completeness are united in a joyful union of opposites. In Chinese philosophy, the Tao (the Way, both of the universe and of man) is a whole made up of the harmonious union of opposite principles: yin, representing the shadow side of the mountain, the moon, the feminine, the dark, the receptive, the yielding, as of water; and yang, representing the sunny side of the mountain, the sun, the masculine, the light, the active, the unyielding, as of rock. (Holmes explained that the Chinese term for "landscape" is "mountain-water picture," implying "yang-yin picture.") That union of equal opposites, usually imaged in the yin-yang or tai-chi symbol, is here represented by the colors in which Adam and Eve are painted. The reversals brought about by the return of Aquarius include the reversal of the colors associated with male and female: The new Adam is here painted in cool yin colors and the new Eve in warm yang colors. Holmes said, when the Messiah comes, the moon will be as bright as the sun (alluding to Isaiah 30:26). The reversal of the soul's exile from the harmonious natural world is celebrated in joy, completing the alchemical transformation that spirit works in the lives of men.

Perhaps now Holmes' terse description of the work will make sense to you. She writes:

We move backward through the Zodiac: Taurus, Aries, Pisces; each constellation dominant for two thousand years to make up the Great Year.

Now Aquarius stands on the burned earth pouring the divine energy, the water of life, from one pitcher to another. On the far right the precursors, the Bull, the Ram, the Fishes live in the dawn world, at one with earth and sea, in a garden with a shepherd and his dog. The shepherd foresees the exile, the loss, when the sweet companions will be gone and the waters spilled on the sand.

What sacrifice will allow the Unicorn to carry the soul to the sky? The virgin must be devoured by the Dragon.

Then the water can rise and white birds fly. All now shall have the flame and shall stand in the living water. Even the two, bound together by their difference, will frolic in the trees.

So the world moves through the constellations and so we move, in a day, an hour, a moment of time, from Paradise, innocent as animals, to isolation and despair, to a little death in the belly of the dragon. Yet through that alchemy lifted on the Unicorn to the Divine presence of the Water-bearer.

Now again we can celebrate. The waters rise, the beloved tree contains us.

The poet Philip Thompson, a devoted friend of Holmes, recorded his understanding of the mural as follows:

The Return of Aquarius is an epic achievement in the endeavor as Mary describes it "of making the invisible visible." The mural depicts a spiritual journey from Creation to Redemption. It is a journey both broadly historical and intimately personal.

Imagery and ideas from Judaism, Christianity, astrology, and alchemy are woven together along with her own pictorial inventions to draw us through the narrative. Water is the central image. We follow its movement across the mural from right to left.

In the painting's myth the coming of the great astrological year of Aquarius to succeed that of Pisces is equated with the arrival of the dispensation of the Holy Spirit that follows the ages of the Father and the Son … and establishes an earthly heaven of peace, perfection, and spiritual fulfillment. The astrological fable is a good one since in the old poetic tradition of the zodiac, Aquarius, the Water Bearer, stands for clarity, vision.

The journey begins with a single person in a lush garden setting of numinous innocence. We move through a desert of exile and despair to the point of being devoured by the dragons of life. But in that "little death," the process of elevation can begin. The central figure, Aquarius, the water bearer, presides over this transformation to new life by filling the empty vessel with thirst-quenching waters. Revived, the young girl is carried off triumphantly by the unicorn. The waters that revive also cleanse and refresh—a kind of baptism.

The last stage of the journey is represented by a man and a woman at play and at home, above the world, in the tree of knowledge. Now they are (and we would be) fully cooperative partners in the Divine Plan.

The Return of Aquarius takes us on the journey that each of us travels in a lifetime, in a day, in a moment, delighting and encouraging us with a vision of redemption.

Panel 1 (far right):

A first-Adam, precursor figure, clothed in a skin and holding a staff, is flanked by sacred animals (ram and bull) and attended by his animal brother the dog. Landscape of rich fields, bright quiet sky—the book of the creatures: Spirit and nature indistinguishable in the pastoral imagination, spirit both omnipresent and hidden.

Panel 2 (second to right):

Abomination of desolation: In a wasteland stretching far into the distance a woman empties a vessel of water onto the sand. Man withdrawn from the divine pictured as the divine withdrawn from man and nature (an illusion, represented by a tiny burning building in the background [based on] a Hasidic tale of a Rabbi who, passing by a burning house because he assumed no one was in it, heard a cry coming from the midst of the flames: moral—the spiritual emptiness of the universe is always an illusion.)

Panels 3, 4, 5 (middle, right to left):

Virgin half-swallowed by a dragon (3) is connected by a rainbow-like band of light to the virgin astride a prancing unicorn (5). The rainbow passes behind the head of Aquarius (4), a towering, glowing naked man who pours water between two pitchers and who is enclosed by a ring of fiery light. Here (3) is the penultimate stage of the great alchemical work, the negation of matter that precedes its transformation into spirit. Here (5) is life transcending all destructions of matter and spirit, a world of pure form, intention, meaning. Virgin and dragon appear upon a landscape underneath a large sky filled with strips of luminous cloud—virgin and unicorn are in this sky— Aquarius stands in a supernatural light.

Panel 6 (second to left):

Images of the state of paradise with a feminine theme. Three women half immersed in a stream—baptismal water, moisture on leaves, three aspects of woman: virgin, bride, matron [or rather: virgin-bride, matron, and seer-prophetess]—amid thick shining foliage, a dove hovering just overhead. A world "saturated with spirit" in Mary's words. [In a letter, Thompson wrote about my phrase, "The water, in which everyone has lived for nine months and the human race for nine million years": "[Rather] the water, in which the human form is perfected for its first birth, and which in the beginning received the spirit of God in the first movement of universal creation... (Because we do not allow the theory of evolution in its 'that's all there is to it' form, and that is the form in which the theory is universally expressed and held.)"]

Panel 7 (far left):

Panel 7 represents the new Adam and the new Eve—exchange of attributes: man in yin colors, woman in yang, transcendence of mere sex [compare with John Donne's "A Valediction: Forbidding Mourning"] as sovereigns of a redeemed nature, a dance in repose upon the boughs of a tree. [In a letter, Thompson wrote about the "exchange of attributes upon rebirth": "To portray redeemed humanity as the composer of transfiguring spiritual music rather than as the product of formal variations on a theme."]

With this sketchy description about all one can say is magnificent! moving! inspiring! beautiful! Everything is painted with such strength and beauty and subtlety—light, landscapes, animals, figures—Mary is a miracle.

The last time Philip Thompson visited Cowell College to see Holmes' paintings again, he studied *The Return of Aquarius* for a long while, and, before leaving, deeply moved, said, "Since the seventeenth century, there is Goya, and there is Mary."

Now look again at the images of the paintings. Can you find meaning pouring through them, through your eyes, through your empathic response, into the heart, making visible the invisible reality of spiritual transformation? If not, blame the poverty of art reproduction and make your way, if you can, to Cowell College, UCSC, in Santa Cruz, California, to look at the mural in person. There you may hope to benefit from the miracle that was Mary Holmes.[2]

---

2 You may learn more about Mary Holmes at www.MaryHolmes.org.

Other Writings

Two Clocks and Another
[c. 1983]

If Big Brother wanted an architectural style that would eliminate from the physical environment of his subjects every image of significance, thereby proclaiming the meaninglessness of everything but the televised face of their master and the absolute will it represented, he could do no better than to imitate the design of the public high school where I taught poetry on Tuesday evenings for the local community college. To make the school itself suit the purpose he would need only to exchange the pre-1984 built-in loudspeakers on the interior wall of each classroom for a video screen. In all other respects the job is done for him. The buildings are long, low, massively eaved, rectangular bungalows of faded-pink stucco, trimmed (if doors and those vast overhangs can be called trim) in middle-tech blue. All are identical: classrooms, library, offices, janitors' closets, auditorium. The gymnasium is taller than the other buildings, but the architect has done what he could to convince us that it isn't. The uneasy angles at which the buildings sit relative to one another; the covered breezeways linking them, empty but for occasional banks of steel lockers, each with a combination lock; the absence of any image or object upon which to rest the eye (no sculpture, mural, flower, shrub, or tree) or the torso (no bench, step, niche, or windowsill—no windows); the absence, but for the white enamel drinking fountains (three stainless steel spouts each), of any non-smooth, non-rectilinear surface whatever—all contribute in the human observer to a semiconscious Magritte-like foreboding that threatens at every moment to erupt into full-scale panic. The occasional trash can, symbolically decorated in senior-class colors, serves only to heighten the overwhelming dreariness of the void that is its context.

Taking this in on the first night of school, I hurried along the breezeways (which in Southern California substitute for hallways) to my assigned room, externally distinguished from the others only by the black "J-12" in stencil military on the outside of the door, and stepping into it I was temporarily relieved. The teacher who presides in the room during the day seemed to be doing her best to counteract the deleterious effects the school's architecture must be having on the tender imaginations of her charges. Instead of the regulation five rows of six chairs were two semicircles. And the walls were decorated with posters: an orange seashore-sunset, a shady forest, a series of portraits of great writers.

"Poems say with words what cannot be said in words," I began that evening, trying to say with words what cannot be said in words, and went on to introduce what has become a foreign language to people most of whose youthful and adult leisure has been spent in watching Big Brother's favorite medium. It was an uphill battle. The opposition, the students' natural and culturally reinforced resistance to the art of poetry, was familiar, but the hill was a new one: my own awareness that whatever the power of the sounds and images that night's poems might generate, they were (unless something special happened) merely delicacies prepared for the entropic maw waiting outside the door to devour them. And as the weeks passed, it began to dawn on me why so many students turn so young to sexual sensation and to chemically induced hallucination for meaningful experience: Apart from one another and their dreams, they are given nothing meaningful to look at.

We are the first people in history to gather for serious purposes — politics, entertainment, education — in environments totally devoid of images of significant things. The columned town halls, ornate theaters, and sculptured monuments of the commonwealth are preserved as relics if not sold for lucre or pulled down with passionate ideological intensity, while we gather, if at all, only to buy and sell in the darkness visible of shopping malls. In Boston's Copley Square, where once eyes, lifted to the elegant Florentine arches of the old Public Library building and the Moorish Gothic grandeur of Trinity Church, might humble the heart before wisdom and the divine mystery, now eyes are raised six times higher to the sterile, mirror-faced John Hancock Tower and subjugate the heart to the vain preeminence of insurance. And the continent is bracketed by the little boxes on the hillsides of Daly City outside San Francisco (made famous in the Malvina Reynolds song of the 1960s) and the bigger boxes on the avenues of aesthetically decimated midtown Manhattan. Dwelling and selling, we inhabit an architectural wasteland. To all of us, but especially to youngsters locked for six or eight hours a day in such prisons of the imagination as this high school, the images that sexual desire and drugs project on the mind might well seem indispensable.

I was complaining of this one day to a friend, also a teacher. "The sad thing," he replied, "is that the images of reality they get inside the classroom are as soul-numbing as those they get outside." Of course he is right. How could it be otherwise? The buildings and what goes on in most of them are products of the same nihilistic, utilitarian vision of the world. My initial approval of the day teacher's efforts to counteract the influence of the exterior landscape had rapidly faded that first night. The posters, sentimental substitutes for nature and arts as they were, bore in addition supposedly inspirational quotations from the likes of Thoreau and Emerson—faintly familiar, shallow out of context, and useless; the semicircles of chairs were perfectly concentric; and the objects on the teacher's table (which in the succeeding weeks remained positioned precisely as they had been the first night)—roll sheets, one textbook, two pens, three pencils, a pencil eraser, a yellow felt marker, a stapler, about six paper clips, a ruler, a box of Kleenex—included a yellow pad at which on one occasion I peeked and read, in an adult hand, "Thomas Philipson, Tuesday, February 7: minus two points for—" But it doesn't matter what Tom had done wrong. Not losing points for not having done it would have been just as demoralizing.

What is going on in this classroom, with its khaki-prosed, committee-approved textbook, its platitudes dipped in photography like candy bars in chocolate, and its dehumanizing demerit points, if not a laboring in the despair that Kierkegaard says is unaware of being despair, a crushing under the juggernaut of the educational system decorated with the husks of former meanings whose kernels are nowhere in evidence? How can a culture that puts its children to school under the flicker and hum of fluorescent lights, that imagines it can deliver philosophy and the natural world poster-packaged, that substitutes an arbitrary point system and cathode rays for the even scales and half-draped figure of blind justice, in short that teaches art and life as mechanisms of which learning is the oil, financial success the purpose (if any), and joy (if any) an incidental by-product—how can such a culture hope to offer as education anything but the reverberating hollowness of Big-Brotherly advice, the practice of distraction under the pretense of truth? Science, sociology, psychology, history, art, and literature, as they are generally taught, cannot but confirm, intentionally or by default, the proposition revealed so eloquently in the school's architecture—namely that but for the accident of life the universe is a void and that human beings are themselves responsible for all illusions of meaning, illusory meaning being the only meaning possible. It is no wonder that we fail to make our buildings into images of significant things when we are taught by implication and believe too well that the only thing significant enough to make images of is nothingness.

For what that our culture offers him should Tom Philipson postpone or renounce the intense and immediate gratification that sex and dope provide and the relief that death promises? The love boat that is TV and the dry dock that is school? If he does not father an illegitimate child or pay for an abortion, if he fails to drink or drug his brains into sediment or ride his motorcycle into a truck before he is eighteen, no thanks for his preservation will be due to the culture whose vapidities he is obliged to swallow on pain of losing points.

And yet here I was, in the same room, under the same lights and an equally desiccated system, using a textbook anthology, hoping against hope to teach poetry. From whence cometh my help?

During our mid-class break on the Tuesday evening following the conversation with my friend, we heard the prodigious roar of a crowd in the stadium where the high school team must have scored a goal in a nighttime home game. Later, on my way out to the car, I overheard the staccato sports chatter of three fourteen-year-olds using a wallet to shoot lay-ups (till their ride should come) at the painted letter designating the "C" building, the sole image on the one hundred or so yards of ponderous eaves overhanging the sidewalk opposite the parking lot. Beneath the ever-present pretense of cool essential to the adolescent boy's public self, in their attention to each lay-up and the conviction with which it was immediately critiqued or hailed, real excitement flowed. In the midst of the most barren of landscapes these boys were charged with an intensity of life.

What can have moved them to find so engaging a use for a structure so entirely the enemy of engagement, to make a liar of it to its face? On reflection I realized that it was the same thing that had brought the crowd to the stadium and had moved them to shout: the longed-for experience of the perfect shot, the score against the resistance of others and the limits of the self and the physical world. In making or beholding the perfect shot—the bull's-eye that the archer knows is one before the arrow has left him, the winning basket made from mid-court as the buzzer sounds, the 10.0 Olympic dive—all of us, athletes and spectators, glimpse a reality greater than our own, proof of which fills us with wonder and with joy. And for all too many, being where the perfect shot may happen is the oppressive school day's only respite, the workweek's only sabbath. Hence the love, the concentration, the disciplined labor, the fanaticism that sports inspire even in the otherwise dissipated. For there we find access to meaning—to no nameable meaning, to nothing repeatable or otherwise transmittable, to nothing that can be taught, but nonetheless to something incontrovertibly there and absolutely real, something outside of but related to our selves, something therefore profoundly satisfying.

Was it coincidence that on the same evening I had been teaching T. S. Eliot's "Preludes"? I had read the poem aloud, twice, and then asked my usual first question: "What hit you?" Often the silence that follows is laden with the students' fears of being the first, or the only, or the dumbest, to speak. This time it bespoke concentration. I waited. After a while, to provide a form for their thoughts to take shape in, I asked what kind of world the poet was describing and read some passages again:

> Or trampled by insistent feet
> At four and five and six o'clock;
> And short square fingers stuffing pipes,
> And evening newspapers, and eyes
> Assured of certain certainties...

One student, who had not spoken in class all semester, said, "Stagnant." "Go on," I said, and for several minutes he did, suddenly impassioned, to an audience rapt, hearing our own responses and our own struggle with the "masquerades / That time resumes" expressed in his words. ("I wish he would talk more often," said a classmate of his to me later, one rarity begetting another.) He had had "such a vision of the street / As the street hardly understands," such an experience of the poem as all of us reading it and listening to him had shared, even as we had shared, perhaps not understanding it, the harrowing walk from car to class through those hellishly empty breezeways.

> I am moved by fancies that are curled
> Around these images, and cling

said the poet, and in doing so had curled our fancies around the poem and the truth around which the poem itself is curled. Through art the vacant passageways of seemingly insignificant existence had been transformed into significant images, and that transformation had become the vehicle of a transformation in us, had given us what the buildings in which it happened could not, what the platitudes on their walls might promise but could never deliver, what the system they were constructed to serve seemed to forbid: an epiphany, a moment of truth revealing the always true.

> The notion of some infinitely gentle
> Infinitely suffering thing

—a notion expressed in words that cannot contain but can sometimes deliver it—had refuted Big Brother, had breached the unseen wall. Feeling too alive to concentrate for a while, we decided to take our twenty-minute break. It was then that we heard the roar from the stadium.

For me these two kinds of epiphany, that experienced in sports and that in works of art, seemed to have joined forces that night against the buildings and the systems we call school and the culture of which it is a microcosm. Though the simple beauty of the perfect shot conveys one kind of meaning and the rich insight of the moving poem another, both seemed to spring from the same source, through a mediating excellence of gesture and form, into our souls. Eliot and I and my students and the football players and the crowd watching them and the three schoolboys had all been engaged in the same kind of attempt. We were trying to arrange dry words and images, bodies and footballs, wallets and walls, in such a way that through the specific quality of their interrelation would pour meaning, without which, no matter how firmly they believe that they believe in ultimate meaninglessness, human beings cannot and will not live.

* * *

It is said that a man with one clock knows what time it is, but a man with two is never sure. There were two clocks on opposite walls of our classroom. (The room can be partitioned but never is.) One clock ran regularly twelve or thirteen minutes behind the other. Without reference to a third timepiece whose accuracy was proven—and how should we have proven it?—we could not know whether one clock anticipated what we must come to or the other reminded us what we had left behind. Both were self-consistent; both claimed to tell the time with equal authority. But at least one of them was lying.

Our buildings, which picture a destined void, and our platitudes, which recall meanings they cannot deliver, like all our artifacts, tell us the time. But in the absence of outside authority neither can be trusted. Our buildings are images of the invisible world we believe we inhabit. We want them to be as they are. If we did not, we would not build and pay for and use them. (The argument from saving expense is irrelevant. Every age spends its limited resources on what means most to it. We are far more prosperous than the medieval cathedral builders, and while many times the wealth that paid for the old Boston Public Library must have gone to purchasing its new wing, not all the wealth in the world would have made the new building anything but the cavernous mausoleum of the spirit that it is. Precisely that mausoleum is what was wanted, presumably to house a culture we believe to be dead.) But the blank boxes we live and work and play and study in assert that the context of our lives is nothingness and that our lives are also therefore nothing. Meanwhile the platitudes of our public life tell us the opposite, only in a way that we cannot believe. Excerpted philosophical hand-me-downs may and often do prove, when tried, to be truer than true. But presented as formulaic relics professed by unbelievers, whether in school, in Congress, on TV, or (Heaven help us) in church and synagogue, they are as effective in bestowing wisdom as a poster is in evoking the wonder of a sunset. "Today is the first day of the rest of your life" does not atomize the past, nor any saccharine placebo of Kahlil Gibran sentimentalize the present, nor the most transparently self-advertising stump speech trivialize the future more completely than does the desperate resort to superficial quotations of "No man is an island" and the "Desiderata" or of Thoreau and Emerson as substitutes for meaning. Powerless to refute, in their weakness they seem to confirm what the vast blank walls they are pinned to proclaim.

But such as we are, we cannot help being offended by nothingness and by the pretense of somethingness. We crave allness experienced in very truth. Build as we will the embodiments of our despair, repeat as we do the formulas of our lost faith, trust as we may the one clock or the other, we cannot leave off going to games or to dance concerts, shooting baskets or singing songs, writing new poems or studying old ones. For in them we can meet, as we sometimes can in love and in prayer, that outside authority, set to Greenwich and infallible, which into the deadly silences and blasting cacophonies of our daily lives rings the true invisible hour. It comes in its time, this mystery of meaning, not in ours. We cannot make it come. But even in the desert we have made of our cities we can prepare forms for it to dwell in and ready ourselves to greet it. And in the transport of wonder that is at once perception and response, we know two things as powerfully as we know we exist: that we have not created it but it creates us, and that nothingness is a lie.

Little Notes from the Chairman
[June 12, 1989]

Dear G—,

We hope you will accept the position at our school. You will like it here. Please come.

Sincerely,
Jane B—

Dear G—,

We're very happy that you'll be with us next year.

Sincerely,
Jane B—

P.S. Book orders are due next Friday. Let me know as soon as possible which text you want to use for sophomore English.

Dear G—,

Thank you for letting me sit in on your Period 8 class today. Don't despair. It's not your fault. They are the worst sophomores we've ever had. However, you mustn't let them run the class. Perhaps quizzes will focus their attention. And may I suggest that next year you use a high-school-level rather than a college-level text?

Jane

G—,

Don't forget to sign up for the video machines, to attend the department meeting on Friday, to take your classes to the library some time this quarter, to prepare your students for the SAT, to meet with the other teachers of sophomore, junior, senior English to establish essay-grading criteria, to come to the department meeting on Friday, to let me know what equipment you think we'll need to purchase for the department, to get your second-semester book orders in, to teach vocabulary, to assess the attached AP qualifying essays, to come to the department meeting on Friday, to prepare your students for the Achievement Test, to get your fall book orders in, to get your final exams to the academic secretary early, to come to the department party on Wednesday.

Jane

G—,

Please let me know whether you have any objection to your teaching assignments for next year. Please look at the attached professional journal and pass it along. Please sign the attached birthday card and pass it along. Please be especially nice this week to poor Jean, Joan, John, who has a son in prison, a mother with Alzheimer's, a gallstone, a pending IRS investigation, an irrational fear of bearded Jewish intellectuals. Please get some rest this weekend.

Jane

G—,

Your idea is a good one. Very idealistic. But we tried it six, eleven, eighteen, and twenty-two years ago and it was a disaster. My advice is to forget it—but it's up to you.

Jane

G—,

I had a talk with the Headmaster today and made it clear that, what with all your other duties, you should not be asked to head the school's Interplanetary Travel Technology and Moral Purity Committee, to arrange for all student lunar accommodations and karmic reassessment, to compose an astro-financial profile for every member of the school's faculty, staff, and administration. He made no promises, but he did say he'd try to get you off lunch duty.

Jane

Dear G—,

Thank you for your chapel talk today. I can't tell you how much you've meant to the school and to me.

Love,

Jane

Dear G—,

Happy Rosh Hashanah, Hanukkah, Birthday, New Year, Passover.

Jane

Dear G—,

In the larger scheme of things, it doesn't matter all that much. Don't worry about it. All shall be well, and all manner of thing shall be well.

Love,

Jane

P.S. Fall book orders are due on Friday.

Letter to a Freshman: On Studying Anthropology
[October 10, 1993]

A letter from a former student, a freshman in college:

> One fascinating class is anthropology. I believe you're not really big on the subject, so I wanted to tell you about the class and hear your response. It's fascinating because it deals with humans and human nature in a very scientific way. It uses hard evidence and reasoning based on that evidence to probe humanity... My big problem with the course is that it presents humans as advanced apes, and scientifically proves that fact. The only really unique quality of humans from that perspective is their advanced spoken language ability. Supposedly, monkeys can feel love, jealousy, anger, loss, and other emotions that I thought uniquely human. Although we can't prove that, we can't disprove it either. Where does the human spirit come into play? I believe I remember you denying evolution. If you do indeed, how can you with so much obvious evidence and so many bright, real people accepting evolution? Another theory is that the selfish survive and prosper, taken from the book *The Selfish Gene* by Richard Dawkins. Dawkins uses compelling evidence that "selfish" people will prosper in the world. That seems very dismal to me. What of altruism—if it hurts a person's reproducing strategy, it seems destined to fail! This is all very scientific, and, if you have a chance, I'd like to hear what you have to say on the subject.

Here is my reply:

First of all, I am not opposed to anthropology as a study at all. I do find it a little ironic that in your description the science purporting to be the "study of man" seems to focus a lot of its attention not on man but on animals, but let that pass. What I am more opposed to is imagining that what anthropology has to say about man is all there is to say, or is even the most important thing to say. You say "it deals with humans and human nature in a very scientific way. It uses hard evidence and reasoning based on that evidence to probe humanity." That is true. But what you must remember is that that probing can be only for the kinds of things science can probe for, and it can take place only upon the assumptions science makes. Anthropology will learn about man only those things that can be learned by looking at certain kinds of "hard facts," and the questions it answers will be only those questions it can imagine asking.

Here's an analogy: Suppose I have a yardstick and I approach a man to find out all I can about him using that yardstick. I'll measure his height. And when I've done so, I will have gathered the most significant information about him that that yardstick can provide. If I'm persistent, I might measure the length of his arms and fingers and legs and the distance between his eyes. If I'm inventive, I may even measure the circumference of his arms and thighs and calves and waist and neck. If I'm also shameless, and if I can persuade him that in the name of knowledge he should be shameless too, I might even measure his private parts, both when at rest and when aroused, as Masters and Johnson did. As a result of all this measuring, I will have a fund of information and can draw conclusions from it. But I will never even have asked the question whether this man is intelligent or artful or faithful or good. And if I were to entertain those questions, they would soon be rejected as irrelevant because they can't be measured with a yardstick, and a yardstick is all I've got to measure with.

Now if in this analogy you read for the word "yardstick" the words "hard facts" or "scientific method," you'll get my point. The assumptions science makes are that only that which can be weighed and measured is real, a conviction deriving from Descartes, and that any question that cannot be answered through weighing and measuring (or observation, statistics, the discernment of physical causes, etc.) is irrelevant or non-real. Thus man is, by hypothesis, defined as that which anthropology can discern him to be, and the conclusion inevitably reached is that what anthropology observes man to be he is. And that's all he is. Hence you can write the sentence "the course . . . presents humans as advanced apes, and scientifically proves that fact." Of necessity, and by the very assumptions of the science, the course does not permit you to ask questions like "Where do you get the concept of 'advanced'?" "Is what can be proved what is most significant about man?" "What do you mean by a fact? Isn't the concept 'fact' a human concept unavailable to apes?" "If an ape and an 'advanced' ape are so different as we experience them to be, what purpose is served by asserting that the latter is only a version of the former?" "What is the real motivation behind the desire to assert that men are really only 'advanced apes'?" And perhaps most important, "If the course's vision of man were so self-evidently true as it pretends to be, why should so intelligent an 'advanced ape' as you have a problem with it?" These questions anthropology cannot and does not wish to answer.

Yes, we know that monkeys can feel love of a sort and jealousy, anger, loss. If you thought those emotions were what made us uniquely human, you were in error. Not only monkeys but dogs and porpoises and horses and pigs can feel those things, and our empathic responses tell us so. We are kin to the animals. However, you admit language as a distinguishing characteristic of human beings. What about the purposes to which we put language? Man makes things, laughs, is a political animal, desires to know himself—the traditional definitions of man. If nothing else, you can say that man is the only creature that studies anthropology. If the study of anthropology is not enough hard evidence that men are essentially different from apes, it is hard to think of any evidence that would demonstrate it to an anthropologist.

But it is a hard fact that, as my great teacher used to say, "man is no more merely an animal than an animal is merely a plant." The human spirit, whose reality you rightly seek to defend, comes into play just where it always does, in all those arenas that cannot be measured by a yardstick. Consider yourself. If the physicists, chemists, biologists, statisticians, anthropologists, and sociologists all took turns defining you, could they possibly account for the things most essential to you—your love of the people you love, your gift for performing, your mysterious and awe-inspiring good spirits and native good nature, your love of virtue and of truth, your willingness to interpret your fellow man's actions in the most positive light, your optimism? If "advanced ape" defines you, then it seems to me that everything essentially significant lies in the "advanced," about which the anthropologists can say very little. All they can do is to spend their days sitting around contemplating the ape part. You can't measure the human spirit with a yardstick, or with any measure applicable to the apes. So if the only thing you choose to believe in is that which can be measured with a yardstick, does that mean the human spirit ceases to exist?

About evolution similar things are to be said. I don't deny evolution if what you mean by it is that through mutation a species may go through alteration in its characteristics. But I cannot believe that the theory of evolution *explains* anything important, even if it is true. Whatever brought us into being may have done so instantaneously or may have used a long slow process. But that we have any reason to think that that process is its own cause is absurd. Evolution is a hypothesis, widely adopted as fact, by which we seek to describe certain phenomena, though it also leaves out some important phenomena that don't confirm its premises. But the theory is by no means proven, and the best scientists will admit so.

Evolution is an image of how things work, just as the electron cloud or antimatter or the black hole or the big bang is an image that seeks to put into humanly imaginable terms that which cannot be directly experienced. If you remember this, you will not go too far wrong. You will be able to live with the fact that there are realities that that image cannot and therefore does not try to explain. It is only if you mistake the image for the whole mysterious reality that you go wrong, just as religion goes wrong when it takes human images of God for God. In religion we call that idol worship. It is no less so in science. To pretend that even if we did evolve from the ape, as is hypothesized, we therefore know anything very important about ourselves—know the cause or the meaning or the purpose of our having evolved—is to worship a process without asking where it is going or why or by whose will or whether it is any good. It is to assume an ultimate meaninglessness that denies the hard fact of the universal human need to find meaning.

All such questions, the most important ones to human beings, are excluded by science. And the belief that evolution is a fact that explains what we are pretends to lay those questions to rest by assuming their irrelevance. But it cannot lay them to rest really; it can only deflect attention from them temporarily. They come back to haunt even those bright, respectable, real people who think that to believe in evolution absolves them from the duties of being human, from asking and seeking answers to those human questions. When they fall in love, or when one of their children dies, or when they are in the midst of a divorce, or when an earthquake levels their homes, or when they contract a fatal disease, how can their belief in evolution help them? What has it to offer of any significance to their particular human situation?

As for the theory that the selfish prosper, the obvious question to ask is how do you define "prosper"? It is certainly a fact that some wealthy people are virtuous and some poor are selfish. And vice versa, some wealthy people are selfish and some poor are virtuous. But even if we assume that selfishness brings material prosperity, does it bring meaning, happiness, goodness, eternal life? And can human beings be content with any definition of prosperity that excludes those? You say, "if it hurts a person's reproducing strategy, it seems destined to fail." But such a sentence can only be written by one who is stuck in a reality in which survival is the ultimate value. The moment you ask why *should* someone who cares only about survival survive, the whole false reality collapses like a house of cards and the true reality of values that transcend survival—love, kindness, reverence, justice, humility—is revealed once again in its truth and splendor. Genes are selfish because they are only genes, have only selves but no consciousness, no will, therefore no capacity to choose, no freedom. Human beings depend on genes, but they are not genes. They have the freedom and capacity and duty to choose, and they have been shown what the alternatives are. They have been shown that the choice for goodness, kindness, justice, and love fulfills their nature, whereas the choice for evil, cruelty, selfishness, and hate wars against their nature. It is only by setting up a false world in which our real experience is denied in favor of the abstract experience of a gene, it is only by reducing the fullness of our being to the lowest common physical attributes of our being, that such a doctrine of selfishness could be entertained. (Dawkins is a bitter hater of religion in his own life, and it is an adolescent rage that fuels his worship of the idol he has made of evolutionary biology. [See "Richard Dawkins, *The Blind Watchmaker*" in Reviews.]) Ask yourself this: Would you rather exclude all other beings and values from consideration and live only to satisfy your physical desires and survive forever? Or would you prefer a mortal life in which you had the opportunity to find pleasure and meaning in nature, work, art, love, and divine worship? I think your answer will prove that we are more than our genes. They exist for our sakes, not we for theirs.

I want to make clear that nothing I've said is meant to keep you from studying anthropology. It is a valuable study if it is taken for what it is. Only when it pretends to eliminate or answer those questions with which it has no equipment to deal does it go astray, and then you must say so far and no further. The moment it moves from asserting that men may be also this to asserting that man is only this, it is out of court. It contradicts its own reason for being. It has pretended to answer questions

224 | Other Writings

it was not invited to ask and has not asked honestly. I am not against yardsticks. They are useful for measuring height. But one does not go to a yardstick to discover where virtue lies, or meaning. It can't conceive of the question or answer anything to the purpose. And the more it denies the validity of the question, the more dangerous it becomes in reducing man to a merely material thing. That we are a merely material thing is no hard fact but a lie, and our actual experience proves so.

Instantaneous Comprehension, or Charles Dickens Meets IM
[May 7, 2005]

My students are some of the brightest in Southern California. They are so capable that they can be listening to a favorite song on an iPod, talking on a cell phone, playing a remote video game, exchanging instant messages with their friends, and typing their English essays all at the same time. This is real talent. I'll talk about the quality of the resulting essays in a minute.

My students' gift of multitasking intelligence being so prodigious, why is it that when my sophomores open Charles Dickens' *A Tale of Two Cities* to the first page, so many of them feel either "this is too hard for me" or "I am too dumb for this" and immediately fly into the Web, where— at Quicknotes or Read4me or Dumbdown—they get stuck among the shrunken, dried, brittle carcasses of books whose juices have all been sucked out of them by the dot com spider?

It becomes obvious that the book is not really too hard for them, nor are they too dumb for it, because approximately four weeks later, having been forced actually to read the book, nearly all of them will report that they loved it, that they were moved by it, that it got easier to read as they went. So why do so many of them think it's too hard for them? And more to the point, why do they think the proper response to that difficulty is to find a way to make it quick and easy?

My theory is that it's because they've been brought up to expect instantaneous comprehension of whatever they see, hear, or read. Almost everything they have seen on TV, in the movies, or on the computer or video screen, almost everything they hear on the radio or CD or iPod, and almost everything they have been expected to read—websites, instant messages, email, advertising, and nearly every textbook—has been pitched at a level so low, so shallow, so easily absorbable, that *anyone* could get it, and get it instantly.

This low aim is intentional on the part of the pitchers. The easier something is to comprehend, the greater the market share. Pitching something that takes effort and time reduces sales.

One of the corollaries of this marketing of lowest-common-denominator content is that any individual instant of it is boring. Freeze-frame a TV show or study the score or lyrics of a pop song or reread an email or IM exchange a week later and you will most likely find insufferable shallowness. But if things keep moving, you don't notice. You have the constant excitement of perpetual expectation. Of course this moment is boring, but that only increases your hope that the next may be meaningful. It isn't? Well, how about the next? The *next*? (If you want to read more about this subject, check out Jerry Mander's book called *Four Arguments for the Elimination of Television*.)

Given the predominance of the shallow media during their formative years, my students grow up expecting, quite understandably, that everything that comes to them can and should be instantly comprehended. And if no one has taken the time or effort to force them to learn from experience that an hour's time and effort expended on a worthy object (like a good book, poem, painting, or movie) will yield deeper meaning than a thousand hours in the electronic media world, then how would they know it?

Because the culture they are steeped in and their busy parents have left it to machines to train them, is it any wonder that their natural reactions end up conforming to the machine? TV, radio, computer, iPod, cell phone, VCR, DVD player, PalmPilot, even the automobile—all respond predictably, regularly, and effectively and yield instantaneous and perfectly comprehensible (however shallow) results. Why wouldn't kids raised by them think that they should be doing the same?

So it is not my students' fault that they are tempted to rush to the computer to find the explanation for a chapter of Dickens thinking they can't do it themselves. They have not been taught that they can. They have not been trained to think it *normal* to reread a difficult sentence before they get it or to look up an unfamiliar word or to think about a passage before its light comes on. They can be forgiven for thinking that anything requiring that sort of effort must be too hard. Nevertheless, they need to be taught a better way.

What is wrong with instantaneous comprehension is that if you think it's either that or Quicknotes dot com, you cannot believe or even imagine how meaningful—how rich, deep, moving, and life-enhancing—are the rewards of time and effort spent in appreciating a great work of art.

As for those essays I mentioned above, which would you rather read: the essay of a student who thinks that *you* should instantly comprehend whatever he or she has tossed together on a computer whose screen also has open windows showing Instant Messages, a video game, and the notes to a Dickens chapter at Cheat4me.com, or the essay of a student who has taken the time and made the effort to live in the world Charles Dickens creates out of words and sentences (of whose profundity freeze-framing would only reveal greater depths) and who has tried to craft his own sentences to be worthy of them?

Speciesism: The Arrogance of Our Humility
[August 24, 2005]

Center of the Universe

It is often said that medieval man was arrogant in imagining that God had placed earth at the center of the concentric spheres he created to form his universe. The implication is that, by comparison, modern man is humble in thinking of the earth as the third of the planets revolving around a sun whose own place is far from the center of a galaxy quite distant from the imagined point where the universe may have burst into being for reasons we don't care to discuss.

Those who examine the medieval model more closely discover that the men and women who inhabited the planet at the center of the physical universe thought of themselves as separated from the spiritual center of things by their own bad moral choice. No ego gratification was gained by thinking of the earth as the gravitational center of error and sin. The real and celebrated center of reality was beyond the heavens, ineffably hidden behind those starry signs of its perfection. Redemption was available not by means of a conquering knowledge but only through a turning of the will made possible by the gift of grace.

We, on the other hand, have been taught to think of ourselves as the pinnacle toward which all natural processes have moved. Believing that reality is nothing but those natural processes, we take credit for exercising the highest faculty we can conceive of in the universe, namely that of learning to understand them. We claim greater humility than medieval thinkers on the grounds that unlike them, we can admit that we are not a special creation of God but are mere instances of physical laws at work to no end other than their own existence.

But is not the assertion of one's humility a form of arrogance?

The arrogance hidden in this humility is that in clinging to the idea that we are merely natural and not also spiritual phenomena, we seek to abolish any ultimate significance in the experiences that are most important to us. In the name of supposedly humble honesty, we assert that non-physical realities are essentially not spiritual but really only material phenomena generated in our brains by the operation of natural laws. The ideals of justice, kindness, and the brotherhood of man; love of our parents, children, friends, spouses, and nature itself; joy in beauty of form, perfection of discipline, and logical clarity; the imagination of an eternal meaning not constrained by the limits of material nature; even the desire to understand how nature works—all are reduced to secondary phenomena solely dependent on physical processes.

Is it not arrogance that in order to fit ourselves to an idea that makes our lives no more significant than the slipping of a rock into the sea we deny the spiritual significance of what most gives meaning to our lives, including the search for meaning itself?

Speciesism

Fairly often now we also hear people argue that it is arrogant for human beings to think of themselves as being higher than other species. It is implied that in thinking of ourselves as merely one among the many species nature has evolved, we show ourselves superior in humility to the ancients, who believed that man's rationality set him highest upon the scale of nature, and to medieval people, who believed the world and all its species were created for the sake of man. Some even claim that the religious traditions of the West are themselves the cause of our abuse of the other species and the environment.

Again, those who look further will find that for the Greeks, man's position as highest of the natural beings put upon him the special responsibility to use his reason to live in harmony with nature, including his own nature, and that for Jews and Christians, man was charged to husband the natural world with loving care.

Here too the assertion of modern humility against traditional arrogance presents a logical problem. Apart from the grounds that the religious traditions provide, what could justify our assertion that we should not feel superior to the other animals? If we are merely another species doing what species do, which is to behave however they do behave in order to survive, on what grounds should we be compassionate to them? It may be in your nature to avoid killing flies or to protest the industrial torture of veal calves. But if it is in my nature to like killing flies and eating veal, what gives you the authority to assert that I shouldn't do so?

Animals have rights, we are told. But where do those rights derive from and why should we grant them? If the other animals have rights that we do, why should we have responsibilities that they don't? Why are animal rights people not preaching to lions about the rights of gazelles or to eagles about the rights of mice?

The answer is that no animals except human beings recognize, or can recognize, the moral obligations of being not merely nature but rational nature. In telling us how we should behave toward nature, the animal egalitarians depend on grounds whose existence they deny: the moral responsibility of rational beings. If this chop logic is not merely stupid, isn't there arrogance in it? What right have we to deny our own nature as morally responsible beings?

Those who claim rights for animals don't acknowledge where even human rights come from. All rights are built upon the same foundation: faith in the sacredness of life, the brotherhood of man, the virtues of justice, kindness, and compassion that are taught us by our religious traditions—just those values about which mere nature at its work neither knows nor cares. The *only* reason we should not wantonly kill flies or buy immorally raised veal is precisely that we are *not* just another species of animal. Being rational and moral, only we among the animals have the duty to care as best we can for our fellow creatures.

Why Not Be Arrogant?

If the authority of universal spiritual values is denied in favor of mere nature at her work, then there can be no reason not to be arrogant, not to think the world was made only for man, not to abuse other species. If humility is not itself a virtue that transcends nature, then there is no virtue in the humility of admitting that the natural universe does not revolve around us.

Even to oppose geocentrism and speciesism, then, is to value what transcends nature. In saying we ought to be humble about our place in the world, the worshippers of nature are revealing their deeper but unacknowledged belief in man's unique moral responsibility.

Freak Dance and Civilization
[October 1, 2005]

Last week a student wrote anonymously in a school publication to complain that adults had stopped students from "dancing the way we want" at a school dance. In response, the writer says, the students refused to dance at all and pouted away.

Here is why adults *should* stop students from freak dancing, even at the risk of their pouting:

1. It reduces girls from dance partners to sex toys.
2. It reduces boys from artful dancers to public masturbators.
3. It reduces dancing from multidimensional art—the celebration of spirit in form—to one-dimensional sensuality.
4. It reduces a school dance from the civilized celebration of the mystery of eros at the heart of any community to a spiritless mass sensual self-indulgence.

The young are not to blame for this reduction. They are enslaved to it by the ubiquitous bad art of their favorite entertainments. Adults who neglect to draw them out of that pleasant mud are the ones to blame.

But adults too are up against four heavy obstacles in trying to preserve youngsters from their own self-indulgence:

1. The overwhelming quantity of titillating poison to which the young are addicted that goes by the name of popular entertainment (music videos, rock/pop/rap songs, TV, movies, and—all too often—school dances).
2. The lack, in many school communities, of adult moral support for a principled stand against such entertainment.
3. The adults' own fear of not being liked by the young in their charge (arising from a fatal supplanting, in their own psyches, of the principle of duty by that of good feeling).
4. The erroneous belief in the natural goodness of man, an inheritance from the Romantic revolution of the late eighteenth and early

nineteenth centuries, which replaced the venerable doctrines of free will and moral responsibility with that of natural impulse as the principal guide to right mental and social life.

If the young are naturally good and it is society that corrupts them (as Rousseau argued), then to let them follow their impulses without interference from adult society is to let them remain innocent and good. Believers in this doctrine, whose memories usually reach no further back than the 1960s, argue that they themselves were once young and outrageously rebellious in their parents' eyes too and yet turned out okay, that the present-day youth will no doubt turn out okay too. ("Okay" seems not to include the notion that a well-turned-out adult is one who can properly educate the next generation of youth.)

The problems with this doctrine are two: The first is that it ignores the fact that the youth of today are *already* being corrupted by society—in the form of the entertainment poison mentioned above. The second is that the doctrine isn't true. Human beings may be well or badly influenced by society, but man is not now and (since Eden) never has been naturally good. Man either is born morally neutral or is fallen into depravity; in any case he requires labor to resist evil and become good, labor directed at achieving right reason (Plato's formulation), right habit (Aristotle's), or right will (the Bible's). A good education would instruct in all three.

Hence, those adults who stand by and watch as the youth indulge in the reductions of freak dancing listed above are themselves guilty of some combination of the following: titillation at watching what they would never permit themselves to do in public; fear of losing the easy affection of young people whom they ought rather to be teaching how to earn adults' respect; and worship of unconsecrated feeling as the god of their (one hopes unconscious) idolatry.

When such feelings, beliefs, and behaviors reach a critical mass in the community or the culture at large, look for one of three events: a sweeping movement of take-no-prisoner fundamentalist religious or personality-cult fervor, a fall like that of Rome, or the rebirth of a genuine vision of the nature and meaning of man. Hope springs eternal, but the two-to-one odds against the last possibility ought to worry us.

Bravo to those proctors who set a limit on public human animality. And if you are one who can enjoy no kind of dancing except freaking, you might take a good look at male-female dance forms from waltz to swing and then inquire what has so impoverished your imagination.

Cutting Corners on the Quad
[November 13, 2005]

Except for the newest one, the buildings at our school are built around a grass quadrangle. It is a long-standing school rule that no one walk on the quad before 12:00 noon. Because we are near the ocean and therefore on many mornings of the year are under clouds or in mist, and because when the sprinklers operate they do so before dawn, the grass of the quad is damp in the morning. The rule protects the quad, and the carpets of the buildings, from becoming a muddy mess.

As a result of the rule, during the five-minute passing periods before noon the cement walkways around the quad are rather more crowded than they are in the afternoons. Because people are both hurrying then and feeling obstructed by the numbers of persons in front of them, some will cut the corners of the quad on their way to class. They will put one foot into the right angle made by the perpendicular walkways or perhaps risk two, three, or more steps to trace a longer hypotenuse across the grass.

The practice is common enough that some seem to be unaware that the letter of a law is being broken. Others are no doubt either hoping not to be caught by an adult rule enforcer or feeling that, given the crowd and the limited time, the spirit of the quad law permits them this mitigation so that they will not break the letter of the law against tardiness to class.

The result is that in the corners of the quad the grass is nonexistent. It is worn away or pressed into the hard, flat, lifeless mud by a hundred feet per day. No matter how often the gardeners dig up, replant, and cordon off the corners, so soon as the corners are green again and the cordons come down, down come the corner-cutting feet, and in a matter of days the corner grass is trampled into oblivion.

Partly because of what the gardeners go through to restore the grass there, partly because the quad rule is just and reasonable, and partly because the aesthetic order and harmony of the campus are marred by right triangles of brown mud where green grass should be, it is somewhat irksome to see people thus cutting the corners before noon.

But there is another reason that, if I happen to be on the walkway myself before noon and see someone cutting the corner, I'll say something:

The muddy corners provide a perfect visual aid for teaching Kant's categorical imperative.

The philosopher Immanuel Kant believed that the structure of the human mind was such that every honest rational being who asked the following question about any particular situation would come to the same conclusion: Can you will the principle of your action in this matter to be a universal principle? If the answer is yes, you may conclude that the action would be right. If no, it would be wrong. In this way Kant sought to restore faith in universal principles of value to an intellectual world that seemed (with the help of philosopher David Hume) to be dismantling them.

At the corners of our quad, it is very easy to see the consequences of ignoring the categorical imperative in the matter of the quad rule. In response to the precocious eighth-grader or sophomore or senior who says, "I'm just one person; my stepping on the grass doesn't hurt anything," all I have to do is to point to the triangular mud-flat he or she has just stepped on and say, "But could you want everybody to think like that? Look what happens when they do. See?" And they see. They can't not see. If you can't will that everyone should think like that, Kant maintains, then to think like that is wrong.

So there's one tiny lesson in individual responsibility taught in the midst of a busy day filled with struggles to learn, to avoid unpopularity, to get to class on time, to survive the pressures of adult supervision. Maybe the eighth-grader will find that the adult corrector is uncool, the sophomore that he's a busybody, the senior that he's an anal-retentive. But maybe they'll also think twice before stepping on the quad before noon. Maybe they will even remember the lesson and, at some point when it counts more, make the choice to do the right thing.

Or maybe I'm dreaming. My little lessons in the categorical imperative don't seem to make much difference in the greenness of the corners of the quad. But a teacher must not measure his success only in visible outcomes. Could I will it to be a universal principle that, whatever the consequences for the corners themselves, teachers should *not* correct corner-cutting students? No.

Is Man Naturally Good?
[December 4, 2005]

A reader of my blog commented on a quotation from me:

> "…the erroneous belief in the natural goodness of man": That makes me so sad. What a pessimistic view … I'm probably just confused, but shouldn't that mean that when you get a new batch of students you trust none of them? You would expect them to lie, steal, kill, cheat, and otherwise sin until they've proven you otherwise. Haha I do think I'm mistaken sorry. Will you explain what you mean? The goodness of man is one of my primary beliefs, and I don't understand how it's so easily dismissed. I automatically trust people and believe they will strive toward good until they disprove me. And even if they do disprove me, I still have hope for them.

I'm very glad the commenter has written because it provides a good opportunity to point out the importance of dialectic reasoning. Please notice that I did not say "the erroneous belief in the goodness of man" but "the erroneous belief in the *natural* goodness of man."

The key is the differences among

a) the idea of *natural* goodness;
b) man's goodness as a creation of God ("And God saw every thing that he had made, and, behold, it was very good"); and
c) man's goodness as a function of his own free moral choices.

Of course I trust students until they show me I shouldn't. Of course I'm optimistic. (One can't keep teaching for long if one is truly pessimistic; why bother?) And of course I have hope even for those who disappoint me, just as I have hope for myself when I disappoint them, which I'm afraid, being human, I do all too often. But I trust and hope because my students have, in varying degrees, been taught the value of choosing to be good.

However, when Jean-Jacques Rousseau asserted that man is *naturally* good and it is society that corrupts him, he altered the picture significantly.

This is not the place for a full lecture on the destructive influences of Rousseau and Romanticism from the late eighteenth century to the present. (They have had some good influences as well.) But if we believe in the *natural* goodness of man, we begin to think (wrongly) that "getting back to nature," "following our impulses," being guided solely by our feelings, letting children decide what they should learn, and freak dancing are the best way to preserve individual goodness from the evil of society, not noticing that all these notions have been embraced and are taught by our popular culture—i.e., society!

I believe, instead, that we are created to be good, but that our goodness is hard won, the result of education in the difference between good and evil and of the myriad choices between good and evil that we are called upon to make between the age of moral responsibility and the age of senility.

Now keep thinking dialectically: I'm not saying all feelings and impulses are bad or that we should never follow them. I'm only saying that they need to be governed by the reason and the will, so that we follow the good ones and resist the bad ones.

Why would anyone write a blog if he thought man were *naturally* good, and why would he think anyone should listen to him? He'd only tell people, as pop singers and beat writers do, to ignore him and drop out, go with the flow, let it be, follow your bliss, etc. But have you noticed that even pop stars and beat writers don't drop so far out that they refuse to let society publish and distribute their words? And who but society is persuading us to gobble them up?

Neither mind nor goodness is merely natural, and though nature is good, it doesn't itself care about goodness. Man is created to be good, but we all need help in learning what is good and in striving to pursue it.

Science and Intelligent Design
[July 7, 2005]

Part 1

A colleague of mine wrote a paper on intelligent design and asked for my opinion of it. The paper treated the concept as the enemy of science, and I raised some objections. Accused then of holding a variety of irrational opinions that I don't hold, I decided to try to articulate what I do think is true on the subject.

Some Christian groups want to substitute the teaching of intelligent design for the teaching of evolution in schools. Many scientists respond by protesting all reference to intelligent design in discussions of science because it is "not science."

The Christian groups fear that philosophical materialism disguised as science threatens the biblical teaching of creation. Scientists fear that ascribing causation to an intelligent designer threatens the rational exploration of natural phenomena. Each group fears that the other will bring on a new dark age of ignorance.

Neither fear is groundless. But where scientists and traditional believers live in fear of one another, no one is well served with truth.

Intelligent Design Is Not a New Idea:

The concept of intelligent design is not new. Almost every scientific discovery before the early twentieth century took place within the context of belief in a divine creator of the order of things. Science itself presupposes an order of things—it must, or the empirical method could not operate—though many contemporary scientists reject the idea of a creator of that order. Yet belief in a creator did not prevent Copernicus, Galileo, Kepler, Newton, Darwin, or Einstein from making their discoveries, for they all shared it.

It is true that particular scientific discoveries and kinds of research have been obstructed by religious institutions at various times, but it was not the concept of a creating intelligence that got in the way of scientific discovery. Likewise, some contemporary scientists maintain an ongoing attack on religion, but it is not science itself that threatens religious faith.

Intelligent Design Is Not Unscientific; Materialism Is Not Science:

Materialism, the idea that everything that exists—whether particle or force—has a material (as opposed to non-material or spiritual) cause, is a theory. That the origin of the physical universe lies in material reality cannot be proven or disproven empirically. Scientists who believe in materialism with complete conviction do so on faith.

Intelligent design is also a theory. Unlike materialism, which offers no original cause for the existence of physical things and forces, intelligent design posits an original divine cause for all that is. But like the theory of materialism, the theory of intelligent design cannot be either proven or disproven empirically.

Rational arguments for both theories have been debated by the greatest minds of Western thought: The Bible, Plato, and Aristotle began the conversation, followed by Epicurus, Lucretius, Hobbes, Hume, Freud, and others on the materialism side and Augustine, Maimonides, Aquinas, Locke, Newton, Kant, C. S. Lewis, and others on the design side. The arguments are about postulates—givens based on insight and faith—not about propositions susceptible of proof.

None of the claims of evolutionary theory constitutes proof of either materialism or intelligent design. Whatever material causes for evolution may be identified, there may or may not be behind them an intelligent designer. And however active the intelligent designer may be, there may or may not always be physical phenomena at work (in the functioning of the design) that we have not comprehended.

Confused scientists claim that the theory of intelligent design threatens the scientific method. It does not. What it threatens is the theory that material causes account for everything, which, being a form of faith, has no more scientific authority than belief in intelligent design or in God. Literalist interpreters of the Bible claim that science threatens belief in God. It does not. It is materialism, not scientific knowledge, that from the religious viewpoint is the idol of false worship.

In other words, neither materialism nor intelligent design should be equated with science. And since either theory—or a combination of both—*might* be true, neither should be banished from discussions of the foundations of science. If intelligent design is forbidden from the classroom, so must materialism be forbidden. If a science teacher believes in materialism, he or she ought to make clear that the credentials of intelligent design are just as valid.

The Limits of Materialism:

Believing, with Lucretius, that everything has a basis in matter or natural forces and that there is no such thing as spirit, materialists will say that it is only because of lack of sufficient experimental evidence that such things as love, hate, and free will cannot be materially explained. Ideally, given enough time and permitted the right experiments, science will "explain" every mystery in material terms.

There are two problems with this assertion: one logical, one moral.

The Logical Limit of Materialism:

Let's say I toss a rose up into the hand of my beloved on a balcony above. Or let's say I hurl a brick from a balcony onto the head of my enemy below. Measuring weights, trajectories, air resistance, etc., scientists can describe what is physically happening with great—actually awe-inspiring—accuracy. If they add in physiology, meteorology, astronomy, and relativity, they can know even more about what is going on in either of these gestures, whether the chosen context is the atom or the human body or the earth or the galaxy or space-time.

But the moment that, based on these observations, the council of scientists assert that they have "explained" the tossed rose or the hurled brick, they have stepped beyond their realm. Even if they attach electrodes to the brains of my beloved, my enemy, and me, they cannot possibly know the whole cause of the phenomena, for some of that cause lies in my unmeasurable mind and will, and beyond too—for even I cannot know everything that has gone into my own motivation.

Since they take place in the context of mystery (the origin of things, the ultimate limits of human comprehension), to assume that all the physical science in the world brought to bear upon these gestures will completely explain them is to pretend to a knowledge that science does not and cannot have.

For data cannot by itself explain anything. All scientific evidence is significant only within an underlying system or organizing theory that gives it meaning. To "explain" means to translate from one system of description to another, to render one kind of evidence significant in terms of another—muscularity in terms of weight lifted, quantity of knowledge in terms of letter grades, the flight of my rose or brick in terms of velocity.

It would be foolish to pretend that by having interpreted the movement of my hand and the motion of the rose or brick and the electrochemical activity of my brain in physical terms we have entirely explained the phenomenon. Just as it would be foolish to pretend that the rose landed in my beloved's hand or the brick on my enemy's head *only* because I willed it to do so, without reference to gravity, weight, air, my nervous and muscular systems, and so on.

That we are empirically aware of non-material realities—love and hate and free will—does not mean that the physical world is not governed by physical laws whose operation may be better and better understood. At the same time, that science "works" in explaining physical phenomena does not mean that there is nothing *but* the material world at work in the material world. Just as the material is real, and knowledge of it matters, so the spiritual—the realm of belief —is real, and knowledge of *it* matters.

Beliefs therefore are not the enemy of science. In fact, science itself is based on spiritual beliefs. Here are some of them:

- Pursuit of truth is good; pursuit of truth about the material world and its operations is good;
- Reality is orderly and consistent; the physical laws that govern the universe are orderly and consistent (I am told that even chaos scientists cannot find empirical evidence of chaos);
- Our sensory experience corresponds to reality; the more that empirical evidence is consistent, orderly, and reproducible, the more it may be trusted;
- Helping our fellow man is good; discovering cures for human disease and easing human suffering are good.

Take away these beliefs, and the reasons for scientific study—to know, to help—disappear. Yet none of them can be proven by scientific experiment. Our trust in their truth is simply fundamental to our being human. They are self-evident.

Thus, while denial or falsification of data based on prejudice is the enemy of science, belief is not. Prejudice may corrupt conclusions based on *any* belief, materialism as well as intelligent design.

When a scientist tells me that a rainbow is the refraction of light by water droplets, I believe it on good authority. When the same scientist tells me that a rainbow is *only* the refraction of light through water droplets and therefore *not* a sign of God's promise to refrain from flooding the world, the scientist is overstepping the bounds of science, just as it would be misuse of the Bible to claim that the refraction theory is false because Genesis calls the rainbow a sign of God's covenant.

To assert that there can be no influence of a non-material will on evolution or the formation of the universe is to claim what science, given the terms of its language, cannot know. Similarly, to assert that God could not, if he willed, use evolution as his mode of creation is to claim that the Bible is the author of God and not God the author of the Bible.

The Moral Limit of Materialism:

The moral problem with the materialist dogma is that, carried to its logical conclusion, in the name of scientific knowledge it would destroy every *other* human value, including, eventually, the love of truth, upon which its own validity rests.

Let's say that materialist science can learn a great deal about the mind by measuring exactly what happens physiologically when a bolt is driven into the head of a monkey, causing severe agony. Can materialist science also measure what is happening in the soul of the scientist who is doing the experiment? Would it if it could? Allowed to continue in the name of gaining knowledge, such experimentation would have two inevitable results:

First, the scientist would find that the mind is nothing more than the brain and its physical functions. This is inevitable because he can admit into his body of knowledge only that kind of information which he set out to look for in the first place. Non-material information is excluded from the start by his underlying materialist assumption.

Second, he will have broken the universal moral law against unnecessary cruelty and put his own soul, if he has one, into jeopardy while abolishing all grounds for thinking that he might have done so.

Such a scientist has departed from the human community and betrayed the very values that make human life, including the study of science, meaningful.

As I pointed out above, science is not responsible for our knowing that love of truth, on which science is based, is a value. That value is an axiom, a fundamental assumption, a self-evident truth, an absolute given—like justice, like kindness. If the one is a value, so are the others. If the others have no absolute authority, neither has that. (For the best discussion of this, see C. S. Lewis, *The Abolition of Man*.)

Because of this equality in fundamental authority, just as people can go astray believing scientific nonsense in the name of religion, so people can go astray believing moral and spiritual nonsense in the name of science.

Practically speaking, science can tell us how dogs behave when we tear their legs off, as Descartes (whose mind-body split laid the foundations for modern materialism) had no objection to doing. But it can't tell us whether we *ought* to do so. Questions of significance and rightness can be answered only by philosophy or religion, not by science. When scientific materialism threatens to decide such questions by ignoring them, the human community must either correct it or risk being destroyed by it.

"Truth Shall Spring out of the Earth and Righteousness Shall Look Down from Heaven" (Psalms 85:11):

Even for those who are as certain of the evolution of species as they are of heliocentrism or the germ theory of disease, the theory of evolution does not and cannot explain its own existence. Science can show *that* molecules and organisms behave thus and thus, but it cannot explain *why* they do, or why they exist to do so. Whether or not God's hand is in any or every molecular event of the universe can never be known by science.

Those who fear that the scientific investigation of evolution threatens biblical truth forget that no amount of human knowledge can reduce the great mystery of creation or the Bible's importance in our relating to it. And those who attack every discussion of intelligent design as a threat to the scientific enterprise are materialist proselytizers practicing exactly the kind of dogmatism they disapprove of in popes who silence Galileos.

True faith is not threatened by knowledge of the physical world, nor honest science by the recognition of its foundation on faith. Being fully human means acknowledging the authority of both kinds of knowing.

It remains an open question whether in the long run science without religion does more damage than religion without science. But our ideal must remain the right practice of both material and spiritual knowledge and discernment of their right relations. To run from either in blind fear is to run toward the darkness.

Part 2

In response to some of the ideas in Part 1, a friend asked the following:

> I wish I were wrong, but I think that we will never know if the universe has real spiritual meaning, if there is a God, and if there really are absolute values. So there are two end point possibilities, and if there is only the material (and I admit we cannot know this, but it is either true or not true), what would that imply about the things we know and how we know them?

Here is my response:

There are various kinds of "knowing." We can never scientifically or mathematically "know" that the universe has real spiritual meaning because nothing spiritual can be corralled into the kind of knowledge (like scientific knowledge) that depends on our own preexisting categories and sense experiences.

However, there are other kinds of knowledge that are based on spiritual experience and on aesthetic and moral insights. If we give these any validity in human life, we *can* know that there is a spiritual meaning. But that knowledge will never submit to being tested in the arenas of the other kind of knowledge.

It would be like trying to prove to my dog that the U.S.A. exists [see "Seeker, Snooper, Teacher, Tale" in High School Homilies]. But my dog certainly enjoys the real benefits of being a dog in the U.S.A. (as opposed to parts of Asia, where people eat dogs). Similarly, we enjoy the benefits of living within a spiritual reality which we cannot perceive by using only those senses useful for perceiving the physical world.

And if, as a philosophical experiment, you want to posit (with the radical philosophical materialists like Richard Dawkins and others) that reality is only the product of physical things, matter and forces, with no spiritual content, then the only possible conclusion is that nothing means anything. Meaning itself being (or being perceived to be) a spiritual phenomenon, it can be nothing but an illusion thrown onto our illusory minds by the illusion-producing physical world. And if that is the case, then all conversation is moot, including all arguments against the compromise of scientific education by religious fundamentalism.

I would argue that since we do *not* feel such conversation is moot, since we *do* value truth and crave and experience meaning—in fact won't live without it—it makes no sense to assume material reality is all there is. If it is, it makes no difference that we invent spiritual realities for ourselves, for under this idea truth itself, a spiritual illusion thrown up by a meaningless material reality, has no spiritual meaning anyway. Only if the physical isn't everything is it meaningful to think about whether it is everything or not. It is Pascal's wager carried to the extreme foundations of philosophical thought.

Most people who refuse to believe in God do so because they can't bear the idea of believing a falsehood. But if there is only the material world, then what difference does believing a falsehood make? Why do they care to avoid believing a falsehood? Because they love truth, which means they love what is not merely material. To believe that truth is better than lies *is* to believe in spiritual realities.

In short, if there is only matter, nothing matters. It makes no difference whether we believe in God or not, and there can be no meaningful reason *not* to do so. If there is God, it does matter that we believe in him. A thorough belief in materialism as the totality of reality is meaningless. A thorough belief in spirit has at least the advantage of being consistent with our actual daily experience, which includes our inescapable craving for meaning.

If nature made the world by accident, then our desire to understand the world and ourselves and nature is meaningless. To believe this is to remove all reason for studying science, let alone religion. Only if the Creator made the world is our desire to know the truth meaningful, including our desire to avoid believing in a fictional Creator.

All things, even atheism, testify to the glory of God!

Part 3
[January 8, 2006]

Two Stealth Movements:

Charles Krauthammer might be the smartest man in Washington. But his latest formulation of the Intelligent Design controversy[1] raises questions.

Krauthammer is right this far: To the extent that Intelligent Design is

---

1 "Phony Theory, False Conflict: 'Intelligent Design' Foolishly Pits Evolution against Faith," *Washington Post*, Friday, November 18, 2005, Page A23. Full disclosure: Krauthammer was a personal friend.

a smokescreen for a fundamentalist agenda of biblical literalism, it has no business in science class. Built upon faith in universal laws of nature, natural science cannot admit capricious supernatural explanations of what in principle might be scientifically understood but is not understood yet. Among respectable thinkers, Intelligent Design may be more than "today's tarted-up version of creationism," but where it rushes to fill gaps in scientific knowledge with the "empirically disprovable" theory that God is the explanation, it discredits itself.

God may be "behind every hydrogen atom in electrolysis," writes Krauthammer, "but that discussion is the province of religion, not science. The relentless attempt to confuse the two by teaching warmed-over creationism as science can only bring ridicule to religion."

Fine. But here's my question: Why isn't it equally ridiculous to make God the enemy of science? Shouldn't the unquestioned assumption that atheist materialism is the only permissible religion for scientists and students of science bring exactly the same ridicule to its proponents? Yet for years our science classrooms have been bathed in this other religion, positivist materialism, masquerading as science. When will the ACLU go to court to prevent teachers from promoting *that* religion in science classes?

Evolutionary biologists like Richard Dawkins and the late Stephen Jay Gould, whose materialism is as strict and totalitarian a fundamentalism as that of the most committed creationist, can admit no place for religion in their version of the enterprise of human learning. Indeed, philosophically Dawkins has not progressed beyond the beliefs of Antoine Nicolas de Condorcet, the reason-worshipping *philosophe* who perished in the French Revolution believing that science, triumphing over religion (which he equated with superstition), would bring about heaven on earth.

Despite the cataclysmic villainies of the twentieth-century atheist dogmas of National Socialism and Soviet and Chinese Communism, Dawkins and other evolutionary biologists write as if religion (which he too equates with superstition) were the greatest source of human ills and as if science founded on human reason alone were their cure.

Leaving aside the question of whether or not the more responsible promoters of I.D. have raised scientifically legitimate questions, is it not true that much of the energy of the I.D. movement has been evoked by the atheist materialism of scientists like Dawkins and stealth proselytizing by science teachers of their stamp? Are they not striving equally to convert the general culture to their brand of fundamentalist faith that matter itself is the cause of its own being and organization?

Can We Get Along?:

The age we live in is one of conflict between different fundamental images of the nature of reality. There are fanatics and polemicists on both sides, and both sides have their stealth promoters. But just as between true and honest believers in materialism and true and honest believers in God there may be open debate without rancor or mutual threat, so dishonestly disguised proselytizing, whether from Christians or from materialists, leads to fear and thence to polarization, rancor, irrational polemics, and, eventually perhaps, violence.

Let's pull back from that brink and try to reason together wisely. Let's not assume that all uses of the term "intelligent design" imply the intent to pollute science with phony scientific theories, and let's not assume that to be a good scientist requires one to embrace materialism as the ultimate reality.

Aristotle's Four Causes:

As Aristotle, the founder of Western science, would have pointed out, and as Dorothy Sayers reminds us in a very fine essay on education ("The Lost Tools of Learning"), both those who think of biblical creationism as a scientifically demonstrable theory and those who think science proves matter to be the sole ground of the nature of things are confusing material and efficient causes with first and final causes.

Let me try to explain with an example: What is the cause of an omelet? Based on Aristotle, we can say that there are four causes of an omelet: The **formal cause** is the plan for the omelet in your mind, the concept "omelet" and the knowledge of what omelets are, without which the omelet would not come to exist. The **material cause** is the eggs: The omelet can't exist without them either; their nature allows omelets to exist and they are what the omelet is made of. The **efficient cause** is the mixing and the pouring of the eggs, the introduction of heat from the fire under the pan, the removal of the pan from the heat before the eggs skip being an omelet and become charcoal, and so on—what you are doing to the eggs that turns them into an omelet. The **final cause** of the omelet is the ultimate purpose for which it exists, the reason you have brought the efficient cause to bear upon the material cause guided by the formal cause. We could debate whether breakfast or hunger or nutrition or survival or service to God is the final cause of the omelet. That would depend on the omelet-maker's ultimate reason for making it.

Material and efficient causes are the proper study of science. But science has no access to the discovery of formal or final causes. They are accessible, if at all, only to thought, not to experimentation, to reasoning but not to material proof.

The material and efficient causes of the phenomena described by the theory of evolution may be studied scientifically. But neither their formal and final causes, nor whether those causes may be material or spiritual, can be determined by science. This is why the question whether evolution is the result of material nature or of intelligent design is a philosophical question, not a scientific one.

At the same time, this is why it is just as offensive to believers in God to use science to promote materialism as it is offensive to positivist-materialists to use science to promote Christian fundamentalism. In both cases, the study of material and efficient causes is being hijacked to teach a particular doctrine of final causes to which science has no access.

Let us agree that the right place for a discussion of the material and efficient causes of evolution is science class and that the right place for a discussion of the final causes of evolution is philosophy or religion class.

Where Can We Study Their Relation?:

Where is the right classroom for a discussion of the *relation* between evolution's material and efficient causes and its possible final causes? Where is the border crossing between the separate provinces of science and faith to which Krauthammer has respectively consigned discussions of matter and mind? Where can those who respect both science and religion hear a discussion between scientists and religious believers on the relative merits of non-phony ideas about intelligent design and atheist materialism?

Thanks to Descartes, we have inherited a view of reality according to which there is mind and there is body, and never the twain shall meet. Our universities have enshrined this split in the division of the arts and humanities from the sciences. At Stanford they call students of the former "fuzzies" and of the latter "techies." Consideration of the formal and final causes of material facts is forbidden to science lest it contaminate the scientific method; consideration of the material and efficient causes within the Creator's design is forbidden to religion lest it tyrannize over science.

Materialists deny the Cartesian split by arguing that the mind is just the body doing its thing. Religious fundamentalists deny the split by arguing that scripture records the only facts that signify. The rest of us are supposed (by modern education) to accept the split itself as dogma.

But greater minds than that of Descartes have found ways of transcending that split, of finding unity where he found division, without denying either matter or spirit. Where can we go to seek such a unity again? Where, oh where, may any conversation take place on the subject of the relation between the truth of matter and the truth of spirit? Apparently not in school.

Both science and religion are built on faith. Science is built on faith in the universality of the laws of nature, in the reality and consistency of cause and effect, in the validity of perception by the human senses and their instruments, in the ability to disprove a bad theory by the use of experimentation, in the authority of the replication of experiments, etc. Religion is built on faith in the reality of more than meets the eye of the body, a reality that may claim some authority from experience but that is not subject to rational proofs because the rational human mind is in this respect the contained, not the container; because, as Wendell Berry puts it, "we can't comprehend what comprehends us."[2]

Cannot we human beings, who are a union of matter and spirit, find a way to agree that since both human enterprises are founded on faiths of these two kinds, there is value in honest conversation between them unmarred by fundamentalist superstitions on either side? Why must I be labeled a threat to science because I want to consider how the facts of science might exhibit intelligent design, or a threat to religion because I want to consider how God's plan might include evolution? Is there no common room in the university of the modern mind where science and faith may meet to discuss, without fear or rancor, the nature of things in general?

2　See footnote, page 78.

Pop Music and Quality in Art
[March 14, 2006]

As promised [in a previous blog], I am to say something about popular music. But rather than defending myself against the accusation that I like only old stuff or debating the quality of Paul Simon's music or the relative merits of classical vs. pop, I'd much rather expand the discussion by contemplating the subject of quality in art. Let's consider some general principles (which I first learned from my teacher Mary Holmes, though any errors should be ascribed to me not to her).

1) Art is not nature; nature is not art. Art is anything made by human beings; nature is anything not made by human beings. Paintings, movies, popular songs, computers, furniture, kitchen spoons, and spaceships are works of art. Babies, seashells, sunsets, dreams, people, and sneezes are not art, though any of them can be used in a work of art. (If you tattoo a baby, glue seashells to a mirror, photograph a sunset, write an interpretation of a dream, get dressed, or record a sneeze, you are making art.)

2) Therefore, "art" should not be used as a term of praise. That something is art just means that it is something made by human beings, is the result of human choices. The significant question is not whether something is art but whether it is any good at conveying something valuable into our experience.

3) Statements about a work of art based on quantitative dichotomies (old/new, popular/unpopular, modern/ancient, famous/unknown, etc.) are significant only in that they provide context for judging the work. They say next to nothing about the work's value. What is significant in judging a work's value is the discernment of the work's qualities given its context: Is it deep or shallow; illuminating or opaque; vital or dead; authentic or sentimental; fresh or derivative; serious or frivolous; uplifting or demoralizing; etc. Is it universal or parochial; self-conscious or naïve; classical or romantic; tragical, comical, historical, or pastoral; idealistic,

pathetic, or critical; hopeful or despairing; religious or skeptical; elegant or rough; civilized or primitive; harmonic or melodic; etc.

4) All such judgments involve the beholder, and it is true that no two beholders will have identical experiences of a work. At the same time, the idea that a work of art may mean anything that any beholder thinks it means, or be rightly or reasonably judged in any way a beholder chooses to judge it, is ludicrous. Of course thought is free; people can think what they like. But works of art are made to serve certain functions, cause particular experiences, evoke certain responses, convey meaning, incarnate essences. The more successfully the work of art fulfills its intentions and the better the quality of those intentions, the better the work. And the better the work, the more the need for interpretation. But while a great work of art may bear many valid interpretations, there are always a great many more possible interpretations that would be invalid. There may be various right ways to interpret a play by Shakespeare, let us say, or a song by Paul Simon. But there may also be many ways that are totally wrong. (Someone who says *King Lear* is mainly about how much fun life can be is a fairly long way off the mark.)

5) Hence, judgments of works of art may themselves be better or worse, depending on how accurately the judge's perceptions reflect the reality of the work being judged. This is why Mary Holmes used to say "the work of art that you judge judges you." To judge that a shallow or sentimental work is great and profound is to reveal one's own shallowness or sentimentality; to judge that a great visionary work is weak or foolish is to be convicted of weakness or foolishness of vision. If it were not so, then *all* judgments (not only legitimate and reasonable ones) would be equally valid, merely the expressions of feelings, neither right nor wrong. And if this were so, then the assertion that all judgments are equal (neither right nor wrong), being itself merely a feeling, would have no more merit than the assertion that judgments may be true or false to the thing being judged. All grounds for disagreement, persuasion, and learning would disappear.

6) Agreeing, then, that judgments of quality in works of art may be better or worse, we can also see that every such judgment depends on three elements: the quality of the *work* being judged; the quality of the *judge* doing the judging; and the quality of the judge's *experience* of the work, on which his or her judgment is based.

Works of art may be good or bad in a myriad ways; judges may be good or bad in as many ways; and each particular experience of a work will be in one sense unique, in a second sense very much like every other experience of that work by that judge, and in a third sense very much like anyone else's experience of the same work. Some works exist to evoke different responses in different sorts of people; others exist to evoke the same response in everyone. Variety in these matters is almost limitless. Yet there remains an inescapable difference between the judgments of an experienced and educated taste and that of a blind or willful ignorance.

7) Since, like works of art themselves, judges may be better or worse, and particular experiences of particular works may vary, there is no final and absolute (human) judge of any work of art, nor any stage of learning at which one has attained perfection as a judge. There is rather the endless deepening of one's capacity to make sound judgments, a deepening that depends on the increasing mastery of the grammar of aesthetic judgment, of the knack of aesthetic appreciation, which is based on the combination of many gifts, including insight, comprehension, responsiveness, clarity of mind, knowledge, memory, and so on, and of the will to put those gifts to good use.

8) Finally, as regards popular music, instead of sweeping generalizations about rock or pop or hip-hop or reggae or rap or any particular musician, let us instead agree that the best judge of any particular artist in any of these forms, and of popular music in general, would be that person who could best combine the following: knowledge of the nature of music, music history, classical and popular forms, and the technology of music production; aesthetic responsiveness to sound; imaginative participation in the language and intention of the artist; lack of narrow prejudices; clear vision of the variety and possibilities of human expression; subtlety; perceptiveness; insight; varied and rich experience; and wisdom.

That's a tall order. But that's what we must aspire to, not in order to enjoy a work of art but in order to judge it well. Only if we can agree on these principles can we have meaningful conversation about any particular work of art. Without them, any discussion of art would be reduced to an endless stream of unjustifiable and shallow opinions—I like it; I don't like it—among which agreement or disagreement would be merely accidental and therefore nugatory. Only by embracing these principles do we preserve the possibility that conversation about art may result in the growth of appreciation.

More on Pop Music: Emo and Scene
[September 13, 2006]

Another classroom discussion of popular music led to the request that I discuss the styles of teen music, dress, MySpace postings, and self-image called "Emo" and "Scene." After a little reading on UrbanDictionary.com, I realize that these styles are deeply uninteresting to one who has seen it all before in various incarnations. They are the newest clothing of the oldest of Romantic clichés: ironically lockstep uniformity in worship of the individual, of emotion for its own sake, and of rebellion against the villain "society."

Though the various styles of music sound different, nearly all the styles of teen-popular music at the moment are versions of the same thing: a mostly shallow and ignorant Romanticism driven by unexamined passions and prejudices expressed in music of painfully ear-piercing noise or Lethe-like, spirit-dulling sentimentalism. My initial grown-up's response to nearly all of this music is "Get real."

This is not surprising. Most music in any age is not much good. The great classical composers remain in our consciousness because of their greatness, but thousands of pieces of classical music are deservedly lost to us. Same with most jazz, most classic rock, most anything. However, different ages too have their characteristic qualities, and it is not unheard of for the art of an entire age to be deservedly forgotten for its banality or dullness or shallow sensationalism. To me, we seem to be in the midst of such an age.

But I don't want merely to discount my students' attachments to their favorite songs and favorite artists. Their feelings matter to me and their attachments are real. But I also have a calling to help them see the meaning in their attachments. So I propose that anyone who would like to persuade me of the seriousness, depth, value, beauty, or truth in his or her favorite songs or musicians, first read "Pop Music and Quality in Art." Then you are welcome to try to persuade me of the value of the pop music you enjoy.

Senioritis
[March 19, 2006]

What we're doing now, if we've done it a lot and don't really love it, always looks drab compared to what we imagine doing in the future. Especially when we're young, but even later, most of us want to imagine life getting better rather than worse. What are the results for high school seniors already imagining being in college? "Why bother"; "Hanging out is more fun"; "I'll do it later"; etc.

But spend a moment trying to imagine what your future would be like if all it consisted of was looking further toward the future. Will you spend your college days thinking about your future employment, your working years thinking about retirement, your retirement thinking about death? If we all really wanted to go to heaven that badly, such a life might make sense. But in the absence of a profound mystical calling to contemplate eternity, living in the future itself soon becomes rather drab. Spend the day thinking about tomorrow instead of today? Been there, done that.

Near-death accidents and life-threatening diseases are well known for focusing our attention on the preciousness of the present moment. But they are not the only cure for senioritis. There's one other.

Take a moment to contemplate exactly what you think is going to make and keep you happy next year in college. I don't mean the temporary thrills of staying up till all hours or being able to sleep till noon or reinventing yourself. (The first two will wear off when you get used to them, and the third usually fades when you discover that you take yourself with you wherever you go.) I mean the kind of thing that you imagine will really make college life meaningful, rewarding, uplifting, deepening, joyful, the kind of thing you're not getting enough of. Then do something to make that happen *now*.

You're looking forward to meeting new people and sharing deep insights with them? Well, share a serious thought with someone you already know. (Did you really think that you had already garnered every significant insight anyone you know had to share?) You're looking forward to reading a book that captures your imagination and changes your perspective on the world? Well, read one now. (Chances are it has already been written.) You're looking forward to being the one to write it someday? Start writing now. (You can toss it if it's no good.) You're looking forward to articulating at last that philosophical dilemma you've been rolling around in your mind but never discussed with anyone because it might make you seem uncool or less in control? Find someone with whom to discuss it now. (What's the worst that can happen? You can start looking cool all over again in September.) Learn a new dance or craft or sport or language or food, not necessarily to master it, just to experience what you haven't experienced already.

I don't mean you always have to be busy or that there is intrinsic value in overloading your life with activities. But have you even learned just to do nothing, to do it *really*—with attention and honesty and joy? Will there be a better time for it than now?

In the *Ethics of the Fathers* Rabbi Hillel is quoted as saying: "If not now, when?" If you want to be wise, or knowledgeable, or popular, or excellent, or good, or happy, or kind, or joyful, what are you waiting for? Will it be easier tomorrow than today? Is freshman year in college any more "now" than senior year in high school?

Of course I know that reading this won't in itself cure you of senioritis. Not even reading Rabbi Hillel will necessarily do that. But actually asking yourself Rabbi Hillel's question is another matter. Honestly ask yourself "If not now, when?" and layers of drabness peel away, "been there, done that" ceases to exist, and echoes of the question's implication deepen into revelation. Arm yourself with Hillel's question and senioritis doesn't stand a chance.

A Fundamental Either/Or
[January 29, 2006]

Here's an either/or proposition that cannot be resolved by human reason:

Either: Temporal nature is the foundation of all reality, the source of all experience, the cause of all being, which, through the phenomenon of complexity, takes the form of minds, their awareness of themselves as functions of nature, and their illusory ideas of meaning, purpose, and eternity;

Or: Eternal mind is the foundation of all reality, the source and cause of nature, which it brings into being as the medium through which minds may come to discover their meaning and purpose, to know themselves as dependent on their own and nature's source, and to imagine and long for the eternal.

All the evidence of the senses enhanced by all the means at the disposal of reason and science cannot decide between these two versions of the foundation of reality. Whether we embrace the one or the other view, or both alternately—as, for example, the "either" in the lab and the "or" in church, museum, or hospital—must itself be a function of either nature at its work or mind at its.

In other words, we believe what we believe about this either/or either because nature has caused us to do so or because mind has created us to do so. And there is no way to know which. The evidence of nature at work cannot disprove that mind is its source. The evidence of mind at work cannot disprove that nature is its source.

We live by faith: either faith that our faith itself is but a natural phenomenon or faith that our faith binds us to the supernatural source of all phenomena.

Look outside at the trees, hear the birds sing, notice the clouds and the sun moving in the blue sky. Which do you believe: that for no reason or purpose nature has caused you to exist, to become aware of and love nature, to contemplate nature's and your own meaning, and to imagine and crave eternity? Or that for some reason some eternal One has caused nature to exist and caused you through nature to exist, to become aware of and love nature and its source, to contemplate nature's and your own meaning, and to imagine and crave eternity?

Some might ask, "What's the difference, since we can't know?" It's a good question, and to this one I think careful observation of your own experience can supply an answer. If you truly believe the "either," the answer is there is no difference. If you truly believe the "or," the answer is all the difference in the world.

"And Is He a Man to Encounter Tybalt?"
(for all my former students now serving our country in the military)
[November 15, 2006]

Last week I was subjected to a rapper's hyperbolical and foul-mouthed diatribe against U.S. Military recruitment on high school campuses. The rapper made a variety of false claims, the central ones being a) that a cynical U.S. Government uses false pretenses to trick American teenagers into joining the U.S. Military; b) that these duped teenagers are sent to foreign countries to kill innocent families and to be killed; and c) that if only we all say no to campus recruitment, military service, and war, there will be no wars.

The rap song was applauded by a number of seniors who attend a comfortable college prep school in a wealthy and relatively safe neighborhood and who look forward to entering good colleges, graduate schools, and professional careers without the help of the military. Of the military's part in ensuring their ability to pursue their careers under the rule of law and free from persecution they seem less than fully aware. I found myself hoping that they would remember their history before we are all condemned to repeat it.

Several days later, I had to pick up a book at the local upscale mall where many of these same seniors often shop. There I saw a clerk with a huge red-and-green spiked Mohawk haircut, another clerk with metal-studded black leather clothing and a metal-studded face, a bevy of barely-teen girls in "goth" costume giggling pseudo-witchcraft cant about evil spirits, and hundreds of people between the ages of twelve and thirty wandering into shops to buy overpriced trinkets and clothing imprinted with cartoon images of skulls and monsters.

According to the pop voice of teenage rebellion, we are to believe that war is never a defensive action against villains who wish to oppress or destroy us and other civilized peoples, that if only imperialistic corporate America would behave itself, the Stalinist and jihadist dictatorships of the world would magically shrivel up and blow away. At the same time,

America (by this reasoning) having no real enemies, we seem to need instead to cultivate imaginary enemies, like those pictured in the video games, movies, tattoos, thirty-five-dollar T-shirts, and extraterrestrial costumes that constitute the lucrative entertainments of the malls.

So I ask myself: Is this a culture to encounter the likes of Osama bin Laden or Mahmoud Ahmadinejad? [Update: or Antifa or Putin or the Chinese Communist Party?]

Romeo did not wake up to the real threat of Tybalt until Tybalt killed Romeo's friend Mercutio. Mercutio was killed partly because Tybalt was angry and vengeful and partly because he himself was equally rash. But Mercutio died also because Romeo, blissfully in love himself, thought he could prevent others' violence by being nice. Tybalt stabbed Mercutio under Romeo's peace-seeking arm.

To be sure, the quarrel between the Montagues and the Capulets was frivolous and unnecessary. But that didn't make Tybalt any the less deadly. And though Shakespeare, like our rapper, also hated futile and avoidable quarrels, he recognized, as the rapper does not, that not all wars are rooted in such quarrels. Some wars are caused by the evil ambitions of men like Macbeth and Richard III and need to be fought in the name of justice and of that true peace which is not merely appeasement.

We all hate war and would rather avoid it. But there are wars of villainous aggression and wars of legitimate defense as well as wars based on frivolous quarrels. The refusal to distinguish among them invites conquest and catastrophe.

Plenty of young people in our society die for pleasures promised by drugs, alcohol, promiscuous sex, mechanical velocity, and street-gang revenge of the sort indulged in by Tybalt and Mercutio. Where are the rappers crying over *their* deaths? Where are the rappers praising the real courage and sacrifice of the men and women who risk their lives to defend our freedom to say whatever we like about the military and to buy and wear whatever we like at the mall?

A society whose young men are taught that no honorable common cause is worth dying for is not likely to put an end to war. It is far more likely either to collapse of its own self-indulgence or to be overrun by a society whose young men *are* willing to die—and to kill—for the worst causes of all.

Response to Ten Atheist Myths
[December 25, 2006]

A student has sent me excerpts from Sam Harris's "Ten Myths and Ten Truths about Atheism" (https://samharris.org/10-myths-and-10-truths-about-atheism/) and asked me to comment.

1) Atheists believe that life is meaningless.

> On the contrary, religious people often worry that life is meaningless and imagine that it can only be redeemed by the promise of eternal happiness beyond the grave. Atheists tend to be quite sure that life is precious. Life is imbued with meaning by being really and fully lived. Our relationships with those we love are meaningful now; they need not last forever to be made so. Atheists tend to find this fear of meaninglessness... well... meaningless.

Both atheists and believers may live in fear of meaninglessness or in the conviction of meaning. Some believers believe in eternal life after death out of fear, some out of faith. Some believers believe meaning is eternal whether there is life after death or not. Some atheists believe the question of meaning is meaningless, some that there can be meaning without a metaphysical context for physical life. In short, it takes all kinds to make a world. In my view, the meaning of the word "meaning" is participation in a reality larger or more complete or more real than that which is perceived by limited beings with limited perceptions and intellects.

The resort to words like "really and fully lived" alters the vocabulary but not the essence. The phrase "really and fully lived" is simply a synonym for "meaningfully." If my definition is a good one, then Harris remains a believer in metaphysical significance, whether he believes in God or not. If my definition is rejected, the burden is on him to define "really and fully lived."

2) Atheism is responsible for the greatest crimes in human history.

> People of faith often claim that the crimes of Hitler, Stalin, Mao and Pol Pot were the inevitable product of unbelief. The problem with fascism and communism, however, is not that they are too critical of religion; the problem is that they are too much like religions. Such regimes are dogmatic to the core and generally give rise to personality cults that are indistinguishable from cults of religious hero worship. Auschwitz, the gulag and the killing fields were not examples of what happens when human beings reject religious dogma; they are examples of political, racial and nationalistic dogma run amok. There is no society in human history that ever suffered because its people became too reasonable.

It is true that no society has suffered because people became too reasonable, if "reasonable" means what Aristotle or Maimonides or St. Thomas Aquinas or Kant meant by reasonable. But then some people think Jeremy Bentham or Nietzsche or Sartre are the best exemplars of reason, and I think it can be shown that any attempt to set up a society upon their principles would cause plenty of suffering. To place Hitler and Stalin and Pol Pot in the same category with Moses and Jesus and Buddha is the height of unreason. Harris seems to have no idea how much his image of a society based on reason owes to believers in God or in Plato's Idea of the Good or later philosophers' *Ens Perfectissimum*, and how little it owes to radical atheism.

3) Atheism is dogmatic.

> Jews, Christians and Muslims claim that their scriptures are so prescient of humanity's needs that they could only have been written under the direction of an omniscient deity. An atheist is simply a person who has considered this claim, read the books and found the claim to be ridiculous. One doesn't have to take anything on faith, or be otherwise dogmatic, to reject unjustified religious beliefs. As the historian Stephen Henry Roberts (1901–71) once said: 'I contend that we are both atheists. I just believe in one fewer god than you do. When you understand why you dismiss all the other possible gods, you will understand why I dismiss yours.'

The idea that the atheist "doesn't have to take anything on faith" is simply absurd. He takes on faith that his reason is the only trustworthy absolute. He takes on faith that nothing ought to be believed that cannot be proven to his reason through his senses. And yet that belief itself cannot be proved to his reason through his senses. He treats religious belief as the kind of thing that can be or fail to be "justified" in the court of his own reason, yet his own perfect faith in his own reason and observations is never asked to justify itself in the same court. And for good reason: it could not possibly do so. I don't ask the atheist to believe what he cannot believe. But if he's going to treat every "unjustified" belief as folly, he ought to include his own.

4) Atheists think everything in the universe arose by chance.

> No one knows why the universe came into being. In fact, it is not entirely clear that we can coherently speak about the "beginning" or "creation" of the universe at all, as these ideas invoke the concept of time, and here we are talking about the origin of space-time itself.
>
> The notion that atheists believe that everything was created by chance is also regularly thrown up as a criticism of Darwinian evolution. As Richard Dawkins explains in his marvelous book, 'The God Delusion,' this represents an utter misunderstanding of evolutionary theory. Although we don't know precisely how the Earth's early chemistry begat biology, we know that the diversity and complexity we see in the living world is not a product of mere chance. Evolution is a combination of chance mutation and natural selection. Darwin arrived at the phrase "natural selection" by analogy to the "artificial selection" performed by breeders of livestock. In both cases, selection exerts a highly non-random effect on the development of any species.

A false argument based on false logic. No one is saying that every atheist asserts that everything is created by chance as the atheist defines chance (totally random accident). That natural selection is not purely random is not the point. The point is that it is not directed by any higher mind or purpose than the natural process itself. To put it another way, either the lower produces the higher (natural process without divine purpose eventually results in us, human beings, who think and ask questions and study science and believe things) or the higher is the source of the being of the lower. More simply, either spirit purposefully gives rise to the physical universe or the physical universe purposelessly gives rise to spirit.

Dawkins is in the latter camp, and hates those in the former. His books are not "marvelous" but characteristically angry and nastily accusatory. As might be said about the Bible-thumpers that he hates because he fears them, the evolutionary biologist doth protest too much, methinks. If believers are deluded, why bother to write a book denouncing us? He ought to pity us. But wait, pity cannot be an "ought" in the universe as Dawkins conceives it. I take it back. There are no grounds on which to appeal to Dawkins to be more just, or more honest. For even the truth presumably pursued by scientists like Dawkins is a value whose worth arises from an act of faith. And how can he prove to me that truth is any more worth pursuing than God or salvation or eternal life?

5) Atheism has no connection to science.

> Although it is possible to be a scientist and still believe in God—as some scientists seem to manage it—there is no question that an engagement with scientific thinking tends to erode, rather than support, religious faith. Taking the U.S. population as an example: Most polls show that about 90% of the general public believes in a personal God; yet 93% of the members of the National Academy of Sciences do not. This suggests that there are few modes of thinking less congenial to religious faith than science is.

I pretty much agree with #5, though my conclusion would be different. I would say science (as practiced by believers in an absolute materialism) only seems to be uncongenial to religious faith because it *is*, for many, a religious faith, at least as much so as Harris would accuse communism or fascism of being. The people we ought to be getting to know are those who are both scientists and believers in God. They might have some real authority to speak on this matter.

6) Atheists are arrogant.

> When scientists don't know something—like why the universe

came into being or how the first self-replicating molecules formed—they admit it. Pretending to know things one doesn't know is a profound liability in science. And yet it is the life-blood of faith-based religion. One of the monumental ironies of religious discourse can be found in the frequency with which people of faith praise themselves for their humility, while claiming to know facts about cosmology, chemistry and biology that no scientist knows. When considering questions about the nature of the cosmos and our place within it, atheists tend to draw their opinions from science. This isn't arrogance; it is intellectual honesty.

I certainly do not think that all atheists are arrogant, and I don't know who does think that. But the statement that "pretending to know things one doesn't know ... is the life-blood of faith-based religion" is pure calumny. Religious faith is not about the knowledge of unknowable facts. The language of religion is perforce metaphorical, using imagery from the created universe in order to talk about the invisible divine because there is no other way for human beings, bound by time and space, to talk about anything. But to say God created the universe is not to pretend to know some pseudo-scientific fact inaccessible to science. It is a way of talking about the admittedly unknowable, of trying to relate to the source from which, and the context in which, time and space have their being.

As for "people of faith praising themselves for their humility," this is pure nonsense. There are arrogant believers in God as in science, and there are humble ones. But what truly religious people praise is the value of humility itself, not themselves for being humble. And if Harris didn't agree with them that humility is to be valued, how could he consider praising oneself for humility to be a fault?

7) Atheists are closed to spiritual experience.

There is nothing that prevents an atheist from experiencing love, ecstasy, rapture and awe; atheists can value these experiences and seek them regularly. What atheists don't tend to do is make unjustified (and unjustifiable) claims about the nature of reality on the basis of such experiences. There is no question that some Christians have transformed their lives for the better by reading the Bible and praying to Jesus. What does this prove? It proves that certain disciplines of attention and codes of conduct can have a profound effect upon the human mind. Do the positive experiences of Christians suggest that Jesus is the sole savior of humanity? Not even remotely—because Hindus, Buddhists, Muslims and even atheists regularly have similar experiences. There is, in fact, not a Christian on this Earth who can be certain that Jesus even wore a beard, much less that he was born of a virgin or rose from the dead. These are just not the sort of claims that spiritual experience can authenticate.

"What atheists don't tend to do is make unjustified (and unjustifiable) claims about the nature of reality on the basis of such experiences." This is hilarious! The atheist's faith in his own profound experience of human reason, observation, experiment, and proof leads to claims precisely as unjustified and unjustifiable as any made by religion, the most extreme being that there is no "justification" for religious faith and that, in the absence of such justification, faith is folly.

All fundamental acts of faith are equally justifiable or unjustifiable because there are no underlying terms in which they can be justified. If you believe in human reason as the deepest reality there is, you will not allow that there is any court in which reason itself may be called to the bar to justify its validity. As with religious faith so with faith in human reason: axioms cannot be proven. As C. S. Lewis reminds us in *The Abolition of Man*, they are premises, not conclusions. The argument is not between those who do not think religion is reasonable and those who do. It is between those who believe in human reason and those who believe in God as the more fundamental reality. And where is the court in which such a case could be impartially tried?

8) Atheists believe that there is nothing beyond human life and human understanding.

Atheists are free to admit the limits of human understanding in a way that religious people are not. It is obvious that we do not fully understand the universe; but it is even more obvious that neither the Bible nor the Koran reflects our best understanding of it. We do not know whether there is complex life elsewhere in the cosmos, but there might be. If there is, such beings could have developed an understanding of nature's laws that vastly exceeds our own. Atheists can freely entertain such possibilities. They also can admit that if brilliant extraterrestrials exist, the contents of the Bible and the Koran will be even less impressive to them than they are to human atheists.

From the atheist point of view, the world's religions utterly trivialize the real beauty and immensity of the universe. One doesn't have to accept anything on insufficient evidence to make such an observation.

Once again "our best understanding" is offered as the only goal of all human discourse. It is a great and noble goal, but it is not the only one and may not be the most important. The existence of extraterrestrial beings, smarter or dumber than we are, would not need in any way to undermine faith in God for a believer, though certainly such a discovery would call everyone, atheist and believer alike, to rethink our place in the created universe. But once again the atheist is stuck in the realm of factual knowledge with no inkling that the Bible is about more than worldly knowledge. It is equally imaginable that extraterrestrials might benefit from and be grateful for exposure to the moral laws and spiritual insights of the sacred texts of human religion as that they might be indifferent to them. Harris is absolutely caught in the trap of thinking that religion is just bad reasoning, entirely unaware that his worship of human reason is itself a form of religious faith.

9) Atheists ignore the fact that religion is extremely beneficial to society.

> Those who emphasize the good effects of religion never seem to realize that such effects fail to demonstrate the truth of any religious doctrine. This is why we have terms such as "wishful thinking" and "self-deception." There is a profound distinction between a consoling delusion and the truth.
>
> In any case, the good effects of religion can surely be disputed. In most cases, it seems that religion gives people bad reasons to behave well, when good reasons are actually available. Ask yourself, which is more moral, helping the poor out of concern for their suffering, or doing so because you think the creator of the universe wants you to do it, will reward you for doing it or will punish you for not doing it?

No rational believer thinks that "good effects" *prove* the validity of religion. This is another false accusation based on ignorance of what real believers really believe. The validity of religion is a matter of faith, not proof or demonstration. Again, premises must not be mistaken for conclusions. The question posed is based on a false dichotomy: "Which is more moral, helping the poor out of concern for their suffering, or doing so because you think the creator of the universe wants you to do it, will reward you for doing it or will punish you for not doing it?" Helping the poor out of concern for their suffering is precisely what is willed by the creator, and if there weren't a long religious tradition that has taught that truth to our culture, the atheist could never have thought of using the value of concern for the suffering of the poor as an argument.

It is true that some people do good deeds merely out of self-interest, as some scientists do what they do out of selfish desire for a government grant. But as the existence of government grants does not prevent the devoted lover of truth from doing good science, so belief in the existence of divine reward and punishment does not prevent the believer from loving his neighbor for the right reasons, reasons which only religion and not science can have shown us to be right.

10) Atheism provides no basis for morality.

> If a person doesn't already understand that cruelty is wrong, he won't discover this by reading the Bible or the Koran—as these books are bursting with celebrations of cruelty, both human and divine. We do not get our morality from religion. We decide what is good in our good books by recourse to moral intuitions that are (at some level) hard-wired in us and that have been refined by thousands of years of thinking about the causes and possibilities of human happiness.
>
> We have made considerable moral progress over the years, and we didn't make this progress by reading the Bible or the Koran more closely. Both books condone the practice of slavery—and yet every civilized human being now recognizes that slavery is an abomination. Whatever is good in scripture—like the golden rule—can be valued for its ethical wisdom without our believing that it was handed down to us by the creator of the universe.

It is true that the Bible and other sacred books tell stories in which cruelty appears, even the cruelty of the supposed exemplars of the good. But Harris is making two significant errors: first, he is equating the religion with the book, and second, he is ignoring the context of the stories within the books themselves.

In his wording, however, Harris gives his real faith away: "If a person doesn't already understand that cruelty is wrong..." tells us that, knowingly or not, the writer is himself a believer in a book, or rather in the ragtag leftovers of several books, written by Jean-Jacques Rousseau. He believes, without questioning it, that man is good by nature, that his naturally evolved reason demonstrates the self-evident good of concern for the poor and the self-evident evil of cruelty. And this is a faith that no amount of observation of human beings and no amount of rational thought could have instilled in him. Once again it is a premise, adopted because it seems to be true to one who believes it to be true, susceptible of no proof and no demonstration to the rational faculty.

His example of slavery is a smokescreen. Slavery in the Bible was never, except among the Egyptians, what it was in America in the nineteenth century, and it is the Bible's assertion of the obligations of the master to the servant and of the brotherhood of man that formed the moral foundations for the abolition of slavery in modern times. The abolitionists were fueled not by some natural recognition arising from a natural progress but by the universalizing of their religious faith in justice, love, and the fatherhood of the creator. Belief in man's natural progress leading necessarily away from religion to an ideal world of reasonable and virtuous human beings is at least as unfounded as, and far wilder than, anyone's belief in hell, purgatory, or heaven.

The atheist is living, without admitting it, on the capital of several thousand years of religious teaching and moralizing. He believes that moral man springs whole from the bosom of nature and that religion (as Enlightenment *philosophes* like Condorcet believed) is the enemy of knowledge, upon which alone virtue is founded. Apart from the communist's belief in a utopian future, it is perhaps the greatest example of wishful thinking that modern history has exhibited, a far greater leap, because history offers so much contrary evidence, than belief in an afterlife, for which there is no more negative evidence than positive.

The atheist and the believer agree that the golden rule is built into the nature of things and that its value is, or ought to be, self-evident. The difference is that the former believes it is there arbitrarily, as a function of natural process naturally unfolding, while the latter believes it was meant to be there from the beginning and that in obeying it we come into touch with the foundations of reality. As I've said before, neither will ever convince the other by argument. But, as the atheist would I hope agree, it pays for neither to be reductive or stupid about what the other believes.

Art: Oooh, Uh-huh, or Aha!
[February 19, 2007]

Oooh:

Oooh is compelling, may be extreme and intense, thrilling or shocking, but it doesn't stay with you. It gets old fast and then a newer and more intense oooh is demanded. So oooh is addictive, temporarily distracts but cannot satisfy. Oooh is the product of the Romantic worship of the merely emotional—of the natural, of the individual, of impulse, of feeling dissociated from rational thought and tradition, of spontaneity, of originality, of extremes. Devotion to oooh makes a Jackson Pollock the most expensive painting ever sold. A naked *Hamlet* is all oooh. Its name is sensationalism.

Uh-huh:

Uh-huh is safe, reassuring, and obvious, even when it is demanding and difficult. It is certain, firm, widely shared. But uh-huh becomes personally irrelevant. It is devoted to the already accepted and does not reach paradox and mystery, where the self actually lives. The uh-huh made T. S. Eliot think Dryden a greater poet than Shelley because Dryden's beliefs were truer. Uh-huh conveys dogma. It may be the product of the Enlightenment, of worship of the rational, the scientific, the tested, the obvious. Or it may be the product of a religious tradition or of the political right, or the political left, or of any shared hobby horse. It may be truth or it may be propaganda, but it soothes without moving.

Our age (perhaps every age) labors under both these erroneous goals of art—often in the same work. Individualism and impulse have become dogma. People exalted the impulsive gestures of a Jackson Pollock till abstract expression became an -ism. The formerly oooh becomes uh-huh.

Aristotle said that virtue is a golden mean that lies between the two extremes of excess and deficiency. The oooh is excess worship of impulse and nature and emotional abandon; the uh-huh is excess worship of familiarity and safety and mental control. At the same time, the oooh is deficiency of universal rational significance and the uh-huh is deficiency of personal emotional relevance.

Aha!:

Aha! is a golden mean, though it cannot be achieved by mere balance of reason and impulse, as if it were itself a quantity. It is original, but not because the artist has pursued originality, for the pursuit of originality decays into mere differentness. It is true, but not because the artist has packaged received truth, for the packaging of received truth decays into mere platitude.

Aha! is achieved in a visionary incarnation of the universally true in the authentic here-and-now particular. It appears in the space between — between the artist and the made object, between the object and the audience, between meaning and form. It effects (in Martin Buber's terms) an I/Thou moment. It rings true, and not only our emotion or our mind tells us so but our whole self—body, heart, mind, and spirit—as one.

Why should we settle for less?

And now, here, look: My title is oooh. My paragraphs are uh-huh. Where is aha!?

On Selfishness
[April 22, 2007]

More than a few times over the years I have heard students claim that everyone is selfish. According to this belief, even people we call selfless, good, or self-sacrificing are "in reality" pleasing only themselves. That they get pleasure from being "what society calls good" does not mean they are any less selfish than those who get pleasure from being bad.

This pseudo-doctrine has settled upon the modern imagination as a noxious fog, exuded when the mixture of Jeremy Bentham's utilitarianism (good is pleasure minus pain) with Nietzsche's moral solvent (good is envy in disguise) in Freud's psychoanalytic cauldron (good is superego's rationalization of ego's survivalist suppression of id) spilled into the popular press. The result: behind every good move is a "real" motive, which is invariably selfish.

In fact the actual adoption of the belief that every choice is a selfish one can lead to nothing but boredom. Once we agree that everything we do is for selfish reasons, what else is there to say? It is an assumption that recognizes no distinctions, evokes no practical or moral or spiritual discussion. It is the end of conversation. Which is why the young would be so disappointed if one were simply to agree with them in accepting it. Without the presumption of resistance, the selfishness doctrine dies of its own vacuity.

Let's accept for a moment the hypothesis that we are all essentially selfish. I am; you are; Einstein is; Descartes is; Mother Theresa is; Saddam Hussein is. Now what? What am I to do about being me, or you about being you? What choices are left us to make? And why would any choice be significant? If all motives are selfish, then choice is only illusion, the selfish preference of this form of selfishness over that. Whether I should apologize to you or hit you again harder is a question exactly like whether I should order vanilla or chocolate. Who could care about anyone or anything if we really believed in this universal selfishness?

If we are all only selfish, then talking about selfishness is like talking about our need for oxygen. We all need oxygen, saints and sinners, our beloveds and the villains who torment us. So what? Shall we ignore everything about people except that they need oxygen? Wouldn't that go against our natures, which, whether or not they are totally selfish, certainly militate against boredom?

Now let us entertain an alternative assumption. Let us say that all creatures are mostly selfish but potentially unselfish. They are selfish in various ways, in accordance with their natures, and yet they have an area of freedom in which they are capable of choosing either to be consistent with their own natural selfishness or, alternatively, to sacrifice their own selfishness in certain limited respects in the name of some value or principle other than selfishness that they find to be meaningful.

If this alternative assumption is true, it is not wrong to say that all creatures are selfish, but it is wrong to say that all creatures are *only* selfish. Now there is space for us to distinguish between good selfish beings and evil selfish beings, between kind selfishness and uncaring or brutal selfishness. If despite being rather selfish we still have some freedom to be more or less selfish, selfish in better or worse ways, or even unselfish, then we can begin to talk about things that matter to us. To solve for x, we cancel out the common factors on both sides of an equation. Similarly, only in agreeing to leave our common selfishness aside can we discuss what besides ourselves we may value. Only then can we find interest in being human.

This more complex assumption also has the advantage of corresponding better to what we actually experience in life. For almost no one, including one who believes that all human beings are only selfish, actually behaves or judges himself or others as if that assumption were true. In practice we all make moral distinctions as well as factual ones. Who would be content to say, "Out of selfishness he stole my wallet; out of selfishness I didn't want him to"? Whether they say so or not, most people will also believe "He was wrong to steal my wallet" or "His selfishness is immoral; mine is not."

Nothing that simply is can be morally bad. Only beings that can freely will alternatives based on moral imperatives can be said to be bad or good. If we are merely nature following our natures, whatever we think we're doing, then even the word "selfish" is meaningless. We are just being what we are being, wanting what we want, and freedom is illusory, discussion is vain, and the assertion that we are all selfish is pointless.

There is undoubtedly a measure of selfishness in most of our choices, but the word "selfish" has meaning because we use it in the context of the freedom not to be selfish. And only belief in that freedom is consistent with our actual experience. We are, by nature and in practice, choice-making beings. We judge, decide, pick, and prefer constantly throughout our waking lives. By our choices we fill our lives with meaning, and in comprehending our choices and their consequences we slowly come to comprehend who and what we are. To say that all our choices amount to the same choice—selfishness—is to say we make no real choices at all, that we already know all there is to know about ourselves.

The belief that there is not also a measure of freedom to choose the good despite our measure of selfishness, that there are not better and worse ways to please the self, not higher as well as lower satisfactions—this belief dissolves all culture, art, and civilization, all discussion and argument, all human conversation. A universally selfish world is a universally boring world in which souls are but belly-feeders and mind is a waste of matter.

If at the end of his life a man discovers, on reflection, that he has been selfish all his life, that is a meaningful discovery only if that selfishness has been chosen, only if another route had been possible. Similarly, if a young person argues that selfishness is all there is, we are not in the presence of logic or wisdom or insight or experience. We are in the presence of a devil's advocate, an intellectual faddist, or a soul in despair. Knowingly or not, all three crave healing refutation.

Holding the Line with Grammar
[July 28, 2007]

If you don't pay a monthly water bill to the City Treasurer, you may not know that the great bureaucracy constituting our city government is looking out for the common interest with regular reminders to monitor the amount of water we devote to landscape. (The City's lack of care to limit property development to what our water resources can sustain is apparently an unrelated issue best kept from the attention of the rate-payers.)

In the lower right corner of each month's water bill is a space reserved for notices relevant to our water use. For about three years, that space has been devoted to the same message, framed in several ways.

From October 2004 to April 2005, the space contained the following sentence:

Fall is a good time to tune-up and turn down the irrigation.

This was followed by the offer of a free survey of one's water usage, available to anyone calling the phone number provided.

Having taken that message to heart when it first appeared, I gave it little attention thereafter, cutting the Water Department some slack for the grammatically inappropriate hyphen. My bill for May 2005, however, in the same space contained the following revised version of the message:

How much water does your lawn, flowers and trees need?

"Ha!" thought I. "Somebody's going to get a wrist slapped for that one." I confess to letting the subject slip out of my mind between water bills, but when the same sentence reappeared on the June bill, I decided to keep an eye on that corner to see how long it would take for someone to catch and correct the grammatical error. July? Nope, same sentence. August? Nope. When the sentence reappeared in September, I couldn't take it anymore.

I called the Water Department, probably in off-hours, and left a message of my own, no doubt sounding like an overwrought eccentric. But I didn't care. I had right on my side and was determined to hold the line. Amazingly enough, on the October 2005 water bill the sentence stood corrected:

How much water do your lawn, flowers and trees need?

Hurray! Chalk one up for the squeaky wheel and extend our lease on the English language!

The Water Department ran along grammatically in its bureaucratic groove, winter, spring, summer, and fall, with neither false hyphen nor agreement error in sight—until June 2007, when suddenly, there it was again:

How much water does your lawn, flowers and trees need?

The error's reappearance could not have been the result of the fresh copy of a newcomer. Everything else in that corner space was identical. No—someone had looked at the correct sentence, decided that it sounded wrong, and silently (as editors say) emended it, no doubt feeling "There, that sounds better; I've done a good deed today."

No more second or third chances now. I gave the Water Department only one. When the bill came for July?—"does." So I called. But this time I held the line (in the other sense) in order to speak to a customer service representative. When she heard my English teacher's hysteria—"Here we English teachers are doing our best to teach our students grammar, and there you are sending out millions of ungrammatical water bills, setting a terrible example to any customers who happen to be paying attention, not to mention any of their children who might want to practice their reading on the monthly water bill, just as if grammar didn't matter; how do you expect us to take the trouble to conserve water when you won't even take the trouble to conserve the language?" etc.—she behaved with exemplary patience and offered me the direct phone number of the Water Department's Supervising Public Information Officer.

I call, leave an equally passionate message, and—wonder of wonders!—he calls me back. Not only that, he sustains my objection and reports that he has given order that no water bill blurbs will henceforth go to press without being read and approved by himself. "We all need an editor," he says. I agree, without adding that some need more editing than others. But I am confident that the friendly and obviously intelligent Supervising Public Information Officer is more than capable of correcting "does" to "do" when the subject of the sentence is plural, even in a direct question where normal word order is inverted.

Why am I telling you this? Not only because at times I feel like the only squeaky wheel in the city and want company. Not only because the Supervising Public Information Officer of the Water Department deserves credit. I want to illustrate the necessity and the possibility of holding the line.

"Holding the line" this time means taking a stand for grammar and civilization, even when the scale seems daunting. It's not really cities we are up against, or even water departments. They are abstractions—real, but not to be conversed with. Actually we are up against potentially reasonable supervisors of imperfectly educated clerks who may respond well to reason and truth if they can be reached.

I know that the Water Department's Supervising Public Information Officer is a public servant and ultimately answerable to the people, and no doubt he is paid partly for dealing with cranks like me. It might have gone harder with AT&T or Microsoft. Still, we have to hold the line (in both senses). Why? Because either lawn, flowers, and trees *does* need water, or they *do*.

If they *does*, then it's good-bye to precise human discourse, the medium of communication about anything significant to the naturally social beings we are. It is by nature that animals preserve the grammars of their own forms of communication. But the nature of human beings is that we must hold the line by choice. And if we fail to do so, not only education, literature, and politics are at risk: Whom does us think am going to get them its water?

Sexuality and the Moral Code
[September 9, 2007]

An alumnus writes:

> I was wondering if you could share your opinion about scholarship dealing with sexuality. Is it good or bad that scholars have been critiquing the old—what to call it?—Judeo-Christian moral code that in its various guises condemned premarital sex, homosexuality, and masturbation?

My reply:

Let's examine the premises on which your question depends.

First, "Is it good or bad?" is a falsely narrow question. There is of course likely to be some good in the worst of the offenders as well as some bad in the best of their critics. But that is obvious. The question really implies that I am to reveal myself as either an old-fashioned moralist (hence a condemner of all who engage in premarital sex, homosexual sex, and masturbation) or a critic of the entire Judeo-Christian moral code (hence a defender of the unexceptionable moral status of those three behaviors). Well, I can't accept the either/or straitjacket. Morality, like life, is complex and challenging. The traditional moral code stands, *and* I won't engage in blanket condemnations.

Second, to call the Judeo-Christian moral code "old" implies that it has been supplanted by a newer and presumably a better one. What would that code be and on what grounds does it rest? You yourself are apparently opposed to condemning premarital sex, homosexuality, and masturbation. Fine. On what moral grounds do you stand to defend them? Justice? Kindness? Individual liberty? The rights of man? Which of those is not rooted deeply in the moral codes of the Jewish and Christian traditions? It is not Hobbes or Nietzsche or Marx or even Freud who would defend the sexual behaviors you list, and Darwin the man (though the theory of Darwin the scientist offers no grounds for doing so) would have been upset to hear them defended. If you believe in the sacredness of the freedom of the individual conscience, which are the grounds upon which I assume you stand to overturn the sexual taboos you mention, you too are within the Judeo-Christian moral tradition.

Third, "various guises" is a rather cavalier reduction of the vast complexity of the religious traditions of half the world. Why don't we talk about the particular times and places and cultures in which your three kinds of sexual behavior have been condemned, how, and by whom instead of tarring all of Western religion with the same brush? Certainly you cannot claim that either Judaism or Christianity has in the last one hundred years succeeded in constraining very many in America from guiltless premarital sex, homosexuality, or masturbation? Are you talking about particular periods and places characterized by moralistic persecutions? Puritan colonies? Rural small towns? The Scarlet Letter is about adultery, not premarital sex, homosexuality, or masturbation. Did you want to add adultery to the list of unforbidden behaviors?

In the Old Testament, the act of premarital sex with an unmarried female is disapproved of because it directs one's sexual potential away from marriage, which, except in cases of incest, can itself usually repair the moral damage. Premarital sex with a married female is adultery, and that is severely punished because, among other things, it is a direct attack upon the sacred bond of matrimony. In the New Testament, Jesus protects even a woman taken in adultery from stoning to death and tells her to go and sin no more. By his example we are taught to distinguish between condemnation of the sin and of the sinner. In both testaments much of the moral code exists to protect women from predatory men.

Only a society that has become confused about the meaning and potential of human sexuality, about the differences between the genders, and about the value of sexual restraint as an enhancement of the sexual relation within marriage could even imagine that unregulated premarital sex was morally speaking a good equal to sex within marriage.

In any case, on what grounds but those of the Judeo-Christian moral code would you argue that premarital sex is not of lesser moral standing than sex within marriage? On grounds of the sacredness of the individual's freedom to live as he or she chooses? But that sacredness is as deeply rooted in the biblical religious tradition's articulation of the brotherhood of man and fatherhood of God as the sexual taboos themselves. In a non-religious, purely natural world, there could be no possible moral grounds not only for asserting a higher meaning to sacramental than to premarital sexuality, but also for protecting women from predatory men. Do away with the "old" code, and for every woman freed to engage in sex however and whenever she wants, ten will be forced to engage in sex purely for the man's pleasure with no protection in sight. For every male enjoying all those freebies, probably two or more children will be forced to grow up without a father. (Why do I put this in the future tense? Isn't that what is happening now in our most "enlightened" cities?)

Similar things might be said about homosexuality and masturbation, about which the rules given exist to assert the higher moral value of heterosexual sex within the bounds of matrimony, which is also a way of saying to assert the higher value of the human soul in a community-sanctioned relationship than of the body in individual sensual gratification. We may advance in broad-mindedness to acknowledging the value of committed and loyal homosexual relationships. But that we recognize such relationships as superior to the multiple-partnered, anonymous, and public sex of the gay so-called community we owe to the Judeo-Christian moral code. And most rabbis are not running around trying to stop bar mitzvah boys from jerking off in private. If responsible rabbis and priests and ministers have anything to say about masturbation, it is likely to be that the ultimate purpose of the gift of the sexual body is the joy of sacramental love and reproduction, and that hormone-driven youth ought to know it for future reference.

To abolish the Judeo-Christian moral tradition is to assert that there is no hierarchical relation between soul and body, that nature is as valid an authority as spirit, that pleasure and pain not good and evil are the fundamental terms of human life. Such things can be believed, of course, and many do believe them. But one ought to recognize what one is tossing out in adopting the "new" morality, which, as Lewis argues in *The Abolition of Man*, is not morality at all but impulse in disguise.

"Scholars" have been critiquing the biblical moral tradition for thousands of years. The race/class/gender and Marx/Nietzsche/Freud folks are neither the first nor the wisest of those who have questioned, examined, and enhanced the moral tradition of Judaism and Christianity. But in order to discover the shallowness and folly of the tossers-out of the "old Judeo-Christian moral code," one must make a little effort to see exactly what it is they are tossing out. No one with even minimal awareness of the arguments about sex, love, freedom, marriage, and the human soul in the Talmud, St. Augustine, Maimonides, or St. Thomas Aquinas could possibly be tempted to jettison the Judeo-Christian moral code in the name of justifying premarital sex, homosexuality, and masturbation. And it remains to be seen whether a society that embraces those behaviors untinged with any guilt about human fallibility can provide a better or happier world than did those admittedly fallen and flawed cultures governed by the "old" morality.

The alumnus responds:

"To call the Judeo-Christian moral code 'old' implies that it has been supplanted by a newer and presumably a better one." I totally agree. There is a common supposition that the traditional sexual code has been replaced by something "modern." I don't believe this to be the case at all.

Americans are still far more puritanical, in thought if not in action, than most of us realize. Some Americans break the traditional sexual code quite often, but all do so with overwhelming consciousness of having "broken the rules." Even the gayest of the gays, the most radical of the feminists, and the most adulterous among us is overwhelmingly conscious of the Judeo-Christian sexual code, and nearly all have adopted it as a sexual standard whether they realize this or not. In fact, these people are probably more conscious of it than the average. The Judeo-Christian code *is* the modern sexual code.

I believe that this current state of sexual affairs—willingness to acknowledge the rules' existence but widespread refusal to follow them—results in many, many of the unhappier aspects of American culture. By the way, I say "American" because I have found that Europeans are very slightly less conscious of Judeo-Christian sexual mores, and they seem happier and their societies seem the tiniest bit more functional as a result.

I'm sure you'll disagree with my conclusion that most sexual standards are very arbitrary and that the traditional sexual code is likely far from the best (codifying what I mean by best will have to wait), but I assume you'll agree that it is absolutely essential for everyone to adhere uniformly to a sexual standard.

My reply:

The response is welcome. I do indeed disagree that sexual mores are merely arbitrary. But I do not agree that "It is absolutely essential for everyone to adhere uniformly to a sexual standard." This is a utopian dream, even if the standard were flawless. Let's say it is essential for a society to promote the aspiration to an ideal standard of sexual behavior. "Uniform" adherence to anything is beyond human capacity, individual or social, and to try to achieve it opens the door to tyranny. On the other hand, traditional sexual standards, far from arbitrary, generally prove themselves to lead to mental and social well-being far more than does the total freedom to follow one's impulses. I do not take the word "puritanical" to mean "repressive" or "bad" or "inhumane" as you seem to do. As with any standard of behavior, society must find the middle path between total license and total repression, both extremes leading to trouble. If some Puritan communities pushed too far in one direction, that hardly justifies our present worship of the opposite extreme.

I agree that too great a disjunction between what we value and what we do is detrimental. But to set Europe up as an example is folly. Europeans may "seem happier," but their society is far from "functional." Once traditional European families are now not having children, and soon there will be too few Europeans to sustain the culture of entitlement that Europe has fallen into. Not having children is a sign of cultural and social despair. Unless one defines happiness as total individual self-indulgence without regard to the commonwealth or the future, Europe can hardly be seen as a place of greater happiness than America, nor can it be called a functional society. (This is to say nothing of the moral collapse evident in the fact that there are some neighborhoods into which the police forces of the "happy" Europeans will not go in uniform or without extensive reinforcements and some in which the persecution of innocent Jews and the rape, genital mutilation, and murder of girls and women have been engaged in with impunity.)[1]

In general, substituting sexual indulgence without guilt for the spiritual, social, and practical values of traditional marriage seems a poor exchange indeed. And as I suggested, I don't believe any true measure will find human beings happier under the regime of untrammeled impulse.

---

1 Some news media have claimed that the idea of literal "no-go zones" has been debunked. For a more nuanced view, see https://www.intelligencefusion.co.uk/insights/resources/intelligence-reports/europes-no-go-zones-fact-or-fiction/.

Moral Absolutes and Relativism
[September 30, 2007]

An alumnus writes:

> The funny thing is that you've campaigned for years the importance of absolute morality and frowned upon relative morality. However, numerous times when your opinion is asked on something such as homosexuality, abortion, etc., you state that such issues are too complicated to give a yes or no answer to. It's almost as though you are stating that one cannot see the world in black and white but shades of gray. That seems like moral relativism to me. Is there some key subtle point I've missed or am I drawing connections where none exist? Please elucidate.

My reply:

With pleasure, though not without difficulty.

You are missing a point whose degree of subtlety to you depends, I suppose, on how easily you come to recognize it. You have got stuck on false meanings for the words "absolute" and "relative" when applied to morality. "Absolute morality" never meant totally clear black-and-white solutions to all particular moral problems. "Relative morality" never meant recognizing that sometimes the right moral path is not clear.

Belief in absolute morality means belief in certain fundamental principles that are universal and unquestionable, premises that cannot be proven and are not subject to discussion. Example: Justice is good. There's no gray there. Accept this premise, you are a moral absolutist, and then we can discuss how best to achieve justice in this or that situation. Reject it—justice is not good, justice is sometimes useful but may be irrelevant—you are a relativist, and then all discussion about how to behave justly in this or that situation becomes moot. Without the shared underlying value, there are no grounds for proving one position superior to another.

Absolute values include justice, mercy, temperance, truth, fidelity, kindness, courage, wisdom, love, patience, humility, and similar universals. A moral absolutist believes these have value in all situations. To be moral is to try to apply each universal value in such a way that no other universal value is breached. This goal defines an ideal, perhaps impossible to achieve, but worth striving for. A moral relativist believes that there are no absolutes of this kind, therefore there is no ideal to strive for, therefore there is no point in arguing about which action would be better than another. There is no better and no worse except in light of absolute values that we agree are unquestionably good.

Thus, there is a huge difference between recognizing the complexity in applying the fundamental rules of absolute morality to particular situations and believing that all morality is relative. I am a moral absolutist only in the sense that I believe these universals are always values, no matter the culture or the age or the particular situation. This does not mean that I always live up to these ideals or always know how to do so. Perhaps no one does. But unlike the relativist, the absolutist believes the values exist as qualities toward which to strive, as guides to choice-making.

The challenge of human life is how to apply these universals in particular situations without betraying any of them. This is why we need the Bible and the Talmud and the *Summa Theologica* and the English Common Law and the U.S. Constitution and the *Divine Comedy* and *Hamlet* and school rule books and many another human effort at clarification. That the application of the universal values to particular situations is difficult is not a sign that the universals don't exist.

It is not moral relativism to recognize that one must not punish with identical penalties similar crimes committed by a small child and by a willfully bad adult. It is justice tempered with wisdom. It is not moral relativism to see a difference between helping the poor as best you can and impoverishing yourself and your family to do so. It is kindness tempered with prudence. To make such distinctions is not to say that morality is relative. It is to say that the proper application of universals to particular situations requires every bit of wisdom and knowledge we can muster. The relativist would say that there are no grounds even for using the word "proper" in the previous sentence.

How one may judge a case with both justice and mercy is a moral problem. How a government can courageously defeat its enemies without failing to recognize their humanity is another. If such questions had simple and absolute answers, there would be no need for the human mind to have to make choices, to figure out the right thing to do. And there would be no need for the thousands of years of moral and legal codes and revisions of codes and preserved historical precedents to try to apply absolutes to particular situations in ways consistent with the other absolutes. Absolutism about moral values means believing there is a meaningful difference between the better and the worse way of deciding such questions. It does not mean that finding the best way is always easy or clear.

There may be actual moral relativists who participate in the debates about abortion and about so-called gay marriage. But I would say that most people, on either side of each issue, are arguing for what they believe to be right, about which they would not claim to be relativists. This does not make the debates themselves easy. But it does make them valuable. If the opponents were true relativists, there would be no grounds for arguing at all. But most who support the freedom to choose abortion, like most who oppose them, believe in values: life, justice, and kindness. How to apply those values is the problem—hence the debate.

I personally believe (consistent with rabbinic tradition) that abortion is wrong except in cases where, in the opinion of a competent medical authority, the actual life of the mother is at stake—that is, until the head of the infant crowns during childbirth, whereupon the lives of mother and child are equal and both must be fought for equally. This may seem like a shade of gray. But it is not. Killing an innocent human being is bad in principle; saving a human life is good in principle. There is no argument there. These are absolutes. The question is what happens when the life of the fetus conflicts with the life of the mother? The rabbis' resolution is an attempt to be true to both values at once. One might reasonably take a different position—arguing that abortion is proper even when only the health of the mother is at stake, or is improper even if her life is at stake—without being a moral relativist. Those positions may be different attempts to apply the same universal values. Even confessing uncertainty about where one ought to stand on the issue is not necessarily relativism. It may be an active embrace of the universal value of humility in the face of a moral problem too difficult for an individual alone to solve. It is people who deny the premises of the debate—the absolute universal value of human life—who are the relativists. With them no discussion is possible, for they reject the very grounds on which any moral argument must be based.

A similar point needs to be made about homosexuality. Rooted in the biblical tradition, in almost universal human cultural practice, and in the natural principle that only through the union of opposites is creation possible, Western civilization has enshrined the value of heterosexual marriage. Acceptance of this value means recognizing that homosexual behavior represents a departure from that ideal. It is not, in other words, a neutral "alternative life choice" of equal value. On the other hand, the same civilization has grown to enshrine individual liberty and equality as essential to justice and holds persecution, particularly for qualities over which an individual has no free choice (skin pigmentation, parentage, etc.) to be unjust. How then in the matter of homosexuality is a society to proceed? And what stand are individuals to take?

The society might try to define sexual orientation as a function of choice and forbid not only homosexual behavior but homosexual feelings; it might accept a person's homosexual orientation but forbid homosexual behavior; it might countenance both orientation and behavior but forbid proselytizing against heterosexual marriage; or it might give up belief in the superior value of heterosexual marriage altogether (as the Roman aristocracy seems to have done at some point before Rome's collapse). Individuals may range in behavior from persecution to laissez-faire disengagement.

The moral path here, which I believe is the middle path, is lit by the golden rule. We ought to do unto others as we would have others do unto us. We don't want others to busy themselves pointing out our failures to live up to moral ideals. Neither do we want them to lie to us by pretending that we have lived up to them when we have not. One must therefore neither persecute one's neighbor for being homosexual nor pretend that homosexual behavior is morally equivalent to marriage (any more than one ought to pretend that pre- or extramarital heterosexual behavior is morally equivalent to marriage). One must treat every human being as one wants to be treated, with both kindness and truth as the situation may demand.

I am not a relativist just because I believe in the universal value of heterosexual marriage even while recognizing that many people cannot achieve it. I am not a relativist just because I maintain that gay marriage is not marriage even while accepting, in the name of justice and kindness, the validity of legal domestic partnerships for homosexuals. A relativist would say, "Do what you want; it doesn't matter." The key here, as in so many modern American dilemmas, is to recognize that equality is not identity, that equal justice under the law cannot abolish nature. There is no good to come of proud, moralistic condemnations of homosexuality.

(Are heterosexuals attracted to the opposite sex because of virtue?) At the same time, a society that has given up on heterosexual marriage by failing to see the essential differences between it and homosexual relationships, like a society that has a 50% divorce rate, like a society that sees children as a time-drain and a cash-drain, like a society that performs millions of abortions each year, like a society that abandons its children to a poisonous entertainment industry or to the culture of the street gang—such a society is in love with death despite the universal moral value that commands us to love life.

I remain a moral absolutist in the sense that I believe in the absolute moral values. But no one in his right mind would claim to know infallibly how to apply those values to all particular situations. The moral life is not easy. We live in shades of gray, believing in the purity of the absolutes, striving to be guided by their light toward the Light.

Sophomore Argument Essays
[October 25, 2007]

Several weeks ago I gave an assignment to my sophomore classes: Write an essay in which you make a persuasive argument about some issue that you care about. No major public issues allowed—the war, immigration, abortion—lest the arguments descend to warmed-over popular clichés. Only something you are personally involved with and know something about.

When the essays came in, I saw a trend:

"The amount of homework at our school should be reduced."
"The school week should be four days."
"Teachers should not assign busywork."
"There should be no homework over vacations."
"School should start later in the day."
"There should be no homework on the days before athletic games."
"Students should be able to take courses in subjects that interest them instead of required courses."
"Having more electives better prepares students to find their life direction and career choice."

I have partly to agree with some of these theses: Students have better things to do than busywork—assignments with little or no educational value. If students work hard during the academic year, relaxation on vacations should be part of their reward. Students in upper grades should have some opportunity to take elective courses in addition to required ones. And a later start to the day would be a blessing to all—if only sports teams could be persuaded to give up a comparable amount of afternoon practice time.

But two assumptions common in my sophomores' essays were troubling: a) students know better than teachers what students should be learning, and b) less work and fewer required courses would make for a better life.

Not too surprisingly, considering the age of the writers, the idea that adults might know better than children what prepares children best for life did not appear in any of the essays. But neither did the idea that excellence requires sacrifice. The notion that, given a limited number of hours in the day, one might have to give up a degree of academic excellence or mastery of skills in order to gain more time for sports, fun, or "just hanging out with friends" did not occur to any of the young authors, though they felt acutely that doing homework and sitting in classes significantly impinges on athletics, recreation, and "just hanging out."

When I was in graduate school in the 1970s, I ran across a similar attitude, but there the relaxationists were members of the faculty. Like other universities, mine had suffered from the student revolutionary fervor of the late 1960s, and the graduate English faculty, succumbing to the call for greater relevance, had revised its curriculum such that candidates for the MA and PhD degrees had but one required course—how to do research. We were free to elect or bypass any other class so long as we completed the requisite total number of classes. It became possible to earn a PhD in English and American Literature without ever having taken a course in Shakespeare.

In various forums I would challenge the powers: "You are the professors; we are the students. It is your responsibility to tell us what we ought to know in order to earn the degree you are granting us." But they had been too much battered by students more forceful than I to return to hierarchical and paternalistic ideas of education. "Personally I think you should probably take courses X and Y, but take whichever you like and we'll see how it goes."

Now many of my sophomore students seem to think that much of high school history, English, math, science, foreign language, art, and music can be dispensed with in favor of psychology, computer graphics, and pre-engineering, as the student's interest may dictate. One student held that if a student is interested in biology, it is unfair and counterproductive to force him or her to study physics too.

This mentality is partly a result of the wrong kind of pressure on students, from parents and peers' parents, to think about careers and future earning power, and hence to specialize too soon. It claims justification from the mistaken idea that one's career is determined by absolutely autonomous free choice and that therefore the earlier a choice is made the better. In reality, I believe, most who end up having successful careers find them in response to being moved—"called" as people used to say—by the unexpected and often the unimaginable. And how better to prepare them for such a calling than with the skills and knowledge taught in the standard required courses?

What was not in evidence in my sophomores' essays was the awareness that some knowledge and skill in history, English, math, science, foreign language, art, and music will be useful on *any* career path. Still less evident was the idea that education is something more than job training, that it is the only way to fulfill what Aristotle calls man's *telos* or purpose: the proper use of the rational intellect in accordance with virtue.

My dedicated colleagues and I are thus surrounded by lovers of freedom from intellectual and cultural responsibility. Behind us are professors, and before us students, who believe that it is the heirs who should determine whether and how the endowment of centuries should be inherited. If they had their way, none of us might even have heard of Aristotle.

Luckily, however, despite the temper of the times, I and others like me were fortunate to have some professors—the few but honorable bearers of cultural tradition and of the principle of learning for its own, civilization's, and our sakes—who felt obliged to pass on what they had received and took joy in doing so. They expected us to learn as much of what they knew to be important as possible first, and only then to go off on our own to enhance or criticize that body of knowledge as we wished. They were not hesitant to assert the requirements for excellence in their disciplines; neither did they refrain from judging those who chose not to make sacrifices to achieve it.

Thank God for such professors. They set the bar high. And whether or not we have approached it, we have them to thank for knowing where it is.

So will our students if my responsible colleagues and I have anything to say about it. Sophomore arguments or no sophomore arguments, our students have teachers who, if we cannot pass the culture on to them intact, will at least die trying. And if the students want less homework and more leisure and fewer days of school, they can find someone else to tell them their education will not suffer for it. If they stick with us, even their sophomoric arguments for ease had better be written in unified, developed, coherent, clear, honest, grammatical, and, if it please the muse, inspired essays. Their responses to literature had better be based on careful reading and serious thought and be subject to revision based on increasing knowledge. And their drive to master their salaried futures had better be put on hold while they discover to how rich an inheritance they are already the heirs.

To expect anything less of them is to succumb to sophomoric arguments against the principles laid down by our own best teachers, Aristotle included, whose wisdom is rather harder to refute.

Process vs. Product
[February 4, 2008]

In an informal conversation at a school function I happened to note the challenges our students face because there is limited space in the regular rotation of required academic courses for arts electives. (The issue was on my mind because we are in the midst of conversations about revising our schedule.) A student artist must often pursue his or her interests with more talent (however little or great that may be) than experience or training. To this observation my well-meaning interlocutor replied, "Well, it's the process, not the product." I left the sentiment unchallenged, admiring the implied commitment to making lemonade from lemons or a silk purse out of a sow's ear or... But the next morning I awoke thinking, "No. If the product doesn't matter, there *is* no process!"

I began to wonder what underlying assumptions about the nature of school and of society lie behind this weighting of process more than product.

Of what value is a process if its reason for being is not also valued? In the absence of product, can process really count? Of course process is meaningful. It matters not only that something is done but how it is done: winning an argument through rhetoric without logic, or winning a game through cheating, is not really winning at all.

But there are limits to the value of process in the absence of valuable product. On the subject of leaving the rearing of young children and moral responsibility to amateurs, G. K. Chesterton wrote, "If a thing is worth doing, it is worth doing badly." Unfortunately, many who quote that quip are too quick to apply it to everything. But some enterprises demand professional product over amateur process. You wouldn't say to your surgeon or your house painter, "If a thing is worth doing, it is worth doing badly." So where is the line between amateur and professional in the matter of the education of children?

Certainly the process of teaching young people to act in a play or paint a painting or dance a ballet or sing an aria is valuable in itself. But its value comes from inspiring in them also a vision of excellence, a longing for quality of product which only quality of process will achieve. Without that vision and that longing, there are no grounds on which the quality of the process can begin to be judged.

Every day, students are motivated to undergo grueling processes in the name of their concept of product. If we teachers value process over product, are we content to be duping our students by allowing them to pretend that the product matters when we ourselves wisely but secretly know that "it's process, not product"? At what point are we to stop lying to them for their own good and confess that what they were aiming to achieve never had more meaning beyond the fact that they were aiming? And why, after that point, should they trust anything else we may say to them?

On the other hand, the sentiment that asserts the value of process over product does have some rational justification. My interlocutor was no doubt trying, by setting a virtuous example, to do his part to correct a culture that measures value by grades, scores, college acceptances, income, and net worth. Here we certainly agree. Quality lies in quality rather than in quantity. In my own English class, as my students hear often repeated, it's the process of reading appreciatively more than the product of getting an A on the test that really matters.

But let us clarify our definitions a little. We should rather say that it is the attainment of the capacity to appreciate literature (product) rather than the taking of reading quizzes (process) that counts. Without the goal of appreciation, the quizzes would be meaningless. The only value of the precise means that is a quiz is the imprecise end that is education. We don't think learning is an expendable excuse for engaging in the valuable process of quizzing. Indeed the very word "learning," being a gerund (that is, a verbal noun), contains both process (its verbal aspect) and product (its noun aspect)—the acquiring of knowledge and the knowledge acquired. Are we to split the unsplittable gerund and say that learning (in the former sense) matters but learning (in the latter) does not?

At a deeper level, the valuing of process over product is an outgrowth of the age of Romantic sensibility, whose doctrines we inherit, consciously and unconsciously. One of them is that nature is process, and is good, and that human departures from nature are error—indeed the only error. Nature doesn't care what comes of what it is doing; it just wants to keep on doing. And human beings, if they're going to be worth anything, need to get back to nature, our mother, our guide, our measure, and our only judge. "Go with the flow." "What's your gut reaction?" "Be true to yourself." "Let nature take its course." "It's genetic." As Rousseau argued: man is naturally good; it is society that corrupts him.

But is this true? Notice that the phrase "if they're going to be worth anything" depends on a doctrine that finds the value of a process in its fruits, not in itself. Even if Rousseau were right, there would be no way to judge whether a person had succeeded in "getting back to nature" or "going with the flow" if we didn't have some consciousness of the difference between natural process and human judgment of results. And on what grounds can Rousseau argue that the most complex social institutions of the world (state, church, and school) are not simply nature doing what it does with human beings? Maybe society is nature's way of getting human beings to "go with the flow."

In any case, the "process not product" sentiment is our attempt, without realizing the consequences, to do to ourselves what cannot be done to a gerund: that is to cut ourselves in half, severing activity from judgment; quantity of process from quality of product; body, sensation, and feeling from mind, aspiration, and virtue, as if we were nothing more than animals or plants with the irrelevant and often irritating appendix called consciousness.

But the severing operation will not work. Cannot work. After a dull and poorly acted play that has bored and exasperated its audience, the cast may stay till the cows come home describing in a forum how moving and profound and illuminating the rehearsal process was. For the audience the experience of the play itself remains unredeemed. The forum itself may become a very entertaining high-quality product, of course, especially for believers in process. But the existence of dull, stale, tired forums refutes the notion that process in itself is enough.

After a lifetime of seeking meaning, a saint might discover that the deepest meaning lay all along in the searching. But do we who are not saints have the right to jump to his conclusion? Or worse, to use his conclusion as an excuse to give up our own search for meaning?

The poet Philip Thompson (in a letter to me dated January 28, 1980) has articulated the truth about process and product, which, in more general philosophical terms, he calls means and ends:

Can a means be employed in the absence of ends? Particular ends are indeed the means to further ends, but each individual end (a house, a marriage, a poem, a farm, a friendship, a meal) must be approached and completed for its own sake before it can be known as a means.

294 | Other Writings

If there are only means, there are only ends, and thus we work in a wilderness of equal and contradictory ends served in conflict, to our mutual confusion. And how would we know that the world itself was not an end if we did not possess an intuition of the end transcending it, and thus of the particular means it is? . . . [C]onsideration of the community's well-being must start with the definition of proper ends (say, *good* houses, *good* poems, *good* farms, *good* meals).

At any given time men's minds bring the same values to the whole variety of their actions. Corruption of craft is the law in a society that does not serve particular luminous ends, and every work made by such a society corresponds to the Navy's meals and houses: "our works are not ends in themselves, they are simply the means of organizing for..."

We need only add ceramic pots, paintings, plays, and choral, instrumental, and dance performances, and athletic contests to Thompson's list to see why the processes of learning, practice, and rehearsal cannot be rightly valued without acknowledgment of the value of *good* pots, *good* paintings, *good* plays, *good* performances, and yes, *good* games. "It matters not whether you win or lose but how you play the game"? Well, after the fact, yes. But the aim to win defines what good athletic practice and good playing mean. (Let no one misunderstand me: I don't mean winning at all costs. Playing dishonestly isn't playing the game at all.)

Human beings find meaning not only in trying to achieve a great performance but in the greatness of the performance achieved. It is the concept of that goal that gives the trying whatever meaning it possesses. There is no serious chef who does not care how the meal finally tastes, no serious violinist who believes the quality of the practice is more valuable than the quality of the performance, no serious writer who doesn't care whether his book ends up being any good. Following Rousseau, as much as we want we can pretend to worship nature and its making; in the end we cannot *not* care about the thing made—what it *is* and whether and how it moves us. It is that caring alone that makes us care how it comes to be.

As every child knows, praise for bad product lavished in the name of fostering self-esteem is hogwash. The child knows it, as we all do within our respective capacities, because human beings are those beings who can tell the difference between bad and good quality, and who love the good. We care about the quality of the things we make and achieve because of the highly unnatural, perhaps supernatural, but in any case uniquely human gift of consciousness that takes the form of a driving and inescapable need to find meaning in things. We will find meaning or die. To the extent that my interlocutor was trying to find meaning in process without product, in activity without purpose, he was trying to do what in reality cannot be done. The meaning of a means lies in whether and how it achieves its ends. Without product, process is futile.

So let us be honest with our students and challenge them to quality process in the name of quality product. Let them strive to make a *good* play or picture or performance, and let us find the time and means to train them in how to do it. The value of our own teaching too lies not alone in putting our students through the process of learning. It lies in the greatest attainable quality of learning—knowledge, understanding, skill, wisdom, and virtue—that they have achieved when our part in the process ends at graduation.

ETs and Environment
[March 17, 2008]

A colleague writes:

> There are more stars in the universe than grains of sand on all the beaches of the earth. Think about that. The only logical conclusion to be drawn from that stat is not merely that there are other "Suns" and "Earths" out there, but billions, if not trillions. What are the odds that not a single one of them developed life, or that a single one of those which developed life did not develop a technological species? For us to assume that we are so special as to be the only "intelligent" species for 13 billion light years is the height of human bombast, and symptomatic of all our other problems—the Medieval notion that we are somehow above nature, or that nature will look out for us because we are so special. Yes, religions teach that, but I could use your demand for proof in reverse: where's the evidence for divine providence? Trillions of trillions of stars make for more hard evidence for proof that life exists throughout the universe than a stack of Bibles or Korans or Torahs can provide for the existence of life on earth only.

My reply:

The "conclusion" that given the hugeness of the universe the odds must be that there is life on other planets is based upon the assumption that life on earth came about by a purely material process entirely accounted for by the laws of physics plus time. This assumption is precisely that, an assumption, unprovable. It is, in more traditional language, an act of faith. If one grants that assumption, your conclusion is perfectly reasonable.

However, since your argument gives no account of how the laws of physics came about, one is permitted by reason to make an alternative assumption, namely that there is a mind—utterly incommensurable with the human mind, and one that seems to have revealed a part of its purpose to human beings in unaccountable ways—behind the very existence of the universe and its laws of physics. Under that assumption, it is equally reasonable to conclude that the universe exists partly in order for our minds to exist and that until and unless we find evidence for life in other worlds, there is no reason to assume its existence.

It does no good for us to argue conclusions unless we can agree on premises. And since our two premises are different and both are unprovable acts of faith, all attempts to convince one another of our opposite conclusions by means of reason are pointless. We must just agree (for the sake of peace, which is both a natural and a moral value) to allow one another our different faiths.

I have never argued that the existence of God can be proven by reason or empirical evidence. On the contrary, my references to empirical evidence are to show that it is not incompatible with either of the above assumptions.

Finally, your attack on the "bombast" of the medieval period is a false accusation. The religious traditions you are attacking (as distinct from some of their ignorant followers) never taught that "nature will look out for us because we are so special" nor that human beings are "somehow above nature"—except in one sense. They taught that we are special precisely because we are not merely nature, that being a combination of nature and spirit, we have duties to behave morally that nothing else in nature has.

In fact, your whole moral passion about saving the natural world from the depravities of man could not exist if it were not built upon the assumption that man has not only a vested interest in treating his environment with respect but also a moral duty to do so. When you labor to make the abusers of earth, air, and water feel guilty for their actions and exhort them in the name of truth and righteousness to go green, you are doing so, like it or not, on the assumption that human beings make choices for which they are morally responsible. If we were merely nature doing its thing, you would have absolutely no grounds for complaining that we are destroying our own environment. So what? Environments change, creatures come into existence and go out of it, and nature continues. Why get worked up about it? But you do, and that is because, will you, nill you, you are a moral being and believe in your heart that it is not only a matter of self-interest to preserve the environment, but a moral obligation to ourselves and our posterity. And about that I agree with you.

As I say, there can be no rational or empirical proof one way or another whether we are merely nature doing its thing or whether we are created to be responsible beings. But whatever you think, you are behaving as if you were the latter and expecting others to behave so too. In this, your character seems to me (given my assumptions) to be superior to your reasoning. To attack the religions that tell man he is a morally responsible being is, in the realm of human decision-making, exactly like attacking the environment that sustains our natural life. It is to cut the ground out from under your own feet.

John Adams on Equality
[May 27, 2008]

Against the argument, made by Anne-Robert-Jacques Turgot, Baron de l'Aulne (1727–1781), for a single legislative body, John Adams argued for a bicameral legislature.[1] In doing so, he considered the question of what is meant by equality in a way that we might all do well to ponder.

> M. Turgot tells us our republics are "founded on the equality of all the citizens, and, therefore, 'orders' and 'equilibriums' are unnecessary, and occasion disputes." But what are we to understand here by equality? Are the citizens to be all of the same age, sex, size, strength, stature, activity, courage, hardiness, industry, patience, ingenuity, wealth, knowledge, fame, wit, temperance, constancy, and wisdom? Was there, or will there ever be, a nation, whose individuals were all equal, in natural and acquired qualities, in virtues, talents, and riches? The answer of all mankind must be in the negative. It must then be acknowledged, that in every state … there are inequalities which God and nature have planted there, and which no human legislator ever can eradicate.
> [In Massachusetts,] there is, it is true, a moral and political equality of rights and duties among all the individuals…; there are, nevertheless, inequalities of great moment in the consideration of a legislator, because they have a natural and inevitable influence in society.

After discussing inequalities of wealth and birth, he adds,

> It will be readily admitted, there are great inequalities of merit, or talents, virtues, services, and what is of more moment, very often of reputation. Some, in a long course of service in an army, have devoted their time, health, and fortunes, signalized their courage

---

1 John Adams, *Defense of the Constitutions of Government of the United States*, 1787.

and address, exposed themselves to hardships and dangers, lost their limbs, and shed their blood, for the people. Others have displayed their wisdom, learning, and eloquence in council, and in various other ways acquired the confidence and affection of their fellow-citizens to such a degree, that the public have settled into a kind of habit of following their example and taking their advice.

There are a few, in whom all these advantages of birth, fortune, and fame are united.

These sources of inequality, which are common to every people, and can never be altered by any, because they are founded in the constitution of nature; this natural aristocracy among mankind, has been dilated on, because it is a fact essential to be considered in the institution of a government. It forms a body of men which contains the greatest collection of virtues and abilities in a free government, is the brightest ornament and glory of the nation, and may always be made the greatest blessing of society, if it be judiciously managed in the constitution. But if this be not done, it is always the most dangerous; nay, it may be added, it never fails to be the destruction of the commonwealth.

What shall be done to guard against it? Shall they be all massacred?

Adams discusses the disastrous consequences of such a policy—we can hardly help thinking of the French Revolution and the likes of Stalin, Mao, and Pol Pot—then goes on to argue for two houses of legislature, a senate made up of that "body of men which contains the greatest collection of virtues and abilities" and a house of the people's representatives, both houses separate from the executive and from the judiciary—the famous balance of powers later established in the U.S. Constitution, largely under Adams' influence.

Hence, as Adams argues, total equality is neither a natural condition nor an absolute ideal. Nor is it the purpose of democratic representative government to secure for its citizens either fantastical goal.

The Declaration of Independence, in stating the revolutionary concept that "all men are created equal," did not mean equal in all ways. It meant that all human beings are created to be equally human beings, equally entitled, therefore, to the fundamental rights with which the Creator has endowed them, among them the right to "life, liberty, and the pursuit of happiness."

But as Larry Arnn, the estimable President of Hillsdale College, has pointed out,[2] those rights, which government exists to secure, themselves depend upon the shared belief in "The Law of Nature and Nature's God." When the shared belief in that foundation declines, how are arguments about what constitutes equality to be settled?

Ignoring all contrary evidence, we steadily expand our illusory faith in our own power to redefine nature. That expansion is fed by a paradoxical combination of two ideas: our increased control of the physical world through machines, and our belief in perpetual evolutionary progress. So we set about gene manipulation, cloning, and sex-change operations. But with every additional declaration of our independence from "The Law of Nature and of Nature's God," the foundation upon which our rights themselves are built is weakened.

Examples abound: Is it a Law of Nature that there will always be rich and poor? Marxism denies it. All people must be equal in wealth. Does Nature's God decree that marriage is a sacred bond between man and woman that cannot apply to two men, two women, men or women and their siblings, men or women and animals, men or women and robots? The movement to legitimize gay marriage—I am not speaking of domestic partnerships—denies it: All people have a right to marry whomever they love. Do the Law of Nature and of Nature's God imply that freedom of religion does not extend to the forced covering of unwilling women (to say nothing of honor killings of unwed pregnant teenage girls)? Certain Islamist fundamentalists couldn't care less. In this we have a real problem, an exaggerated right to freedom of religion coming up against the right to the liberty of dressing as one pleases.

To illustrate the point only partly facetiously: With the ongoing demotion of natural and divine law, what is there to prevent the legally enforced removal of all urinals from men's bathrooms on the grounds that it is unfair for women to have to sit to urinate when men may stand? How dare government not see to it that the lines outside the men's and women's bathrooms at all public concerts and ballgames be equal in length?

John Adams did not have to face precisely these questions because his society still believed almost universally in "The Law of Nature and of Nature's God." But where in our time can we stand to debate these

---

2 Larry Arnn, *Liberty and Learning: The Evolution of American Education* (Hillsdale, MI: Hillsdale College Press, 2004), pages 6, 11.

questions if we cannot begin by agreeing on universal first principles? Equalization of income, gay marriage, purdah, honor killings, the dying in combat of military females, and the competing of biological males in women's sports are claimed to be "rights" under the doctrine of equality.

But the claimants forget, or don't understand, that their concept of equality rests upon still more fundamental ideas which the society that invented them once agreed upon. In the absence of that shared faith in "The Law of Nature and of Nature's God," the very word "rights" becomes nonsense. Rights become merely the self-interests that one group can browbeat another into acknowledging. This is to make the securing of rights into Hobbes's war of all against all.

Fact, Feeling, and Myth
[June 17, 2008]

Being heirs of both the Enlightenment and Romanticism, we suffer from a kind of cultural schizophrenia. We alternate between the conviction that everything can be comprehended rationally through science and the compulsion to escape from the resulting aridity into a world of feeling however fantastically inspired. As if we were two different beings at different times, we might spend countless hours mastering the technical facts about HD plasma TV and then escape into the emotional roller coaster of an adventurous, romantic, or violent movie.

This condition is an extension of the natural difference between our reason and our emotions. But it is pathological to the extent that, in the absence of a unifying principle of meaning, the two parts of ourselves are not related in fruitful tension but divorced. By day in the lab we think of the unborn fetus as two accidentally joined cells subdividing according to the laws of physics, chemistry, and biology that we know. By night at home we feel empty without the caress of an unconditional love. Rarely do we consider how both can be true of the same being. Our humanity is thus reduced to an unsteady either/or state.

Yet our nature being what it is, we crave to transcend this schism between facts and feelings. We want to be whole, fully human beings, even as we discredit the very things that have the power to unify us.

One of the contributors to the schism is our daily exposure to the cliché antithesis between "myth" and "fact." Every political partisan, science journalist, and commodity advertiser will one time or another try to shame us into abandoning the myth (meaning a falsehood) for the fact (meaning what he wants us to believe instead). Examples taken almost at random: "King Tut Curse: Myth or Fact?" (ThinkQuest NYC); "Is it myth or fact? Take our *MythBusters* quizzes to find out" (Discovery Channel website).

We impoverish ourselves by the erroneous notion that the ancient Greek myths were childish ways of "explaining" phenomena that "we now know" are caused by this or that principle of physics. Thus ancient myth is relegated to the category of falsehood and then co-opted by the sentimentality of HBO or Disney.

Similarly impoverished are the kinds of religious fundamentalist and the kinds of scientific atheist who read the Bible entirely literally. The former has such faith in the literal historicity of the Bible that he may reject much true scientific knowledge; the latter has equal faith that disproving the Bible's literal historicity is grounds for rejecting biblical religion altogether. Call the Bible "myth" and the former is offended, the latter delighted, because both take the word "myth" to mean "falsehood" and both, in different ways, worship factuality.

The profoundest vehicles of human insight are thus banished before the reductive, either/or choice between hard facts and wishful thinking. We are bounced between dissolving skepticism and sentimental credulity, left to embrace now an emotionless reason that banishes faith, now an emotional faith that flies in the face of reason.

The beginning of healing may lie in recognizing that in reality, myth is not always the enemy of fact. It can be the vehicle of the significance of facts. Nor is it always the servant of feeling. It can be the vehicle of authenticity of feelings. Myths can have the power to engage both reason and emotion, both knowledge and imagination, in a unifying and transcending experience of meaning. Whatever the art form in which they are represented (drama, fiction, poetry, painting, sculpture, music, dance, architecture, film, cartoon, advertising, etc.), myths are valuable because they illuminate realities that engage our whole selves, realities whose meanings cannot be conveyed in any other way.

Consider the familiar sort of myth depicted in the TV automobile commercial. The newest car, the complex product of science and technology, races at high speed through a pristine romantic wilderness somewhere in Utah. Here the mythic image temporarily unites our rational and romantic sides in a single experience that we cannot find in our own lives either by owning a car or by traveling to Utah or both. We can buy the car, but in it we'll as often as not be sitting in a freeway traffic jam. We can head for the Utah wilds, but we'll soon face the cold-turkey terrors of separation from the familiar machine that got us there, not to mention from the computer, the telephone, the water heater, and the light bulb, let alone the flush toilet.

But the myth imaged in the ad gives us the thrill of a desired union of technology and nature unencumbered by deer crossings, power lines, and cops, the thrill of an imaginary redemption from our divided selves.

Is the myth depicted in that TV commercial true? The answer depends on what we mean by "true." The image depicted cannot be realized in practice. But what moves us more—our own car or the commercial? Our car of course moves us physically. But the myth we may carry in our minds for days or weeks or even a lifetime, and it will influence not only our purchase of a car and our vacation plans but our very concept of what constitutes joy.

This kind of myth—driving fast through perfect wilderness in a perfect vehicle—is a self-evident fantasy, bounded not only by practical impossibility (and therefore potentially arousing more frustration than satisfaction), but also by time, place, and culture. Powerful though it is for a modern American, the automobile ad would probably mean very little to an eighteenth-century or a twenty-third-century American, or to a Bedouin or a Sherpa.

But consider the myth of Narcissus or of the serpent in the Garden of Eden. Such myths as these transcend not only our rational knowledge and our personal feelings but our time, our place, our language, and our culture because they go to the heart of what human beings are. They remind us that whatever we understand and however we feel, we are part of a larger reality than we can contain, and yet a reality revealed and accessible to anyone who knows the story.

If we try to say exactly *what* we know from a great myth, we find it impossible. Good luck trying to express in your own words the meaning of the disaster of self-love or of the temptation to be like God in knowing good and evil. You will soon find that any way of articulating such realities falls short of what is conveyed by the myth itself. We may analyze, synthesize, emphasize, and formulate. Nothing gets at the reality like simply retelling the mythic story. But tell the story of Narcissus or of the temptation of Eve and—presto!—the reality is revealed in all its glory and terror.

Is the story of Narcissus true? Is the fall from Eden? Far truer than the evening news. But to ask whether or not in historical time there was ever a boy named Narcissus who fell in love with his own image in a pool, like demanding the medical records of his wasting away, would be absurd. To prove and to disprove his historicity would be equally empty. The authenticity of the myth itself commands us more powerfully than any documentary evidence could do. Similarly, to discover whether our DNA can be traced back to one male and one female human being would be as insignificant as asking for videotape of the serpent whispering to Eve. What could such paltry facts offer in the face of the story of Eden, with its profound implications for our understanding of the meaning of ourselves, life, free will, suffering, and death?

A few weeks ago, walking home from the park with my dog, I was struck by the thought that the most amazing phenomenon in the universe—more amazing than the hydrogen fusion reaction on which all physical life on earth depends, more amazing even than the fact of human consciousness—is the fact that human consciousness can and does conceive of non-physical, non-temporal meaning—transcending but revealed in the facts and feelings of our lives. That is, we are compelled to find in a thing or an action or an experience its quality—whether it is good or bad, fair or unfair, kind or cruel, true or false, deep or shallow, beautiful or ugly—and its significance, its place in the invisible pattern of all things that are.

It is to that apparently miraculous activity of the human mind—the pursuit of meaning—that myth speaks, carrying us beyond our reductive either/or limitations and putting us in touch with reality, whose mystery we can experience but never comprehend.

Choosing a Religion, Ethical Dilemmas, and Just War
[July 20, 2008]

I recently received questions on these three topics from a student on a spiritual search.

> [T]his summer I'd been "shopping" for a religion until [in one of your classes a student] asked you how one should "find" a tradition if one was not raised within a religion. Following your advice that "no birth is an accident" and that one should figure out where one comes from, I did a little research of my own; it ends up nearly all of my ancestors on my dad's side are Lutheran. All this surprised me, since my birth has generally been called an accident and I'd thought I'd come from a fairly agnostic family... I met with a Lutheran pastor in La Jolla and attended services, and since then I've started reading some Lutheran/Christian texts, but I'm wondering if you have any more advice for me, in terms of "finding" a tradition to belong to. I feel like I'm kind of copping out on my "spiritual quest" or whatever you want to call it by just conveniently choosing a religion some people related to me were associated with. It seems too easy and too intellectual and I'm not sure my heart's in it.

The problem with "choosing a religion" is that the grounds upon which you can choose are functions of religious beliefs, even if they are not formal. Let's say you reject Hinduism because of its belief in reincarnation. Well, on what grounds do you not believe in reincarnation? You are already the product of a civilization that rejects the idea of reincarnation and has influenced you in that rejection. But if a Hindu says "On what grounds do you reject reincarnation?" and you say "I have no religion, so I don't know," then how can you justify rejecting Hinduism? Or embracing it for that matter?

My point is simply that it is not really possible to exist so far out of a religious tradition that in the matter of "choosing a religion" you don't have some preexisting elements of faith. If you didn't, you'd have to choose every religion or none, since the judgment of any implies the pre-existing faith in at least some of the tenets of it or of another. And of course "none" isn't possible either. As my teacher Mary Holmes used to say, "All human beings worship. The only question is what they worship."

I think you have begun well. Read those Lutheran texts and see to what degree they speak to you. And I would also suggest that you work backward and read the Christian documents that Luther was revising so you can decide whether his revolution or that which he was revolting against rings more true. You have already seen what Dante has to say. I suggest you read the Gospels, and St. Paul's letters, and the writings of St. Augustine (in particular his *Confessions* and his *City of God*), and then read about St. Francis, and the writings of St. Thomas Aquinas and St. Bonaventure. Then you will be able to see what it is that Luther is particularly energized about. And then you will slowly grow to increasing recognition of where in the tradition you yourself might belong.

> I sure wouldn't have believed it maybe three years ago but more and more lately I've found myself defending your (and C. S. Lewis's) positions to other students here at college—advocates of atheism, utilitarianism, Objectivism. More often than not they attack me with some sort of "thought experiment" like the following: "You must torture and kill one person in order to save an entire city from destruction—what do you do?" And I can't on earth figure out how I'm supposed to answer this sort of question. They all remind me a lot of "Sophie's Choice" which you mentioned ... a long time ago, but that doesn't get me any closer on figuring out how to answer or respond to these types of intellectual challenges. Any thoughts?

I'm very glad that you are defending the rational and true position of ultimate values rather than succumbing to the pressure of the fuzzy-minded crowds.

The first thing to say about the kind of test question they "attack" you with (and it is an attack, because they themselves would not want to be faced with such a question), is that the prior question is why they are asking it. Is it a real desire to know the truth, or is it a scoffer's challenge (like the jailer's question of the rebbe in prison in the first chapter of

Martin Buber's *The Way of Man According to the Teaching of Hasidism*: trying to trip him up with a question from the Bible)?

The second thing to say is that if the questioner does not share your belief in fundamental and ultimate universal values, then the question is pointless. Whether you say "do the torture" or "don't do the torture," the relativist questioner has no grounds for approving or disapproving of your answer because he has rejected *both* the principle of "do unto others as you would have them do unto you" *and* the principle of "he who saves a life is as if he has saved the whole world" (in their various versions). In other words, the question whether you're allowed to cause one man to suffer to save many other men can only have any meaning to someone who believes it is wrong to harm others unjustly and it is right to protect innocents from harm. If you don't believe in those absolute values, you have no moral grounds for preferring one answer of the question to another.

The truth is that only with someone who agrees on the fundamental values and on their universality can engaging in a discussion of the torture question be worth anything. It's like trying to sue in court someone who does not believe in the rule of law.

The real response to such a challenge is to ask the challenger on what grounds he stands to condemn torturers or innocent village destroyers if he doesn't believe in universal moral values? Why *not* torture someone or kill innocents if all values are relative? Then you will come to the real difference of opinion, which makes the question he initially asked trivial by comparison. And you will usually find that he is a relativist when it suits him and an absolutist when it suits him. He's a relativist when he's afraid you are going to hold him to some standard of value, and he's an (illogical) absolutist in being against all moral absolutes.

A central business of human life is to apply the universal values we believe in to each particular situation as it arises. Each such application is a test of what we are and what we believe. And we make our choices not knowing the "answers," not knowing whether we have passed the test of being judgment-making creatures. But we must judge anyway, and we *will* judge, whatever we think, and so we are taking the test, whether we like it or not, despite not knowing anything about how it will turn out. It's what human beings do.

The clear-thinking person strives to discern and then to do the right thing, though it isn't clear or easy. The confused person pretends there are no values to go by and so it doesn't matter and, in practice, judges that it is "better" to avoid making any moral judgments at all. This is a great way of pretending to get off the hook, except that it can't really work, because a) he himself has surrendered any grounds for justifying that "better," and b) in a moral crisis, all decent, non-pathological human beings would recognize who is the more admirable: the man who strives to do good, even at great personal sacrifice, or the man who avoids making a decision and runs from it instead.

Finally, we have been given a long history of wisdom to help us. We know the universal values, and we are *in* the particular situations of our lives. Those are givens. But we also have great men and women and their sayings to guide us in making our decisions. We have Moses and Maimonides and the Baal Shem Tov; we have Socrates and Plato and Aristotle; we have Jesus and Augustine and Aquinas and Francis and Bonaventure; we have Confucius and Lao Tzu, the Bhagavad Gita and the Buddha, Kant and Pascal, Dante and Shakespeare, Austen and Dickinson, C. S. Lewis and Viktor Frankl and Martin Buber.

And we also have one another: I mean those among our relatives and friends and teachers whom we admire and trust and whose own experience often can shed light on the difficulties of the decisions we must make.

Hence we do not have to invent reality for ourselves. Some of these guides speak to us more clearly, more relevantly than others. But the fact that in the abstract one cannot answer the kind of question the challenger asks is no evidence whatsoever for there being no better way to act, and no worse way, in a real-life situation.

> Finally, just war. I've read Buber's letter to Gandhi which you mentioned in Humanities, and I really want to say that war is justified in some cases, but how can you send people off to war when you know that some civilians/innocents will inevitably be killed? How can that be a just war?

The question presumes that we live in a perfect and just world and that if we behave justly, no harm will be done. But this is a false premise. The world is not Eden. It is flawed or fallen or troubled with man's sin, however you want to describe it, and goodness in the world can only ever be an approximation unless one is especially gifted with vision and grace (like Socrates or Jesus or St. Francis or the Baal Shem Tov). Again, one must make judgments. No just person wants innocents to be harmed in war. And yet, though war will inevitably harm some number of innocents, not to go to war may be a far worse choice, resulting in far worse consequences to innocents.

There is a wonderful speech on this subject in Act IV, Scene i, of Shakespeare's *Henry V*. On the night before the battle of Agincourt, one of the soldiers says, in the hearing of the disguised king, that the king will have a lot to answer for because men are going to die. Henry muses then on the king's purpose in going to war (not that his men should be killed) and on the responsibility of each individual soldier for the state of his own soul. It's worth reading.

Any ruler, any people who are voting, *must* consider all consequences and alternatives in every case. But anyone who makes a blanket statement about all wars being immoral, while strictly speaking correct because it would be better if war were not necessary, is denying reality if he cannot also recognize that sometimes war is the more moral choice.

If the choice is between conquering a neighboring town in order to get more land or striving to live as well as possible within one's own boundaries, of course war is the immoral choice. But if the choice is between surrendering the values of justice, liberty, and the rule of law to a conquering tyrant, then not to go to war against him is the immoral choice.

Here again, we must return to the fundamental values and use them as guides to see through the confusing facts of the situation we are in. And of course, we never have the benefit of hindsight when we are making such decisions. They are always an approximation, the best we can do in the circumstances. But that is just what is wanted: the *best* we can do, not just any old thing. (For inspiration here, read the great speeches of Winston Churchill.)

[How can we] reconcile what look like impossible paradoxes[?]

The key thing here is to be very clear about what the paradoxes really are, and then to accept that we must all learn to live with paradox. Paradox is the nature of the world from the viewpoint of man. We are male and female, we want to live and know we will die, we have both selfish and generous impulses in us, we crave meaning and want not to be judged, we have faith and we have doubt. This is the human condition, and I think that no human meaning or energy would be possible if we were not paradoxical beings. But it means there is no single, simple, easy rule to follow in all circumstances that will never lead astray. Always what is required is engagement of the whole self, all we are and all we know and all we believe, all our virtue, in making the decisions we are called upon to make. And that is the true path through life, and I believe the ultimately rewarded path: the path of meaning and the path most pleasing to God.

Studying History
[July 31, 2008]

One of my former students writes the following:

> I've always liked studying history, but it's only recently that I've started to develop actual historical perspective.
>
> An example: I can't remember who exactly said it, but one of the high-ranking admirals in Japan said, after Pearl Harbor, 'I fear we have awoken a sleeping giant.'
>
> Of course it was true, but my historical study (too much of an emphasis on facts I believe) left out the really important part of that statement, that it was a perceptive analysis, and not at all obvious at the time. Only by mentally putting myself into that time frame, while simultaneously suppressing my knowledge of the future, can I really gain some insight into the past...
>
> [L]ack of historical study really hinders us as a society. I think it's especially detrimental to youth, as I felt as I was growing up that all the news and situations in the world at large were bad, and that the reality of any given time was that things are bad now, and they are probably as bad as they have ever been.
>
> I guess what I'm trying to get at is that the past doesn't easily resonate in me, and that's kind of scary. I can spend lots of time learning about ancient Rome, or the Aztecs, but I don't instinctively feel that I am the inheritor of this vast tract of human experience—really, I feel that all that has come before me seems to barely influence me at all. And I feel that this is common in my generation, and perhaps in others. Rather than enjoying our new paths in art and science as additions to the vastness of human experience, I get the feeling that I'm subsisting just on the new as its own, rather than the newest chapter in an epic tale. The feeling that new is good, not because it's better, but because it's all we have.
>
> And I see this extending into avenues besides history and literature appreciation. Particularly in technology this disdain for

the past is rampant. What's heralded today as groundbreaking is mocked tomorrow as archaic.

This is really scary now that I consider it—if we don't appreciate and understand where we have come from, and what is good in that, how can we say that we have gone anywhere? If it's all just a set of discrete points not connected, how can any one point be said to be anything other than that, a random point?

What I'm really going for, I think, is that without the past, my future is pretty much dead. If I don't have Plato and Shakespeare to learn from and build off of, how will I ever better myself in my humanity? To hope that I am some incredibly lucky person who just manages to fit all the pieces of life and meaning together in one lifetime?

Hmmm, maybe that's the really scary thing about my generation, this undercurrent of individuality, that all accomplishments and discoveries must be made yourself, and that study of the past or learning from past masters is useless without the discovery on your own. It's that vibe I seem to feel from this age that worries me—that humanity is just one large rat chasing its own tail for all eternity, refusing to learn from the past out of pride.

Then again, I'm guessing life has always been like this. And rather than worry that my peers aren't reading Plato, I should get to reading myself!

My response:

What you have very truly written can hardly be bettered. The essential thing to add is that your worry about this renunciation of the past is itself a sign that not all is lost. It shows that you don't believe humanity is only a rat. One need only renounce that vibe and try to discern what we are that is *not* the rat, and behold!—the tail-chasing is revealed as a disguise behind which the inquiring mind may catch a glimpse of the unclear but inescapably meaningful story of man.

You are quite right about your generation's apparent divorce from history—real divorce being impossible. Every generation feels something like this. Every age of serious intellectual activity strives to improve on the past, one among many examples being the turning of attention from heaven to earth in the Renaissance: from halos and gold backgrounds to linear perspective and blue sky, from pointed to rounded arches, from *Everyman* to *Hamlet*.

However, not everyone has shared our modern idea of entirely divorcing the present from the past, which is far more extreme. That idea (ironically) is inherited from the age of the American and French revolutions, when the worship of human progress as an inevitable natural phenomenon rose to preeminence in the writings of Enlightenment *philosophes* like Condorcet and of the Romantic Rousseau. In the nineteenth century it took firm hold in the ideas of Darwin, Marx, and many others. Thus it is from the relatively recent past that we inherit our contempt for the past, though the historically untutored don't know it.

In some ways, of course, we are indeed superior to our forebears. The progress of scientific and technological knowledge (not considering social effects) is irrefutable. Computers get smaller and more powerful, and we can go to the moon and back. We abandon older machines for new ones as the fifth-century Greeks melted down archaic bronze statues for material to make what hindsight now calls "developed" sculptures, some of the greatest ever made by human beings. Progress seems to be the way of the world.

Seems. Because technology is so forceful a piece of evidence—every new machine more amazing than the last—people think that (to paraphrase Émile Coué) every day, in *every* way, we are getting better and better (my italics). (Coué's method of autosuggestion shows him to be a true heir of Condorcet, who believed that by the power of reason and science man would soon conquer all obstacles to happiness, including death.)

The rub is that though we can spend a lifetime autosuggesting our own improvement, we can't *feel* that we are getting better in every way. There's a bit too much contrary evidence. Some of those Greek bronzes of the highest period were themselves no doubt melted down to make way for inferior later works in which we can see the signs of cultural decay. In recent decades we have tossed away representational drawing and painting for abstract expressionism, unflagging Dada, and museum pieces involving urine and feces. At my last school taking roll by computer made life easier for the attendance secretary, but it diverted my attention during three of the five daily homeroom minutes from my students to the screen. Newer is better for a while, and then it is worse. The trick is to be able to see the difference in one's own time.

American democratic government and the rule of law are certainly advances over any political forms known in the past. But the last century also saw by far the worst depravities that human beings have ever enacted. In terms of individual human happiness, it's probably a toss-up: we are certainly more physically comfortable (though inhabitants of Darfur and North Korea are not), but we suffer from a severe shortage of ultimate meaning (though there are always some who can find meaning in any here-and-now moment).

The truth is that in some things we progress and in others we don't, and that, as Santayana said, "Those who cannot remember the past are condemned to repeat it." But it's more than that. It is almost impossible for those who do not live responsibly with the past and the future to have a meaningful present. As you wrote so insightfully, "if we don't appreciate and understand where we have come from, and what is good in that, how can we say that we have gone anywhere? If it's all just a set of discrete points not connected, how can any one point be said to be anything other than that, a random point?"

The poet Philip Thompson observed, analogously, that if the work week is a hell whose only solace is anticipation of the weekend, then the weekend is equally a hell whose torture is the anticipation of Monday morning. Only some concept of Sabbath, that is, of a relation between time and spirit, redeems the weekend from mere escapism and the work week from mere drudgery. Likewise, if the past is nothing but what needs to be got out of the way so that we can enjoy the present, then the present is nothing but one more bit to be got out of the way. In fact, from such a perspective there really is no way at all.

Without learning what has been excellent in the past and the ways in which we are both the fruition and the disappointment of past hopes, nothing of the "better" that we hope for our own future can be more significant than a deluding fancy. Only our participation in the human story, which is more than the mere succession of meaningless pasts giving way to new but equally meaningless futures, weaves our lives into a larger fabric of significance.

But such participation is extremely difficult in our supposedly post-historical time. All cultures live upon the lore of the past as conveyed in ritual and story. But most of our rituals and stories promote the value of unexamined technical or natural progress with no spiritual meaning in sight. Notice the TV commercial, our society's most pervasive medium for communicating what is important to it, in which what sells (besides sex) is newness. And the institutions charged with preserving knowledge of the past—academy, library, museum—are now largely in the hands of those whose only use for the past is as a trash can. Few and far between are the teachers and curators for whom the past is the repository of those "monuments of unaging intellect" that teach our souls to sing (as in the Yeats poem "Sailing to Byzantium").

To complicate things, there is no single objective past to which anyone has access. Every history is a version of reality as perceived by a limited mind or group of minds. Believers understand that the whole story of the world, past, present, and future, and therefore of ourselves and our place in that story, can be known entirely only to God. Hence studying the past is always a matter of approaching the truth without ever totally comprehending it. As Wendell Berry has said, "we can't comprehend what comprehends us."[1]

Given the predispositions of our time, rightly reclaiming our inheritance of the past is not easy. It requires the same precious gifts that any good work requires: insight and imagination, talent and skill, conviction and humility, wisdom and love of truth—above all, vision.

Nonetheless, as Socrates said and exemplified, we must never give up pursuing the truth. In that pursuit, even if we fail, we shall become better human beings than those who, daunted by the impossibility of complete success, never even try.

Finally, a little lesson in the importance of facts in your study of history: Here's what Wikipedia has to say about the quotation that got you thinking on this subject:

> Japanese Admiral Isoroku Yamamoto is portrayed in the 1970 film *Tora! Tora! Tora!*, as saying after his attack on Pearl Harbor, "I fear all we have done is to awaken a sleeping giant and fill him with a terrible resolve." The supposed quotation was abbreviated in the film *Pearl Harbor* (2001), where it merely read, "I fear all we have done is to awaken a sleeping giant."
>
> Neither *At Dawn We Slept*, written by Gordon Prange, nor *The Reluctant Admiral*, the definitive biography of Yamamoto in English by Agawa Hiroyu[ki], contains the line.
>
> Randall Wallace, the screenwriter of *Pearl Harbor*, readily admitted that he copied the line from *Tora! Tora! Tora!*. The director of the movie *Tora! Tora! Tora!*, Richard Fleischer, stated that while Yamamoto may never have said those words, the film's producer,

---

1 See footnote, page 78.

Elmo Williams, had found the line written in Yamamoto's diary. Williams, in turn, has stated that Larry Forrester, the screenwriter, found a 1943 letter from Yamamoto to the Admiralty in Tokyo containing the quotation. However, Forrester cannot produce the letter, nor can anyone else, American or Japanese, recall or find it.

In *The Reluctant Admiral*, Hiroyuki Agawa, without a citation, does give a quotation from a reply by Admiral Yamamoto to Ogata Taketora on January 9, 1942, which is strikingly similar to the famous version: "A military man can scarcely pride himself on having 'smitten a sleeping enemy'; it is more a matter of shame, simply, for the one smitten. I would rather you made your appraisal after seeing what the enemy does, since it is certain that, angered and outraged, he will soon launch a determined counterattack."

Yamamoto believed that Japan could not win a protracted war with the United States, and moreover seems to have believed that the Pearl Harbor attack had become a blunder—even though he was the person who came up with the idea of a surprise attack. *The Reluctant Admiral* relates that "Yamamoto alone" (while all his staff members were celebrating) spent the day after Pearl Harbor "sunk in apparent depression." He is also known to have been upset by the bungling of the Foreign Ministry which led to the attack happening while the countries were technically at peace, thus making the incident an unprovoked sneak attack that would certainly enrage the enemy.

The line serves as a dramatic ending to the attack, and may well have encapsulated some of his real feelings about it, but it has yet to be verified.

There is no doubt more to the story, but I quote the passage to suggest how studying the past may deepen understanding. The phrase you remembered may be based on historical evidence of Yamamoto's prescience; it is certainly historical evidence of the moviemaker's justifiable pride in America.

Nonetheless, your insight stands: To study history well requires getting imaginatively into the minds and situations of past thinkers, who had, as we have now, to think and act without benefit of hindsight.

One more thing: You confess to a lack of an instinct for inheriting the past. This makes sense. Interest in the past is a function not of instinct but of intellect in the service of values. Most people have little enough impulse to enter even into the perspective of their nearest neighbor. But why should instinct be our only, or even our main, guide? When you do get back to reading Plato, you'll find that in *The Republic* he helps to place instinct in right relation to reason: Let the mind's wisdom temper the body's impulses through the courageous discipline of the heart. Only then will justice—including our justice to the past and the future—appear.

Free Will and Determinism
[September 9, 2008]

A student of mine now at Princeton sends a link to a long discussion of free will and determinism (in an article called "Luck Swallows Everything" no longer accessible to me) that attempts an analysis of possible rational positions on the subject: we have no free will; we have some free will; we have absolute free will. After pages of Enlightenment argument, exhausting in trying to be exhaustive, the article concludes with a Romantic implication: truth is a matter of individual opinion. This is what happens when one worships human reason. The most annoying passages in the article attempt to assess whether we have "ultimate responsibility" for our choices, as if human free will could ever be ultimate. (However we have come into being, we have certainly not created ourselves.)

Such a discussion may be useful for intellectual training. It is not a path to truth. Here are my own guidelines for thinking about free will and predetermination:

1. *Oedipus Rex* is the extra-biblical world's most powerful articulation of the relation between free will and fate, which, in a mystery, are one. Reading it is humbling tonic.

2. In *The Ethics of the Fathers*, Rabbi Akiba says, "All is foreseen and free choice is given…" He is asserting that God (the only possible bearer of "ultimate responsibility") foresees everything *and* gives man free will. The implication of this condensed statement is that we live in mystery and must live with paradox, and that our mission is not to solve the mystery or resolve the paradox but to choose the good. The sentence concludes, "and the world is judged by goodness and all is according to the amount of work." That is, God is good in his judgment and rewards virtuous deeds, assertions that would be pointless if we had no free will.

3. Dante agrees. In the *Paradiso* he asserts that free will is God's greatest gift to man, that God predestines all things, and that no

created being can comprehend the divine predestination or its relation to our free will.

4. Milton agrees. In *Paradise Lost*, he asserts that God's foreknowledge does not limit man's freedom of choice, the only basis for the justice of reward and punishment, whether human or divine.

5. The modern concept of predetermination depends on the belief that all events are physical, every event being a deterministic function of all previous physical events. But since it is not provable or disprovable that all reality is comprehended by the physical universe, the actual existence of free will remains a matter of faith, not knowledge. The strictly deterministic science of physics itself arrives at quantum theory, which paradoxically contradicts absolute physical determinism. (Jeffrey Satinover argues in *The Quantum Brain* that quantum indeterminacy may be the very locus of our freedom.)

6. Belief in the absence of human free will goes against the mainstream of Western intellectual and religious tradition, and the question of the precise relation of free will to determinism is a profound mystery that cannot be solved by the human mind. (Those who think otherwise, despite their apparent commitment to Enlightenment rationality, are fantasizing.)

7. My teacher Mary Holmes said, "It doesn't matter whether we actually have free will; we *think* we do." We experience ourselves as making choices, an experience not altered by imagining the choices to be illusory. Every participant in the colloquy, however deterministic his abstract picture of reality, will nonetheless be living in practice under the assumption that he is making free choices. Thus it seems silly to embrace a philosophical position that posits that a universal foundation of the thought and behavior of actual human beings—even determinists—is an empty shell. One might as soon believe that desire, language, or breathing were illusory. My advice is to laugh at them.

California's Proposition 8 and the Meaning of Marriage
[November 9, 2008]

I believe in equal justice under the law for same-sex couples. But more is being demanded. We are told that we must call same-sex unions "marriage" and that not to do so is discriminatory injustice.

Since California law already secures for same-sex couples all legal rights enjoyed by married couples, the desire to redefine marriage must arise from the longing for people with a same-sex orientation to feel socially indistinguishable from people with an opposite-sex orientation. Not equality but identity is desired for same-sex couples by those who oppose Proposition 8 (which sought to define marriage in California as between a man and a woman, was passed by the voters, and was later rendered moot by the Supreme Court). This desire to be considered normal is understandable, and in some ways I sympathize. Who would want oneself or a relative or friend to be deprived of something so profoundly meaningful as marriage? Nonetheless, given our natures, defining same-sex unions as marriage in order to avoid feelings of exclusion is an impossible and ultimately an undesirable goal.

The goal is impossible because sex and sexual orientation matter. They do not justify injustice, but neither are they irrelevant when it comes to marriage. Sexuality is so rooted in us that the differences between same-sex and opposite-sex orientation, like the differences between male and female, cannot be willed into insignificance without violence to our inner lives. We might want to re-order our society to eliminate all reproductive, legal, social, emotional, and psychic differences between the sexes and between sexual orientations. But to pretend that we can actually do so is to sacrifice truth to wishful thinking. We may fear and hate, or accept and celebrate, the powerful mystery of such differences, but short of remaking humanity in the manner of Huxley's *Brave New World*, we cannot eliminate it.

The goal is undesirable because marriage is not merely the name for a set of variable historical phenomena. Marriage as defined by the wisdom of civilized traditions is an ideal, an image of the best, most perfect way that human beings may live in the physical body in the world and in society. It is an image of the uniting of all parts of the self by uniting the self in a relationship with another who is both similar and opposite. My teacher used to say that all creation comes by the union of opposites. She meant not only the union of the opposite sexes in reproduction, but of opposite qualities (light/dark, tension/relaxation, movement/stasis, etc.) in works of art, opposite experiences (comedy/tragedy, day/night, puzzlement/enlightenment, etc.) in the mental life, opposite characteristics (daring/careful, rational/passionate, tender/strong, etc.) in human relationships.

Marriage is the archetypal union of opposites: of yin and yang, of heart and mind, of body and soul, of past and future, of temporality and permanence, of the personal and the social, of all that we mean by femininity and masculinity (however mixed in particular selves), of sexual desire and satisfaction, of physical need and help, in the union of two who love one another as individuals physically, emotionally, and rationally, and as potentially fruitful representatives of the past and future of any community. It is the greatest example of the principle of sublimation, in the pre-Freudian sense of the word, of the raising up of all that is lower and including it in the higher. It is an incarnation of the sacramental principle of life, according to which it is man's function to embrace the here-and-now moment and to hallow it.

Homosexuality as a fact of the psyche is a human variation to be acknowledged and accepted and, as an aspect of the individuals we love, embraced. But only heterosexuality makes possible the realization of the potential in marriage.

To many, the above image of marriage will seem like old-fashioned balderdash. That is precisely the problem. The truth of this image of marriage is opaque to those whose imaginations rule out the sacramental in life as purely imaginary. In order to make marriage available to same-sex relationships, they redefine it as a property agreement or a merely personal choice, reducing it from a universal ideal to a social tool of the desiring self.

Yet even such secularists believe in the sacred without knowing they do. They believe in the sacredness of equality and of emotion. Raised to believe in the unlimited reach of human reason and in the unquestioned validity of natural feelings, they cannot see why marriage cannot apply to same-sex couples, since it is nothing but a practical social construct built either on the ownership of property (as reason says) or on the personal desire for love and companionship (as the feelings say). Under these assumptions, the position is perfectly understandable, as is the belief that any opposition to it could only arise from injustice (bad reason) or bigotry (bad feelings).

But if equality and good feelings are sacred, then so are truth and humility. If it is wrong to persecute minorities, then it is wrong to pretend a lie. C. S. Lewis has written (in *The Abolition of Man*), "For the wise men of old the cardinal problem had been how to conform the soul to reality, and the solution had been knowledge, self-discipline, and virtue. For magic and applied science [and, we may add, the effort to redefine marriage, along with many another modern movement] the problem is how to subdue reality to the wishes of men." The abolition of slavery and of Jim Crow laws was an example of the former, an attempt to conform man's behavior to virtue. The effort to redefine marriage is an example of the latter, the attempt to subdue reality to man's wishes. Hence the commonly repeated analogy of same-sex couples to victims of racial prejudice is a false one. The actual legal rights of same-sex couples having been secured, the "right" to "marriage" is a chimera.

Conversely, if reality is to be subdued to the wishes of men, why should the subduers care so much about the word once they have claimed the thing? If marriage is not sacred but is only a name for however people happen to behave erotically at any given moment in history, then why should the right to the word be so fervently demanded for same-sex couples? Where has all the diversity training gone? To foster diversity truly would be to acknowledge that same-sex relationships are something different from marriage and to embrace that difference without prejudice. But here the diversity-mongers balk. Why do they care so much about the word "marriage" that any distinction between same-sex and opposite-sex relationships becomes intolerable to them?

The answer is that those who support same-sex "marriage" want it both ways: They want marriage to mean something profound, universal, redemptive, and sublime so that participation in it by same-sex couples might be hallowed. At the same time they argue that there is nothing sacred about marriage so that participation in it by same-sex couples might be totally accepted. They want to reap the benefits of marriage in society by denaturing them in the mind, to eat that cake and have it too.

Of course it cannot be done, and so arises the impulse to redefine out of existence what cannot be enjoyed. What marches as passion for equality—emotionally genuine, perhaps, but intellectually spurious—begins in envy. Instead of articulating an ideal form of union in which same-sex couples could sublimate their distinct kind of relationship, the impulse abroad is to destroy an ideal to which only opposite-sex couples can aspire. It is sour grapes raised to the level of social revolution. As Aesop might say, it is easy (or rather imperative) to despise what you cannot have.

To be sure, if the sacred ideal of marriage is abandoned by our society, it will not be only—or even mainly—because of the movement to call same-sex couples "married." Fiercer enemies of marriage have long been at work. The invention of the contraceptive pill and the conversion of marriage from a combined spiritual, social, and personal institution into nothing more than a "relationship of two people who love each other" have fundamentally reconstructed the mental landscape in which marriage takes place.

The consequences are perfectly familiar. The acceptability of pre- and extramarital sex has increased. The divorce rate has increased. The numbers of unwed mothers and irresponsible fathers have increased. The rate of reproduction among the beneficiaries of "higher education" (whose institutions have threatened population explosion and preached careerism while denigrating marriage) has declined. The young are systematically misled about the negative consequences of divorcing "sexual activity" from expectations for marriage. The pretense that gender is irrelevant to home, workplace, and church has constituted a de facto war against the differences between the sexes out of which the meaning of marriage arises. Extreme feminists characterize marriage as institutionalized rape.

All of these trends arise from the intellectual falsification of actual human experience, the reduction of the profound mysteries of sex, love, reproduction, nature, and society to matters of equality and power only. The sacred ideal of marriage is thus under siege from many directions.

Finally, we are told—as if it were a rational argument—that we must accept same-sex "marriage" because it will soon be universally approved and all who resist the change are headed for the dustbin of history. Perhaps. But the inevitability of a change does not make the change necessarily a good one. History provides plenty of examples of changes that, to put it mildly, have not meant progress.

My argument is not that the concept of marriage will not change but that, if it does, a true ideal will be sacrificed for a false idea. Future

326 | Other Writings

generations may grow up imagining that there is no difference between same-sex and opposite-sex couples. So far as society is concerned, they will be right, but only because marriage will have become a thing of the past.

*   *   *

[Update: The moment that the Supreme Court found same-sex marriage to be a "right," the social turmoil around the issue disappeared and was immediately replaced by social turmoil around transgenderism. The war against marriage having been "won," the next war is against gender itself, and now not only human institutions but human bodies—including the bodies of children—are being mangled to incarnate a lie.]

Socialism and Virtue
[December 20, 2009]

A former student has sent me the following note and exercise and his friend's response:

The note:

> Not sure if you may have seen this exercise floating around the internet ... but my friend's rebuttal was so good I had to share the exercise and his comment. I am curious [about] your thoughts ... if you could spare a moment.

The exercise:

> An economics professor at a local college made a statement that he had never failed a single student before, but had once failed an entire class. That class had insisted that Obama's socialism worked and that no one would be poor and no one would be rich, a great equalizer. The professor then said, "Okay, we will have an experiment in this class on Obama's plan." All grades would be averaged and everyone would receive the same grade so no one would fail and no one would receive an A.
>
> After the first test, the grades were averaged and everyone got a B. The students who studied hard were upset and the students who studied little were happy.
>
> As the second test rolled around, the students who studied little had studied even less and the ones who studied hard decided they wanted a free ride too so they studied little. The second test average was a D. No one was happy. When the third test rolled around, the average was an F. The scores never increased as bickering, blame, and name-calling all resulted in hard feelings and no one would study for the benefit of anyone else.
>
> All failed, to their great surprise, and the professor told them that socialism would also ultimately fail because when the reward

328 | Other Writings

is great, the effort to succeed is great, but when government takes all the reward away, no one will try or want to succeed.
Could not be any simpler than that.

The friend's response:

Where there is no compassion for the unfortunates and no accounting for luck, there will be a savage race to wealth. The classmates who understood the material and didn't see the value in helping the others understand the material deserved the failing grades they all got.

My response:

I like the intellectual exercise you sent, though I doubt it is a true story. But it makes a good point, and I think a true one, about the hopelessness of the socialist theory as a substitute for individual responsibility.

As for your friend's comment, it is true that compassion for unfortunates is essential to civilization. However, it is essential as a virtue, to be sought individually and to be culturally taught, recognized, and admired. But though such virtue must influence human law, it cannot be secured by law or forced through a political system or dictated from above.

Virtue is called virtue (from *vir*, meaning man) partly because it is to be practiced by an individual human being. When individuals surrender to the state their responsibility for acting virtuously, they will cease to be virtuous and the state will redefine virtue to serve its own interests. (Think *1984* and *Brave New World*; German National Socialism and Soviet Russia; Communist China, North Korea, and Cuba.)

Any theory that purports to substitute a forced system of virtue for individual responsibility for virtue is denying what the Founding Fathers of the United States knew well, that is, the limits of human perfectibility. This is why Marx and all his offshoots are whistling in the wind and why all Marxist regimes sink into utterly *un*-virtuous dictatorships.

The real danger is tyranny wearing the clothes of virtue. Without logic and trained reason, people can be manipulated into believing that in the name of the good they should renounce their freedom to be good or bad. What that leads to, over and over again, and inevitably, is bad.

As a nation we are precariously teetering on the brink of such a delusion now, and I hope that the majority of Americans will bethink themselves and return to the wisdom of the best of their ancestors before they sell their individual liberties and responsibilities to buy a false vision of utopia. The word *utopia* means "no place" for a good reason.

On a Jury
[January 16, 2010]

Last week I served as a juror on a criminal case in federal court. The unpleasantness of having to hear testimony about nasty human behavior was significantly counterbalanced for me by my experience in the jury room, where all the members of the jury, of various walks of life and varying experience, deliberated with care, intelligence, responsibility, and determination to reach a fair and truthful verdict.

The experience renewed my faith in the wisdom of the Founding Fathers' commitment to trial by jury. It occurred to me that most of what we hear about the behavior of the fellow human beings whom we don't know personally is via the news, and most news is about bad human behavior. But here were eleven people whom I did not know, randomly chosen, seriously trying to do the right thing as I was and thereby justifying the Founders' trust in their collective wisdom. It was the opposite of the news. It was good news.

When I returned to school and described the above, one of my colleagues suggested that my faith in the goodness of human nature had been renewed. I said I had no faith in the goodness of human nature. (There's Rousseau again, blowing smoke.) Any particular human being's nature may be good or bad; in general, human nature is plastic, malleable, able to be influenced by training for good or ill, and at least in part subject to the government of the free will. I did not see how one could hear the testimony I heard and still believe that man is naturally good.

But what my experience did renew was my appreciation for the power of culture, tradition, education, social pressure, and law, when they are intact and rooted in wisdom and virtue, to influence people for the good. More specifically, I found that in a relatively random sample of my fellow American citizens, the values of reason, patience, truth, the rule of law, common sense, politeness, honesty, and justice were very much in evidence.

Given the corrupting influences of our entertainments, schools, celebrities, politicians, and the usual news, the likelihood that such values will continue to characterize a random sample of citizens may be doubtful. But the behavior of my fellow jurors on last week's trial persuaded me to hope that perhaps we are not so far gone as a culture as it sometimes seems.

*   *   *

[Update: The above was written before the recent tidal wave of leftist irrationality in the forms of identity politics, deep-state undermining of a duly elected president, COVID-19 panic, anarchist riots, anti-Jewish pogroms, statue razing, cancel culture, and an attempt to assassinate a sitting Supreme Court justice. Can the legal system based on juries of "twelve just men and true" survive in a society whose education system, media, corporate executives, elected officials, and career bureaucrats war against law and justice, nature and truth? For political reasons a Washington D.C. jury has just acquitted a former Hillary Clinton campaign attorney of making false statements to the FBI despite overwhelming evidence of his guilt.]

Left on Down toward Incest
[December 14, 2010]

Thanks to the Drudge Report, we have this inevitable news from Switzerland:

Switzerland Considers Repealing Incest Laws

Switzerland is considering repealing its incest laws because they are "obsolete."
By Allan Hall in Berlin 4:17 PM GMT 13 Dec 2010

The upper house of the Swiss parliament has drafted a law decriminalising sex between consenting family members which must now be considered by the government.

There have been only three cases of incest since 1984.

Switzerland, which recently held a referendum passing a draconian law that will boot out foreigners convicted of committing the smallest of crimes, insists that children within families will continue to be protected by laws governing abuse and paedophilia.

Daniel Vischer, a Green party MP, said he saw nothing wrong with two consenting adults having sex, even if they were related.

"Incest is a difficult moral question, but not one that is answered by penal law," he said.

I say the news is "inevitable" because it represents but one more step in the long march from traditional values toward a future devoted to—well, to what? Let's see where we end up if we plot the course laid out by "progressivist" promoters of social and legal "progress" in recent years.

By "progress" I don't mean legitimate improvements in the justice system or wiser practical balancing of the often-conflicting values of liberty and equality. I am referring, rather, to the Oregon and Netherlands laws permitting assisted suicide and euthanasia; to the push for gay marriage; to the argument that any woman has a "right" to choose to have an abortion at any time; to the promotion of sex-change surgeries in adults and transgendering hormone "therapies" and puberty blockers in children, to the attempt to assert the "rights" of animals (as opposed to the responsibilities of human beings); to the defense of lucrative traffic in addictive drugs, pornography, and sex slaves; to the fringe-group justification of homosexual pedophilia; to the legalization of marijuana; to the refusal of Homeland Security, against all practical reason, to countenance so-called "profiling" while justifying what in any non-government operation would be considered sexual harassment. You may wish to add examples of your own.

All these movements, backed by passionate groups of devotees, are predicated upon the valid principles of individual liberty and equality under the law. They reason thus: If all men are created with equal rights, as they interpret the words, "who is to say" that women can't choose to abort, that two men can't choose to marry, that any man or woman can't be the gender he or she would like to be, that an underage child can't sexually love an older person, that a white great-grandmother or an Asian infant should be immune to the kind of body search more properly directed at swarthy Middle-Eastern Muslim men between the ages of eighteen and forty? Why *not* die when you feel like it or marry your sister if you wish?

The problem is that the backers admit no limits imposed by the same authority by which we claim our rights to liberty and equality, namely "nature and nature's God."

The only traditional reason not to do any of these things is civilized tradition itself, rooted in ancient wisdom, religious faith, the practice of neighbors and nations for millennia. The legalization of incest, whether Switzerland passes the bill this time around or not, is but one more in the long list of rebellions against all tradition in the name of the freedom to make the world correspond to any desire we may conceive instead of having to correspond ourselves to once universally acknowledged rules of human behavior.

But my assertion of the validity of those traditional values need not be repeated. Anyone interested in the fundamental arguments for them may read C. S. Lewis's *The Abolition of Man*, so often referred to in my writing. Today I want to ask instead toward what world the supporters of these various progressive advances imagine they are moving us. How do they picture us living if they should have their way?

I realize that not all those who embrace one item in the list above will necessarily embrace all, or even any, of the others. I also realize that the devil is in the details. But promoters of each of the above changes have in common the similar intellectual stance that nothing may justly hinder anyone from living out his or her heart's desire. Well, let's say government did get completely out of the way, or rather, as is more in keeping with the "progressive" program, enforced society's acceptance of these movements. Where would we be? What would be the practical effects of the success in the "progressive" agenda?

At a certain point in the decline of ancient Rome, if things didn't quite go your way—say you had a rebellious child or lost an election or couldn't pay a debt—you'd get into a warm bath and slit your wrists. Any child of either gender not under fairly careful protection might be subject to sexual abuse by any passing epicure. All the trees of Italy were burned to make hot running water in Rome. According to Suetonius, Caligula threatened to make his horse Incitatus a consul. Is ancient Rome in collapse to provide the picture of our own ideal future?

Suppose all incest taboos were renounced as antediluvian superstition and we were not to suffer a flood of mental and physical impairments or supernatural punishments. Wouldn't something nonetheless be lost? To the ancients, Oedipus was that man to whom the worst thing that could possibly happen to a man happened—killing one's father and marrying one's mother. If our enlightened northwest were to go the way of Switzerland, how many thousands would blaze a new Oregon Trail in order to clear a senile old man out of the path to a trophy mother? If only Oedipus, like us, hadn't had the gods in his way, bugging him for doing what came naturally! Who are non-Oregonians to say that Oedipus didn't deserve a happy life too?

Imagine a child growing up in a world in which he knows that one day his parents will ask him to kill them as he will be expected to ask his own future children to kill him to get him off their impatient hands; a world in which married couples may be any mix of genders or transgenders and of any blood relation; a world in which a boy is taught no sexual responsibility because women can have free abortions any time and children are available for his future sexual needs as he is available at present to those of his elders; a world in which animals may not, but people may, perhaps must, be eaten; a world in which there are no Jewish ethicists, no Catholic confessionals, no Protestant Bible-thumpers curtailing our freedoms and ruining our fun; a world in which no vestigial notions of higher divine authority or higher human calling will be permitted to stand in the way of the satisfaction of any material desire, practical or sensual.

Do the promoters of these perverse ideas of progress really believe that man is naturally good? That without the constraint of law and custom mankind will not fall to barbarism? That the abandonment of all traditional virtues will involve no loss of happiness, contentment, or meaning for the individual in society? Do they actually think that the goods of civilization won from nature in years past are so permanent and secure that all restrictions of individual desire can be safely dismantled? If they do, they must be utterly ignorant of human history, or utterly mad—or both.

We cannot have it both ways. Either we are moral beings, created in a context of neutral nature to aspire to meaning and happiness consistent with goodness by constraining our illicit impulses for the sake of ourselves and our posterity, or we are mere bundles of desire whose mission is to indulge in every pleasure that strikes our fancy until such time as nature itself prevents us, at which point we are free to end our desperate and ultimately meaningless lives before others end them for us.

As Charles Embree put it, "It's either right back up or left on down."

If you agree with me that we are moral beings, answerable for our choices to the power that made us, we had better start drawing some non-negotiable lines—at incest if no closer.

* * *

[Update:

A US first? Massachusetts city votes to recognize polyamorous relationships in domestic partnership policy.
By Elinor Aspergren USA TODAY July 3, 2020

A Massachusetts city northwest of Boston is believed to be the first in the nation to adopt an ordinance recognizing polyamory.

Somerville adopted a domestic partnership policy including polyamorous couples after a unanimous vote of the city council last week, reported the *Somerville Journal*, part of the *USA Today* Network.

Polyamory is the practice of having multiple intimate relationships with the full knowledge and consent of everyone involved, according to *Psychology Today*.

The city's law defines a domestic partnership as an "entity formed by people" instead of an "entity formed by two persons." It also replaces "he and she" with "they," and replaces "both" with "all."

Mayor Joe Curtatone signed the domestic partnership ordinance into municipal law June 29, according to the Journal, after the city council passed the bill June 25.

Right back up or left on down.]

The Educational Downside of Technology
[2011]

I have taught English at upscale independent high schools since 1985. My sophomore syllabus has changed little over the years: *Sir Gawain and the Green Knight, The Canterbury Tales, Macbeth,* and *A Tale of Two Cities* have generally won my students over.

About ten years ago, my sophomores started complaining that the homework burden was too heavy. [See also "Instantaneous Comprehension or Charles Dickens meets IM" above.] In the forty-five minutes that they owed me on four nights per week, they could not get the reading done. I had not significantly altered the number of pages I expected them to read on any given night, and I knew they were not less capable than their predecessors. What was it?

One day it occurred to me to ask for a show of hands: "When you are reading your English homework, how many of you have the computer on?" A majority of hands went up. "iPod?" A somewhat different but equally substantial majority. "Instant messaging?" Nearly all. "TV?" Many. "Video games?" A substantial minority. "Do you have your own phone in your room?" Yup.

I had my answer. They couldn't get a scene of *Macbeth* or two chapters of Dickens read in forty-five minutes because they had no uninterrupted reading time. So I wrote out a page called "How to Do English Homework." It consisted essentially of my saying, "Turn off all electronic devices." I listed all I could think of and have updated it each year—"texting" and Facebook have replaced the antediluvian I.M.

But it gets worse. Recently the problem has become not simply interruptions. Almost all my present sophomores cannot remember a time when they did not have cell phones, and the effect on their minds of their use of electronic screens has been decisive. Nearly all of them—except for the vestigial book lovers or those whose parents shut down electronics on school nights—have an attention deficit. They simply cannot concentrate on any challenging text for more than a very few minutes without feeling the compelling need to look at an electronic screen.

My theory about why this has happened is only reinforced by recent research on how technologies are "rewiring" the teenage brain: Everything a young person sees on a screen—laptop, smartphone, video game, iPad—is instantly comprehended. The medium is pitched so that no degree of concentration and no more than a second or two are required for grasp of its content. Of course concentration is required to advance in video games, and we are told that such activities enhance hand-eye coordination. But nothing in the way of extended thought is required to "get" what is being delivered by a screen. If anything appears that is not instantly grasped, an instantly graspable explanation is only a click away.

The result is that children raised on screens have hours of experience of instant comprehension and *no* experience of the rewards of attention paid to a challenging text over time—even minutes, let alone hours or weeks. When they are confronted by the kind of literature that requires such effort, their first and almost unconquerable reaction is "I can't understand this—it's too hard." Then they a) conclude that they are stupid, b) look for a screen to help them satisfy the teacher's unfair expectations, and (if screens are forbidden) c) quit and wait for an explanation in class.

Raised on screens, the students are not to blame for this response. But it accounts for their feeling that we expect of them too much reading that is too hard, and for their resort to SparkNotes and other online cheat channels that they consider lifelines. They now go online not only to plagiarize essays but just to find out what happened in the story.

Railing against this technological threat to reading, I wondered whether I had become a luddite. Articles like Karen Faucett's "Virtual School" in the June 2011 *Education Matters*, or Jill Newell's "Natives and Pioneers: Digital Education for Students and Teachers" in July, or the Association of American Educators Member Survey in November (in which it was reported that 58% agree with replacing textbooks with "digital content") made me feel like Cassandra. Who is talking about the actual downside of getting with the technology program?[1]

---

1 Mark Bauerlein, professor of English at Emory University, has written bracingly about the lack of ability among college students to understand complex texts. See his article called "Too Dumb for Complex Texts?" (*Educational Leadership* [Volume 68, Number 5, February 2011], pages 28–33) online at http://www.ascd.org/publications/educational-leadership/feb11/vol68/num05/Too-Dumb-for-Complex-Texts%C2%A2.aspx. Professor Bauerlein is the author of *The Dumbest Generation: How the Digital Age Stupefies Young Americans and Jeopardizes Our Future (Or, Don't Trust Anyone Under 30)* (Penguin, 2008).

I am not in principle opposed to the appropriate use of digital technology: I am adept at using the computer in ways I find useful, and I liked having my iPod Shuffle on a recent flight. But then I already know how to read with concentration when I need to. My students do not, and I see nothing in the latest techno-pedagogies that will change that.

Studies are now demonstrating the obvious, as "studies" so often do: The multitasking in which our students are trained by their machines in fact reduces the quality of the work done on any one task. There are studies demonstrating that being raised on screens actually trains the brain *not* to be able to think deeply.

Some of my students confess to spending four hours a night on Facebook. Many are texting all day. Low English grades cause them to ask what they can do for extra credit. My response is often to suggest an experiment: For a month turn off all screens and beeps when doing homework; let's see whether your grades improve. They react as if I were asking them to give up oxygen, but, *mirabile dictu*, in the ones who dare to try it, it often works.

Cassandra or no, I maintain that we must do our best to break our students of their addiction to screens. If we don't, we will bequeath to our heirs a society run by speedily multitasking illiterates.

Appreciating the Paintings of Mary Holmes
[2014]

> Every society recognizes a holy virgin. The nature of
> nobility is that it doesn't interact. (Gold is called a noble
> metal because it doesn't interact.) Nobility (virginity) is
> a condition of isolation, separation. The noble virgin, the
> eternal virgin, is a new life with the potential to bear life
> but not yet entered into that condition. The conception of
> Christ by the Virgin is the great image of the interaction of
> spirit with the world. It is unique in her case, but partly
> experienced by every woman, and it educates *all* of us.
>
> —Mary Holmes

To appreciate the paintings of Mary Holmes one must look at them with
the whole self. The eyes and the senses alone will not do. Nor just the
feelings, nor just the intellect. Only the whole self, including the intuition,
the capacity for insight, the receptivity to gradual or sudden illuminations,
will discern what she is really painting. Hence, to see her work as it is
requires abandoning the distorting lenses imposed upon our vision by
modernist and post-modernist principles of art. Her paintings do not
exist merely to illustrate concepts, to express a self, to evoke emotions,
or to reveal underlying psychological structures or underlying physical
structures. A different principle is at work here.

As Holmes taught, because we are incarnate beings, for whom only
seeing is believing, we need art, and we make art, in order to make the
invisible visible. She also said that whatever the style, age, or degree of
seriousness, every work of art is made by a realist. That is, every artist
strives to give visible form to what he or she knows or believes is real but
is otherwise invisible.

The realities Holmes strives to make visible in her work are the realities
of spirit. To appreciate a painting by her, therefore, is to experience a reality

of the spirit revealed in visible form. Under her brush, the iconic figure, the formal gesture, the symbolic object, the illustrated myth, the richness of nature, above all what Milton calls "the human face divine" becomes a window into the invisible. In her paintings we are able to see, fixed in form for our contemplation, essences to which we would otherwise have no access in concept, word, or image and which we therefore cannot believe in, not having seen them. And yet they are essences which, whether we know it or not, we yearn to see so that we *can* believe in them.

An example: It has been several centuries since serious painters have taken a subject like the Annunciation seriously. We live, we are told, in a post-Christian age. Many feet have developed blisters walking through numberless museum galleries on whose walls are hung paintings of the Annunciation (or the Madonna and Child or the Crucifixion or the Deposition or the Flight into Egypt), and we are, as an age, fed up. Hence Cezanne, Picasso, Duchamp, and Warhol. Why bother depicting a story that cannot signify after Darwin, Nietzsche, Marx, Freud, Einstein, and Sartre? Well, look at Mary Holmes' Annunciation in the small side chapel devoted to the Virgin in her Chapel of the Holy Spirit in Santa Cruz, California. It is not asking you to come to it believing what you can't believe. Just look at it and let yourself, your *whole* self, see what the painting reveals by being what it *is*. You may not come away from it a convert to any creed. But you will have seen and hence believed in the reality of a young woman's readiness to be the bearer of a profound and redemptive meaning that she has neither invented nor understood, a meaning greater than a human self can contain, greater than nature, greater than art, greater than psychology, greater even than history.

Look more. The angel Gabriel addresses the Virgin. In the fiery cloud the prophecy (the destiny of the prefigured child) is made visible to us as it is being made known to the Virgin in Gabriel's words. Holmes has painted the Virgin, who will bear the metaphorical Lamb of God, as a shepherdess. She holds a natural lamb, whose own mother too knows something that the Virgin's mystified puppy does not. Fire is in the heavens and water on the earth, both symbols of the spirit, which enters the world just as the soul enters the flesh through woman in conception and as Christians believe Christ entered the world through the Virgin in the Incarnation. The traditional lily held by the angel symbolizes the Virgin's purity.

Now look at the body of this image, the colors, shapes, relation of forms. Feel the movement of comprehension, of descending grace and ascending receptivity. Study the angel's wings and the Virgin's gesture. Feel the pregnancy of the sky, the circumambient air, the water, the grass, the animals, all poised in this moment to receive the promise of the day of fulfillment. Can you sense that nature in this painting is not a function of Darwinian warfare but a gift of love? That the pain of existing is not the result of an accidental, random, meaningless conflict (survival of the fittest) but rather the fruit of an ineffable grace at work in us? Don't try to believe it. Can you see it? Yes? Then you are ready. No? Then go on. Look at the place where the gold of Angel, vision, and hair meet the blue of water and dress, where heaven meets earth, spirit is made flesh, meaning is revealed in form. Look at the face of the Virgin.

What is made visible in her face cannot be put into words. But look. Keep looking. Are you tempted to name these realities made visible? Humble awe ... loving wonder ... receptive purity ... acceptance of mystery ... foresight in readiness ... innocence on the brink of knowledge ... sadness looking toward redemption ... the gentle pulling of a soul together for a sacrifice and a reward unimaginable? Is not this every mother at her best when she knows she is to bear a child? Is not this the feminine in every one of us at our best when we know at a particular moment of truth that we are stepping from our past into our future? Is this not also what we *would* be at our best if we could, for seeing the good is also recognizing how short of it we have come, though our deepest selves long for it? Is this not a visible reality before which we would not be ashamed to worship?

These paintings do not exist to prove a doctrine, to impose, to convert. Holmes painted them, as she said, because she wanted to see such images and no such images were otherwise available. (C. S. Lewis said the same about the books he wrote: He wanted to read them, but because they didn't exist, he had to write them himself.) If Holmes could have seen them without having to paint them herself, she would not have had to go to the trouble. They don't impose, but they do reveal. And because seeing is believing, is not revelation also invitation, instruction, demonstration, imposition, even proof? Don't answer before you have looked at the paintings of Mary Holmes with your whole self.[1]

---

1 Find more about Mary Holmes at https://maryholmes.org/.

Cum Laude vs. *Cum Invidia*
[c. 2015]

After Tuesday's Cum Laude assembly, I ran into several students who thought the ceremony to be distasteful because unfair. Their argument was that because lots of students at school work hard, some as hard as those honored by induction into the Cum Laude Society, it is not fair to honor only those few. The general attitude represented by this complaint could be called, in John Milton's terms, "a sense of injured merit."

My response to such feelings is fourfold:

1. Cum Laude honors not merely hard work but excellence of achievement in academic subjects.

2. To be consistent, students complaining about Cum Laude induction should complain equally about athletic trophies for Most Valuable or Most Improved players. But they don't.

3. To grudge at others' honors, rather than to celebrate their accomplishments in joy and approval, is a succumbing to temptation. It is a permission of the more selfish and shallow parts of our minds to overbear our higher reason. Since all of us wish to be praised for our own accomplishments, the determination to withhold that praise and celebration from deserving others is unjust as well as inconsistent.

4. One of the Ten Commandments is "Thou shalt not covet." This commandment instructs us not to wish in our hearts for what our neighbor has but rather to be grateful both for what we have been given and for the good of others. The part of ourselves that feels wronged just because someone else has been honored is the part of us that wants to think of ourselves as our own god, the part that fears that our neighbor's advantage is our disadvantage. It is the translation of a false picture of life as a zero-sum game into a habit of malice, which tends toward behavior destructive to self,

neighbor, and community. It is the sin called envy, from the Latin *invidia*, rooted in the idea of looking furtively into others' good in fear for oneself.

In *Paradise Lost* Milton used the phrase "sense of injured merit" to describe the motivation of Lucifer, who could not bear the fact that he had been created by God and was therefore not God himself. His desperate (and of course fruitless) attempt to alter that situation led to rebellion and destruction. As Hamlet might say, "O reform it altogether."

Fact and Faith: Jordan Peterson and Sam Harris on "Truth"
[December 21, 2019]

A friend sent me an edited transcription of the first conversation between Jordan Peterson and Sam Harris, in which they were disagreeing about the definition and foundations of the concept "truth." He thought the debate would serve as a primer on epistemology (the study of the nature and grounds of knowledge).

Here is my reply:

The problem with the transcription of the conversation between Sam Harris and Jordan Peterson is that Sam Harris worships "facts" without recognizing that our knowledge of all facts depends on preexisting assumptions—i.e., on faith. For example, the scientific fact depends upon the preexisting assumption, an act of faith, that the laws of physics are constant and unchanging. This is not a demonstrable or provable fact. We take it on faith. Once we do, we can prove a whole lot of other things. But in itself it cannot be proven. To prove something, to demonstrate its truth, means to translate it into terms which we have already adopted as true. But the most fundamental things we know are founded on faith. We cannot even trust our own reason without believing, on faith, that our reason works and corresponds to reality. So before they try to define "What is truth?" they need to agree on the underlying assumptions that they bring to thinking at all about anything.

The only reasonable unity that can possibly lie behind Sam Harris's longing for truth independent of goodness and Jordan Peterson's longing for truth that is healing to mankind is faith in the source of both goodness and truth (and beauty) in a single divine reality that emanates forth all three principles of value for human beings. Any other idea of the foundation of reality leaves us wallowing in ignorance, confusion, and mere personal preferences, leading to endless unresolvable arguments like the one you've transcribed.

In short, if God is not the source of reason, of truth, of beauty, of goodness, of our capacity to appreciate these things, and of our own longing for them, then we cannot know anything. And, correlatively, only faith in that divine unity behind what can be seen by human beings can serve as any foundation for reasonable argument.

Alphabetical Index to Titles